UNDERSTANDING
CRIME

A **Multidisciplinary** Approach

Susan Guarino-Ghezzi / A. Javier Treviño
Stonehill College   Wheaton College

Foreword by Albert K. Cohen
Professor Emeritus, University of Connecticut

 LexisNexis®

 **anderson publishing**
A member of the LexisNexis Group

Understanding Crime: A Multidisciplinary Approach

Copyright © 2005
Matthew Bender & Company, Inc., a member of the LexisNexis Group

Phone 877-374-2919
Web Site www.lexisnexis.com/anderson/criminaljustice

LexisNexis and the Knowledge Burst logo are trademarks of Reed Elsevier Properties, Inc.
Anderson Publishing is a registered trademark of Anderson Publishing, a member of the LexisNexis Group

Library of Congress Cataloging-in-Publication Data

Guarino-Ghezzi, Susan.
 Understanding crime : a multidisciplinary approach / Susan Guarino-Ghezzi, A. Javier Treviño
  p. cm.
 Includes bibliographical references and index.
 ISBN 1-59345-966-1 (softbound)
 1. Criminology. 2. Crime. I. Treviño, A. Javier, 1958- II. Title.
HV6025.G795 2005
364--dc22   2005003539

Cover design by Tin Box Studio, Inc./Cincinnati, Ohio

EDITOR Ellen S. Boyne
ACQUISITIONS EDITOR Michael C. Braswell

To
Richard Quinney
mentor and friend of a lifetime

Foreword

Albert K. Cohen

How does one go about learning about crime? Whose business is it to study crime, to pull together what is known about it, to construct theories to account for it, and to answer our questions?

Your questions, whoever you are. Your life is somehow touched by crime. Are you a professor of criminal law who teaches students what you think they need to know in order to convict or acquit a defendant? Are you a police officer trying to decide whether to arrest a disorderly person? Are you that disorderly person, who is wondering whether to offer in some unobtrusive but unmistakable manner a small "monetary donation" to a police officer? Are you the police chief whose job includes badgering the city council for money to maintain its police force? Or perhaps you are a parent who worries about the friends your kids hang with or whether, contrary to your admonitions, they talk to strangers? Maybe you are a legislator working on a bill to protect the environment from industrial waste, or an airline passenger resentful of the security inspection meant to protect you from terrorism?

If you want to know all about crime, then you want to know about the administration of criminal justice. Crime and criminal justice occur in a context that comprehends the whole of society, and they are articulated with that society in ways that are far more complex than are illuminated by any one academic discipline. Within these academic domains we find most of the really systematic, "disciplined" work of studying crime, especially concerning the causes of crime: What makes crime happen?

In the early days of criminological theory, during the nineteenth century, there was great interest in biological theories, including the notion of the "born criminal" and the possibility of recognizing him by the shape of his head and his facial features. These early theories did not stand up to scholarly scrutiny; they survive mostly as historical curiosities. This early experience with the biology of crime should not lead us to dismiss the notion that our bodies may have something to do with criminality and that research into the biology of crime is legitimate. We know—some of us from experience—that the chemical substances we pour, inhale, or inject into our bodies can produce behavior that we may not like to think of as "our true self," but which nonetheless is clearly criminal. How about the chemical substances produced by the body itself and that we call "hormones"? We know a good deal about the physiological effects of hormones on our moods and emotions. It would certainly be premature to write off the possible effects of human chemistry on our choices and conduct.

To explain differences in conduct generally, and deviant and criminal conduct in particular, one would expect to learn a great deal from psychology and sociology. Both disciplines try to explain behavior by means of theories of learning, of personality, and of motivation. Sociology tends to place more emphasis on the role of the social and cultural environment in the production of learning, personality, and motivation, and psychology tends to place more emphasis on the internal dynamics of personality. But such a description is very crude, and it is not possible, in a few words, to do justice to the richness and variety of thinking going on in both disciplines.

Economics is the social science largely concerned with the world of work, the production and exchange of goods and services, and the distribution of wealth. But underlying it all is a theory of motivation on the individual level; a theory that explains action as largely determined by weighing the costs and benefits of alternative courses of action and choosing the course that promises to maximize the net gain. Economics does not insist that conduct is totally determined by such considerations, but economic reasoning is never absent in the shaping of human conduct. Certainly the system of criminal punishment is largely premised upon the assumption that the state itself is an economic actor, weighing financial costs about such issues as executing a felon versus locking him or her up for life.

Some events seem to challenge economic theory as an explanation of crime. What are we to say of "suicide bombers" who deliberately and knowingly blow themselves up in order to inflict damage upon an enemy? Can economic theory handle the suicide bomber? Probably you have anticipated me; perhaps his or her sacrifice is to be entered into the equations as a *gain* rather than a *cost*. The suicide bomber is a "martyr" who will be honored by those who survive him or her and will be richly rewarded in the world to come. The example of the suicide bomber suggests that assigning values to the variables of economic theory may require entering into the mind of the actor and appreciating the culture that informs his or her values. This begins to sound more like sociology and psychology, and it reminds us that apparently "autonomous" disciplines may interpenetrate and depend upon one another.

Before we drop the subject of terrorism, consider this question: Are we really talking about crime? The U.S. government thinks so, but does the suicide bomber think so? Or is the "martyr" giving his or her life in a noble cause much as a "soldier" fulfills his or her duty? Suddenly we find ourselves questioning what we thought was already settled: the meaning of "crime" and, by extension, of "criminological theory." Have we stumbled onto the territory of another, relatively recondite discipline, "game theory," where the name of the game is everything?

We have used the word "explain" to account for differences among individuals: Why did I lie about my income to the Internal Revenue Service, but you did not? Explaining differences in rates and quantities of crime is another matter. Why are the per capita rates of kidnapping much higher in Mexico and some other Latin American countries than in the United States? Why have rates for crimes of violence increased in England, but declined in the United States? Why does slavery, defined as criminal in all countries, still exist in places like Sudan? Why is political corruption—the buying and selling of the services of governmental employees—enormously variable among countries and among states, provinces, and cities within those countries? Why, for that matter, are some acts that are defined as crimes in one country *not* crimes in another?

Clearly, we are now talking about crimes as properties of social systems rather than of human individuals. In the latter case we were asking: How do differences among individual persons, their personalities, and the situations in which they find themselves, account for differences in the production of criminal behavior? Now we are asking: How do the *rates* for this or that crime vary as they do for men and women, for persons of different ages, for immigrants and natives? Countries are social systems, but there are systems within systems. Why are rates of cheating different across universities and within universities, among males and females, freshmen and seniors, members of fraternities and nonmembers?

The theories that we were considering before do not provide the answers to questions about the criminality of social systems, but they are not irrelevant either. Theories on the individual level claim to identify combinations of variables, characteristics of persons and their situations, that are productive of criminal acts. Let us call these "criminogenic situations." Now we must ask: What is it about social systems, about their cultures, about how they are put together and how their parts interact, about how people move about within the systems, and about the ways in which resources, opportunities, aspirations, and beliefs are distributed within systems, that explain differences in the ways that criminogenic situations are produced and distributed?

To answer these questions we call upon different bodies of knowledge than we did before. Those that come to mind most readily are political science and organizational sociology. Both are concerned with the study of social systems, how they are organized, how their parts interact, and so on. Both have had some experience with the analysis of such systems, that is, with actually figuring out how the parts interact to produce the behavior that goes on at particular locations within those systems.

We have posed many questions concerning crime and talked about the major disciplines that study crime, do research, lecture, debate, and write about crime. Who else does these things? The answer is: almost everybody.

For example, I wanted to learn more about the Quakers, and so I attended a week-long gathering of the Society of Friends, as the Quakers call themselves. Some of the people in attendance were atheists or agnostics who talked about their shared concerns. The chief of those concerns was the question: What do I say to fellow Quakers who ask me, "If you do not believe in God—a God who knows and cares about you, and wants you to behave, and to love your neighbor and treat him with respect—and if you do not believe that you have an immortal soul, then what is your basis for morality, for disciplining your appetites, for being a good citizen and treating your neighbor as you would like him or her to treat you?" Although I was persuaded that my newfound godless Quaker friends walked as perpendicular in the way of the Lord as anybody else, they didn't know how to answer this question and it really bothered them, just as for many people the question of the legitimacy of the death penalty is essentially a religious question. Clearly, morality and crime on the part of persons and institutions are central concerns of religious thought and find expression in sermons, social action, everyday conduct, and religious scholarship.

Back to my original question: How do you go about the study of crime? How do you *start*? From what I have said in these pages, it follows that you do *not* start by sitting at the feet of the world's smartest sociologist or psychologist or biologist or economist or legal scholar, and you may also include in the list, philosopher and religious studies scholar. I have tried to suggest the multitude of ways in which crime touches our lives, the shapes it takes, and the ways we respond to it; the multitude of perspectives from which it can be approached; the different questions that each perspective raises; the interdependencies among the disciplines that study crime; and the importance, but also the limitations, of what each discipline has to tell us. It follows that one should start by wandering though the world of crime accompanied by specialists, each of whom will see things and interconnections that others will not. It is, of course, essential that they talk to one another so that all of us come out with an enriched understanding of what is, after all, the same object. This is what this book, *Understanding Crime: A Mutlidisciplinary Approach*, does. Actually, it would take a library of big fat books to do it, but let us start one book at a time, and let it be this book.

Table of Contents

Chapter One

Introduction: A Multidisciplined Approach to Crime

Susan Guarino-Ghezzi and A. Javier Treviño

Our attempts at understanding crime are as old as our attempts at understanding the larger subject of human behavior. When Cain murdered Abel, the meaning of the act was dissected for many centuries, for many audiences, and on many levels. Today, crimes of various sorts are predictably frequent subjects in movies, books, in the news, on talk shows, and in the corner pub. Crime is a subject that nearly everyone feels qualified to debate, to have opinions about, to comment on. There are many conflicting views on crime—perhaps because the subject of crime is itself a contradiction. Literary critic Wendy Lesser (1994) has argued that we are drawn to horror films such as *The Silence of the Lambs* because we, the audience, identify with both of the movie's main characters: the detective and the murderer. Even as the diabolical Hannibal Lecter assists in the investigation of the latest serial killer by putting himself into the killer's shoes, Lecter's audience imagines what it is like to be *him*. Contrast that image— of murderous impulses within the investigators—with the criminal justice system. The bureaucratic, "fact-finding" image of police investigation and courtroom trial gives the outward impression of objectivity, of "us" versus "them," the good and bad, the law-abiders and lawbreakers. Yet, the sorting of individuals into moral and legal categories is far from a precise science.

There are those who believe that the criminal is not a distant "other," but is lurking within ourselves. Consider the first line of Nick Lowe's lyrics to "The Beast in Me": "The beast in me is caged by frail and fragile bars; restless by day and by night rants and rages at the stars; God help the beast in me." "The Beast in Me" was played on the highly rated television series "The Sopranos," in which organized crime boss Tony Soprano ruthlessly kills to maintain dominance even as he appears to be living out the "American

1

dream" in his upscale suburban community. Literature scholar R.A. Foakes (2003) suggests that we are fascinated by violence in the media because it provides us with a safe way to identify with it harmlessly, without acting on it, and to release impulses we normally repress. "The beast in me" may be the subconscious magnet for many talk show audiences, and it is certainly the direct subject of such literary works as Robert Louis Stevenson's *Dr. Jekyll and Mr. Hyde* as well as many Shakespearean tragedies.

If crime is indeed about human weakness, are the causes psychological, biological, or purely moral? Mental pathology or a flawed moral-cognitive development seemed to be at the root of the ruthless murders commissioned by 1960s cult leader Charles Manson in California and the 1978 Florida murders committed by serial killer Ted Bundy. There is evidence of a psychology-crime link in the increased numbers of offenders with mental disorders as well. Biological factors including brain function, genes, male hormones, and the effects of harmful addictions have also been associated with crime. Some people view biological and psychological explanations as mere excuses; what about weak moral character and bad choices? Consider the Menendez brothers, raised in affluence, who in 1996 were convicted of mercilessly slaughtering their parents in cold blood. Although they claimed they were sexually abused, just weeks earlier the brothers were glued to "The Billionaire Boys Club," a television mini-series based on real-life events in which a group of young men from Beverly Hills premeditated the murder of two people, including the father of one of the young men.

Psychology, biology, and morality help us to understand individual causes of crime, but they do not tell us the full story. Crime is also the result of *societal/cultural weakness*—society's inability to control individuals, particularly as members of groups or subcultures. Consider the romantic attraction that many Americans have to the "wild, wild west" of defiant gun slingers such as Jesse James, or gangsters such as John Dillinger, whom many rooted for during the 1920s even as the FBI's "G-men" worked to track him down. The ambiguous corporate culture of greed and selective lawbreaking has been blamed for such notorious white-collar crimes as junk-bond specialist Michael Milken's multimillion-dollar violations of federal securities and racketeering laws during the 1980s, or Enron's illegal accounting practices in 2003. Cultures need not be weak enforcers of social control, however. Amish communities in the United States and Canada provide an interesting case of a religious culture with tight-knit families and strong communities that control behavior by separating themselves from the larger society. Similarly, teenagers in Japan have been known for obedience to moral values and internationally low rates of delinquency, although Japan is now experiencing a surge in youth violence (Faiola, 2004). Recently an 11-year-old girl used a box cutter to slit the throat of a classmate and then brutally kicked her as she lay dying. Some Japanese attribute such sudden acts of rage to a long economic slump, soaring rates of divorce, domestic violence, suicide, and violent animated films, comic strips, and video games marketed to children.

shape one's moral's choices

soc. conditions • urban areas w/ unemployment (high)
• gun availability
• violent media images

As the Japanese example illustrates, crime is a societal tragedy—a failure of social institutions like families or schools to intervene and block the negative influences. *Criminogenic* social conditions, which lead to crime, include urban areas with high rates of unemployment, gun availability, transient communities, and violent media imagery. These conditions of the social environment shape moral choices and, if left unattended, neutralize existing social controls of family, religion, and other societal institutions.

Criminal acts also provide insight into the strong spirit of the human will to overcome social injustice. Certain individuals or groups seeking justice have been labeled "criminal" although they were struggling toward a higher purpose—showing political resistance to arrogant power-holders. Consider the fictional character of Antigone, in Sophocles' ancient Greek drama bearing her name from around 400 BCE. After the death of Antigone's brother, her uncle, King Creon, falsely accused the brother of treason and ordered his corpse to be placed on display rather than be given a religious burial. Ignoring the king's threats, Antigone buried her brother and was subsequently condemned to die of starvation. Antigone committed suicide rather than wait to die, and was vindicated when the king's son and wife also killed themselves out of grief. Similarly, under China's strict totalitarian dictatorship, group behaviors that are not approved by the government are banned, with serious consequences for those who persist. Recent reports have described the Chinese rite of Falun Gong, a spiritual practice of group exercise that attracts thousands of adherents, many of whom are mothers and grandmothers. These reports detail how the Chinese government, threatened by any behavior that resembles a religious movement, imposes long-term detention on Falun Gong followers and labels the practice a "dangerous cult," yet support for Falun Gong remains strong among many people.

For complex reasons, citizens as well as governments may be tempted to spread cultural myths about "bad people." Cultural critic René Girard (1989) believes that members of every society have a deep-seated fear of danger by their enemies or natural disasters, and comfort themselves by mimicking the very violence they claim to deplore. This contradiction requires a subconscious creation of cultural myths in which innocent targets—the sinner, the witch, the counter-revolutionary, the Jew—become the scapegoat, or surrogate victim, representing all that is wrong. In anticipation of a crisis such as the great plagues of Europe or a military attack, one type of individual is arbitrarily selected as the "real" source of danger and murdered, "sacrificed" in a religious ritual, or expelled. The scapegoat is perceived as both the cause and solution to violence (Girard and Williams, 1996).

The contemporary U.S. criminal justice system, if unchallenged, would place a great deal of unchecked power into the hands of a few, and unjust laws, corrupt police, or prosecutorial malpractice would never be exposed. Once the law defines a behavior as criminal, there is a tendency to unquestioningly accept that definition and probe no further—to let "justice" take its course. Yet, as philosophers and legal activists tell us, we endanger our

the law defines one behavior as criminal
└ it remains unquestioned

└ we endanger our liberty

liberty if we merely sit back and accept the reach and command of the law. If indeed the criminal law is a way to control the dangerous impulses lurking in many of us, then those same impulses are lurking in lawmakers and enforcers as well.

Consider Joseph Conrad's novel *Heart of Darkness,* on which the film *Apocalypse Now* was based. Conrad tells the story of Mr. Kurtz, an ivory trader who arrived in the heart of the jungle and established a highly successful business. His success was based on his discovery that natives treated him as a supernatural being, a mistaken belief that he exploited to control the natives and amass his wealth. Human heads, of "rebel" natives, were mounted near Kurtz's home to reinforce his power—even though he thought of himself as a benevolent leader. Literary analyst R.A. Foakes (2003:2) observes that "Mr. Kurtz invaded the wilderness, and the wilderness [took] a terrible vengeance on him by invading him." Mr. Kurtz was able to maintain his powerful position by following this sentiment: "Exterminate all of the brutes." Yet Conrad was not only telling a story, but using his twisted character to illustrate the coexisting impulses in all of us. On the one hand, we have a desire to exert benevolence, to achieve the praise of those who look up to us. On the other, we have the desire to exterminate our enemies. Both impulses are prompted by the same "heart of darkness."

If we agree to relax our definitions of "crime," because they may be biased by existing criminal law, and talk instead about "aggression," we see more conflicting points of view. At times aggression is not only acceptable, but encouraged and lauded—as in aggressive sales practices that may at times "fool" or "trick" consumers but are nevertheless legal. Is the law inconsistent? Do most people support aggression as long as it contributes to the functioning of a competitive society, or deals with enemies outside the borders? Perhaps contradictions built into common attitudes about aggression help to explain our fascination with news reports and fictional accounts of criminal or accidental violence.

A Short History of Criminology

Criminologists, as professionals who study crime, discuss, agree, and disagree about different issues than do neighborhood residents kicking back at the pub. While the academic criminologists will study the effect of incarceration on crime rates in society, the neighborhood group might debate how a prison cell could be made more punishing to the individual offender. Removed from the personal and concrete, most criminologists treat the study of crime from a distance, much as chemists might dispassionately write up the implications of a lab experiment.

Generally, criminologists are professionals who study three main areas of crime: (1) why laws are made, (2) why they are broken, and (3) what the societal reaction is, or should be, to the criminal offender. There are two beginnings to the history of the disciplined study of crime, or *criminology*. The first dates from the mid-eighteenth-century Enlightenment contributions of Italian philosopher Cesare Beccaria (1738-1794) and English philosopher Jeremy Bentham (1748-1832). In their era, their ideas were revolutionary because they challenged the existing arbitrary and barbaric system of criminal law and proposed a more rational system of laws and punishments that corresponded to rational views of human behavior. Their ideas constitute what is called the "classical school" of criminology, which assumes that individuals have free will and choose their behaviors based on rational calculations of expected gains and losses.

A century later the second main influence of criminology began. This was the "positivist" revolution, most closely associated with the 1876 publication of Cesare Lombroso's *The Criminal Man*. Lombroso, who was an Italian physician, proposed that the criminal was a biological "atavist"—a throwback of evolution. His claim turned out to be false, but was nonetheless influential because his research applied the scientific method of measurement and experimentation to the study of crime. *Positivism*, or the consideration of observable facts as opposed to philosophical ideals, eventually grew into a mainstream *positivist school*, as criminologists tried to emulate natural scientists by developing and testing hypotheses, measuring levels of criminality, and using their findings to support or refute theories of crime. Unlike the classical school, positivism did not assume rational free will or choice on the part of the individual, but considered how the individual was affected by "determinism," or biological, psychological, and social factors. The notion of *causality*, or cause-and-effect relationships, was introduced as positivist criminologists tested the effects of multiple factors on criminal behavior by studying and comparing individuals. More than other social science disciplines, positivist criminology became known for its multidisciplinary influences from psychology, sociology, law, and biology.

During the early part of the twentieth century, at the same time as positivist criminologists were testing and formulating theories of criminal behavior, classical criminologists continued the classical school's tradition of analyzing the state's response to crime. The most important U.S. figure in this area was August Vollmer, former chief of police in Berkeley, California, whose goal was that police, particularly administrators, "become broadly informed in the entire area of criminology and in the principles of such related areas as public administration, political science, psychology, and sociology" (Morris, 1975:127). Vollmer, in collaboration with law professor Alexander Marsden Kidd, developed a summer session program in criminology at the University of California in Berkeley in 1916. In 1933, the University expanded the program and formed an academic major in criminology, followed in succession by the formation of the Bureau of Criminology in the Department of Political Science (1939), a Master's program in Criminology (1947), and in 1950 the nation's first formal "school" of criminology, with police administrator O.W. Wilson as Dean.

August Vollmer. *With permission of the Berkeley Police Department Historical Preservation Society*

Vollmer also paved the way for the first professional organizations of criminologists. The National Association of College Police Officials (NACPO) was founded in 1941 by Vollmer and six other men, mostly former police officers, who taught "police science and administration" at the University of California at Berkeley. Five years later, the NACPO grew into the Society for the Advancement of Criminology, which defined criminology as "the study of the causes, treatment and prevention of crime" and included studies in crime investigation, prevention, and administration (Morris, 1975:128). The Society for the Advancement of Criminology was later renamed the American Society of Criminology (ASC). A series of newsletters and journals made their appearance during the 1950s. In the 1960s, women began to enter the field. By 1970, an early newsletter eventually grew into the current journal *Criminology*, which was established as the ASC's official scholarly venue. The journal's founding editorial policy described *Criminology* as "interdisciplinary," and that claim remains with the journal today.

While the growing academic discipline of criminology drew from many fields, the meaning and implications of the term "interdisciplinary" were not always consistent. For example, "social work" was one of *Criminology's* allied disciplines at the time the journal was founded, but it is no longer included in the journal's editorial policy. Albert Morris's (1975) history of the ASC suggests that social work's emphasis on "how-to-do-it" courses meant that the social work discipline was too applied for the ASC's more lofty vision of "understanding . . . what is fundamental to human experience." Criminologist Stanley Cohen (1988), however, points out that its separation from social work practice may have cost the discipline of criminology some practical insight.

Morris (1975:162) offers four different approaches on what it means to be interdisciplinary in the study of crime:

4 different approaches to crime

1. *Individualistic application:* Scholars trained in different disciplines apply their specialized knowledge to particular aspects and special areas of criminology. For example, sociologist Edwin H. Sutherland, who specialized in how individuals acquire knowledge through social interaction, studied professional fences who first apprenticed and then mastered the skills needed to buy and sell stolen property. Economist Anne Piehl has used economic theories of rational choice and cost-benefit analysis to evaluate the deterrent value of Operation Ceasefire, a program that seeks to control gang violence by escalating police responses to gang behaviors.

2. *Cooperative application:* Scholars trained in different disciplines bring their respective special knowledge and approaches to bear collaboratively on common problems. For instance, in a volume on violence against children, Joy Osofsky (1997) brought together clinical psychologists, neuropsychologists, sociologists, and educators to examine the issues of child victims of violence.

3. *Exchange and assimilation:* Scholars trained in different disciplines interact with one another in an effort to develop an improved body of concepts and principles. The Model Penal Code, written in 1962, was the product of a consortium of philosophers, legal scholars, and criminologists who worked together to develop a principled, systematic approach to sentencing criminal offenders.

4. *Some combination of the above.*

However, this fourfold typology leaves many unanswered questions. Can a Freudian psychologist studying white-collar crime, who believes that human choices are predetermined at a very early age, ever come to terms with a rational choice economist, who perceives few limitations on human choice? How would a philosopher whose main concern is that the state not exceed its proper authority, or a religion scholar whose work involves interpreting sacred admonitions about crime and punishment, deal with a biologist's contention that violent crimes have a genetic component?

Over the last century, the study of crime proved to be a compelling subject that attracted various academic disciplines to its edge, while it brought criminologists into the margins of various other disciplines. Criminologist Stanley Cohen (1988) astutely observed that the field of criminology drew not only methods, such as statistical comparisons of subgroups, and theories such as learning theory, but also academic credibility from the more established disciplines of law, psychology, and sociology. The pattern was a haphazard assimilation of other disciplines' theories or methods. Some of the mid-twentieth-century sociologists, for example, were particularly good at adapting psychological explanations into sociological methods to form new theories of crime. The ultimate goal of criminology, according to most (but not all) criminologists, was to better understand crime from a scientific point of view, in much the same way that sociology and psychology were producing new understandings of social movements and mental illness.

According to historian Michel Foucault (1980), however, the ultimate goal of criminology was not knowledge-building, but really to create a justification for the exercise of power. For Foucault, knowledge was a tool used by people in authority to maintain their power over others. Foucault criticized prison research in particular for substituting purely managerial principles for theoretical reasoning. Indeed, the field of criminology has grown with professionals who work in the criminal justice system and who may have a vested interest in importing their own organizational and professional perspectives. In challenging the hierarchy of power that is the foundation of criminal justice, "radical criminologists" of the last century, including some of the faculty at the Berkeley School of Criminology who believed that capitalism was the source of social problems such as crime, put themselves in vulnerable positions.

Box 1.1 • Suppression of Free Speech at the Berkeley School of Criminology

The influential Berkeley School of Criminology was closed in the 1970s after losing a political battle with then–California Governor Ronald Reagan, who had campaigned against "campus malcontents and filthy speech advocates" at Berkeley. Members of the University of California Board of Regents closed the school because they had financial interests in corporate and defense contracts and were threatened by the popularity of the "radical perspective" that challenged the Vietnam War and was being taught by some of the criminology faculty (Rosenfeld, 2002; Schwendinger and Schwendinger, n.d.).

Critics of criminology such as Stanley Cohen (1988) and Jock Young (1981) have pointed out that criminologists themselves are actually quite divided on such basic issues as the image of human nature, the basis of social order, the nature and extent of crime, and the understanding of how theory should affect public policy. The diversity of viewpoints among criminologists may not be all that unusual for such a young discipline, particularly given the fact that not only is human *behavior* its main subject, but human behavior that the state is organized to punish (Cohen, 1988). Within the ASC there are several subdivisions that challenge the mainstream: critical criminologists, convict criminologists, feminist criminologists, and peacemaking criminologists, to name a few.

Many *critical criminologists* today contest the traditional assumption that "the criminal" should be criminology's main subject of study. Instead they examine the making of certain laws in the first place and question whether those laws that protect powerful interests, such as those of large corporations, should exist at all, or whether more laws are needed to control those interests. A subgroup known as *convict criminologists* is composed mostly of ex-offenders who pursued advanced degrees in criminology. Some studied criminology while incarcerated in prison. Convict criminologists examine the entire crime-control system—police, courts, and prisons—from the offender's perspective. *Feminist criminologists* focus on gender inequality, and argue, for instance, that punishing female prostitutes, but not their clients, creates a double standard, and that domestic violence such as wife battering is not taken seriously by police or courts. Finally, *peacemaking criminologists* endeavor to formulate a criminology, based on religious and philosophical doctrines, that will promote a more peaceful and just society for everyone. Rather than punishing the offender through punitive retribution, peacemaking criminologists seek a peaceful resolution for the victim, offender, and community through principles of restorative justice. The distinct concerns of these various subgroups indicate one of the major divisions in criminology—who are the "real" criminals? How do we reconcile punishing the lawbreaker with the knowledge that laws are often stacked against those who are less powerful, such as the poor, racial minorities, and women?

Box 1.2 • Peacemaking Criminology

A *criminology of peacemaking*, the nonviolent criminology of compassion and service, seeks to end suffering and thereby eliminate crime. . . .

[C]rime is suffering and . . . the ending of crime is possible only with the ending of suffering. And the ending both of suffering and of crime, which is the establishing of justice, can come only out of peace, out of a peace that is spiritually grounded in our very being. To eliminate crime—to end the construction and perpetuation of an existence that makes crime possible—requires a transformation of our human being. We as human beings must *be* peace if we are to live in a world free of crime, in a world of peace.

Richard Quinney, "The Way of Peace: On Crime, Suffering, and Service" (1991).

Theory and Methods

Scholars in all disciplines—from physics to philosophy—employ certain tools to analyze the phenomena of interest to them. Some of these tools, particularly in the physical and biological sciences, take the form of technological devices, as in the case of microscopes, magnetic resonance imaging (MRI) units, and particle accelerators (atom smashers). There are, however, other, more abstract types of very important "tools" that are widely utilized by scholars in all disciplines. These are *concepts*, or *ideas* that scholars have about some aspect of physical or social reality. Concepts tend to be articulated most often as words, but sometimes as phrases.

In physics, one of the fundamental concepts for understanding the workings of the physical universe is "energy." Every physicist is thoroughly acquainted with the notion of energy—$E=mc^2$—what it is and how it works. A physicist who doesn't know about the concept of energy doesn't understand how the universe operates. Similarly, the concept of "gravity," a force of matter between bodies that have mass, is essential to understanding the motions of all physical objects. Thus, concepts like "personality" (in psychology), "social structure" (in sociology), and "evolution" (in biology) are intended to help scholars gain a better understanding of the phenomenon they propose to study, by naming, through the use of words (that is, concepts), important aspects of that phenomenon. Concepts make up a discipline's vocabulary and are the building blocks of theory.

Theory is an attempt to articulate the relationship between two or more concepts. A sociologist, for example, may want to examine the relationship between certain types of social structure and social behavior. Generally, theory has three aims in regard to a discipline's understanding of its subject matter: (1) explanation, (2) interpretation, and/or (3) critique. While not all disciplines—particularly those that are not sciences, such as philosophy and religious studies—construct theories per se, they all endeavor to explain, interpret, and/or critique aspects of the phenomenon they study in order to achieve a better understanding of it.

Explanation, which is the chief goal of theory in the natural sciences and, frequently, the social sciences, involves explaining why a particular phenomenon occurs under given circumstances. The most common type of theoretical explanation is a "causal" explanation, which has to do with identifying cause-and-effect relationships between phenomena, such as positing that high unemployment leads to crime. *Interpretation*, which has to do with an attempt to understand a phenomenon or object of study by considering it from different subjective points of view, such as female victims' perspectives on crime, is likely to characterize the theories of the social sciences and humanities. *Critique*, or critical analysis, involves understanding a phenomenon, such as the death penalty, by subjecting it to a negative examination aimed at discovering its weaknesses, flaws, and injustices, for the purpose of either strengthening it or proposing an alternative to it. Critical analysis is typically done in the social sciences and humanities.

Theory can take the form of *propositions*, statements (written as sentences) of relationships between concepts, or the form of a *conceptual framework*, a general "road map" that guides the scholar in terms of where to look to better understand the subject matter. Propositions are typically found in biology and other natural sciences and, less frequently, in behavioral and social sciences such as psychology, sociology, and economics. Conceptual frameworks are more likely the provinces of the social sciences and humanities, which includes philosophy and religious studies, and may involve the general theorizing of Marxism (in economics, sociology, philosophy), rational-choice theory (in economics and sociology), and psychoanalysis (in psychology).

Closely related to the abstract thinking found in theory is the empirical data-gathering process that underlies research. Indeed, theory and research are intimately connected in two ways: *deductively*, whereby scholars attempt to test the theory in data, and *inductively*, whereby scholars formulate theory from the data. Either way, in all disciplines, data must be gathered, and research must be done. As such, the various disciplines employ a variety of *research methods*, or specialized techniques and strategies, for obtaining information about their subject of study.

Research methodology can be quantitative or qualitative. *Quantitative research* consists of methods for obtaining statistical or numerical facts from such sources as large-scale surveys conducted by the U.S. Census Bureau, official statistical reports prepared by the FBI, or psychological assessment instruments. *Qualitative research* encompasses a variety of research techniques ranging from literary criticism to ethnographic studies/participant observation, analogical reasoning, and in-depth interviews. Quantitative research is the preferred methodology in the natural sciences and sometimes in the social and behavioral sciences, while qualitative methodology is most often used in the humanities and tends to be used in sociology and psychology as well.

What is a "Discipline"?

Criminology generally claims that it is a "discipline." Let us begin by discussing the meaning of the term. The noun "discipline" has many dictionary definitions, including "controlled behavior resulting from disciplinary training; self-control," but the academic meaning is usually "a branch of knowledge or teaching."

Yet these two meanings are related. As any student who has endured tedious lectures would suspect, the academic use of the word "discipline" has much in common with the other definitions that describe the imposition of behavioral control. From the Latin word *discere,* which means "to learn," came other Latin words including *discipulus,* which gave us the English word "pupil," and *disciplina* (instruction, knowledge), which came to mean the maintenance of order necessary for giving instruction. *Disciplina* evolved into our current English word *discipline.* Thus, the "discipline" that comes to the learner is the result of imposed study habits. The idea of discipline, originally found in teaching, gave birth to a much wider variety of meanings about behavioral discipline and many forms of self-control.

The word roots are interesting when we consider what an academic discipline is supposed to do. Why study an academic discipline? Many students would probably respond, "Because I want to get a job in that field" or "Because I enjoy it." The word roots, though, suggest that we need to study academic disciplines because, unlike our buddies at the corner pub who insist that capital punishment has to deter criminals because they "know" it would deter them, academic disciplines provide structured guidelines for how to view the world. When we take a systematic approach to understanding crime by using a discipline's assumptions, concepts, theories, and methods to question our commonsense notions about crime, we can substitute more rigorously defensible assertions. The more we study a particular discipline, the more we learn how to think about the world using disciplinary assumptions, concepts, theories, and methods such as those described in the six chapters that follow. Over time, students come to "think like psychologists," or biologists, or philosophers, not only because they emulate the approaches of their professors, but also because they begin to absorb the underlying viewpoints or perspectives of the discipline. What is important to the discipline? What is *not* important? While answers to such questions are not usually presented in an explicit way, students gradually develop a "sense" of them. By the time an M.A. or Ph.D. student chooses a thesis topic, he or she must discern which issues and methods are acceptable (i.e., relevant) to the discipline, and which are not.

If disciplinary knowledge offers a way to think systematically about human behavior, then what about multidisciplinary or interdisciplinary studies? We will again begin with a definition of terms. The knowledge that is accumulated by studying a subject such as crime can vary a great deal depending on which discipline is chosen. The process of knowledge-building is also affected by drawing on several disciplines as opposed to one. Let us now consider the language that describes how the disciplines can be used.

Disciplinary. The simplest and most common approach to understanding crime is using one theory within a single discipline, typically sociology. If two or more theories are used within the same discipline, the term used by criminologists is *integrative*. The term *integrative* would also apply to multidisciplinary and interdisciplinary perspectives on crime.

Multidisciplinary. This approach takes a cross-section of disciplines and applies them to a given subject. When the subject is crime, the usual disciplines are sociology, psychology, and biology, but increasingly criminology has considered other subjects, such as economics and philosophy. Each discipline is used for what it might contribute to the understanding of crime. Colleges and universities are traditionally set up as "multidisciplinary" to the extent that a cross-sectional array of disciplines is available to the student, though not usually focused on a single subject (notable exceptions might be professional programs such as business or nursing). If there are faculty from two departments whose expertise happens to overlap on a given subject, it may make note-taking easier, but it is likely to be a pure coincidence. A more deliberate multidisciplinary approach might take different forms. For example, two or more disciplines might focus on one topic while using the concepts, methods, and standards that they share in common. Or two disciplines, such as sociology and psychology, might divide a topic (e.g., studying small-group behavior) into nonoverlapping areas of study.

Interdisciplinary. Interdisciplinary approaches most commonly draw from two or more similar disciplines (such as from the natural sciences, the humanities, or the social sciences), but scholars can cross academic boundaries and draw from disciplines that do not ordinarily intersect, such as biology and sociology. Often there is a hierarchy of disciplines, with one dominating the others. As is discussed in Chapter Two, in criminology, the dominating discipline has tended to be sociology. Yet the ultimate goal of interdisciplinary studies is a balanced treatment of each discipline that leads to a synthesis of new knowledge about a subject. Rather than just picking and choosing one concept, theory, or method from another discipline, the interdisciplinary approach strives for a full understanding of the similarities, differences, strengths, and limitations across the disciplines.

▭▷ Transdisciplinary. Thinking in this way about the disciplines—examining how interdisciplinary linkages work, the knowledge gaps between disciplines, the types of subjects that lend themselves to interdisciplinary approaches—is known as transdisciplinary analysis.

If disciplines by definition have their own distinct identities with well-defined boundaries, vocabularies, assumptions, values, theories, methods, and so on, will problems of communicating across disciplines discourage interdisciplinary efforts? Do certain subject areas compel the use of interdisciplinary approaches despite the inherent difficulties? In the natural sciences, revolutions in thinking take place by reconstituting our ideas about the natural world. Biochemists studying human cells—who previously joined the disciplines of biology and chemistry—now work with physicists and engineers in addition to chemists and biologists. Scientists are now combining their understanding of their subject matter in ways that simply did not exist in the last century. In chemistry, new subdisciplines and inter-disciplines are being generated even now: For example, new fields include geochemistry, astrochemistry, cosmochemistry, and materials science (the study of how electronics interact with other materials, which has become the basis for the electronics industry)—of which the latter is more of an "anti-discipline," without boundaries, designed to be ever-changing so it can build on the latest knowledge.

Why Take a Multidisciplinary or Interdisciplinary Approach?

Blending disciplines to create new area studies is a growing trend in colleges and universities. Some states have designated one of their public university campuses as an exclusively "liberal arts" college featuring inter-disciplinary courses. For example, at Truman State University in Missouri, sociology professor Michael Seipel instructs his students that rural America is best understood by combining and building on the disciplines of geography, sociology, economics, and political science. Or consider Brazilian studies, which is a relatively new interdiscipline. The nation of Brazil lends itself to interdisciplinary studies in large part due to its history of military dictatorship, its rich cultural diversity, and wide extremes between the wealthy and poor. The "party atmosphere" that Brazil is superficially known for around the world is deeply complex and relates to geography, military science, sociology, anthropology, economics, and religious studies, among other disciplines. Many colleges now have well established area studies programs such as culture studies, women's studies, and Latino studies that are interdisciplinary. Recent academic concerns with the problem of terrorism have already stimulated interdisciplinary endeavors.

There are many reasons for taking multidisciplinary and interdisciplinary approaches. In general, the most important rationale for interdisciplinary education is that students need to be prepared to face a world in which boundaries of all sorts—cultural, economic, knowledge—increasingly overlap. They need to be versatile and to learn skills of processing information that will help them to understand and evaluate new developments from fields outside of their own. In addition, studying other disciplinary approaches to a similar problem teaches us the limitations of our own discipline's language, rules, techniques, methods, meanings, and so on.

Contrary to popular belief, most scientific disciplines do not make measured advances in knowledge over time, but instead are characterized by slow progress based on increasingly outdated assumptions. Not surprisingly, this state of affairs eventually leads to an intellectual crisis within the discipline, perhaps because scholars cannot ignore discrepancies between theory and fact, or because changes occur in their area of study that the discipline cannot explain (e.g., why the space shuttle fails). Recently, Cambridge University astrophysicist Stephen Hawkins retracted his once-leading theory of black holes because it does not fit into the more widely accepted string theory in physics. The response to such a retraction is what philosopher Thomas Kuhn (1962) called a "scientific revolution," in which the previously closely held assumptions are relaxed and the rules loosened. In some cases the key scholars within the discipline become convinced that a new set of assumptions should replace the old ones.

What can we say about the discipline of criminology, which not only failed to predict the substantial decline in crime during the 1990s, but made headlines predicting the opposite of what really happened: a sharp *increase* in the crime rate for the same time period? The inaccurate predictions were based on a simplistic assumption made by criminologists: that crime rates are directly related to demographics, particularly the number of adolescents and young adults. When the baby boomers' "boomlet" children would hit the streets in the 1990s, blood was expected to flow. Although the number of predicted young people was correct, the surrounding context changed dramatically. During the 1980s, the crack-cocaine "epidemic" spawned a "handgun generation" of urban juveniles who were lured into the drug trade by adult distributors seeking to evade stricter drug sentences themselves. However, despite rising numbers of young people, the drug-related street violence declined steeply during the 1990s and largely disappeared by the end of the decade as demand for crack-cocaine dissipated. After the dramatic downturn in crime occurred, many tried to explain why criminologists had been so wrong in their predictions about the crime rate.

Why did crime, notably street violence by juveniles and young adults, decrease during the 1990s? Was it the result of stepped-up efforts by police to achieve "order maintenance" by removing graffiti and strictly enforcing disorderly conduct statutes against "undesirable" individuals such as the homeless, intoxicated persons, and prostitutes? Was it due to the development of computerized mapping systems used to mobilize police forces to "hot spots" or high crime areas? Was the downturn in youth crime court-related—a result of early intervention with first-time offenders, increased incarceration rates, or use of the Racketeer Influenced and Corrupt Organization Act (the RICO law) by federal prosecutors against drug gangs? Did it have to do with the increased use of personal electronic protection devices such as home security systems? Was it due to the fact that, while the numbers of young people increased, the number of older adults also increased, thus contributing to more stable neighborhoods? Was it because of a robust economy and growth in jobs? Was it the result of efforts to support youths and families through domestic violence services and after-school programs? Or was the decline in youth crime completely unrelated to any planned intervention, but instead the result of murders of such influential rappers as Tupac Shakur and Biggie Smalls that changed young people's attitudes toward violence?

How might a true cross-section of academic disciplines explain the recent and unexpected decline in violent youth crime? How would other disciplines build on existing knowledge to help prevent crime increases such as the one that occurred in the 1980s? Drawing on Thomas Kuhn's ideas, philosopher Paul Feyerabend (1993) suggests an answer. He argues that new "paradigms," or general assumptions that direct the discipline, are typically not introduced by scholars with a deep understanding of their own discipline, but by scholars outside of the discipline who are not experts in the subject area itself. This has led some to advocate for scholarship that is unrestricted by disciplinary criteria—essentially having to worry about *no* restrictions on disciplinary thinking. A recent news item about advances in genetic engineering confirms that there may be wisdom to this approach.

Box 1.3 • Physics Professor Surprises Biologists

The natural sciences are characterized by interdisciplinary studies, but this has not been the case until the 1990s. Then, interdisciplinary projects were given a tremendous boost by the Human Genome Project, which mapped the genetic properties of the human body and provided a foundation for new assumptions about chemical and physical properties of cells. For example, a physics professor at Boston University was previously "blown off" by the biology faculty when he first inquired about the possibility of using engineering to address medical issues, but he fortunately persevered. He is now using his in-depth understanding of physics combined with a newly acquired understanding of biology to develop programmable cells that can be turned "on" and "off" by manipulating their genes (Allen, 2004).

Multidisciplinary and interdisciplinary approaches enable students to understand perspectives that might not appeal to them initially. Educational psychologists have demonstrated that there are distinct "learning styles" that influence how we select and process information. For example, psychologist David Keirsey (1998) has identified four such styles, which can be assessed by testing students with a written exam. Some students are drawn to people, others to abstract ideas, some to step-by-step solutions, and others to learning by experience. These differences might affect a student's choice of major, and then the training in the major may entrench, rather than balance out, their learning style, making them even less open to ideas outside of their major. Professionals who work with criminals or victims have not necessarily studied any of the disciplines to be discussed in this book. Although many criminal justice professionals probably have specialized in sociology or psychology, most of them have not ventured deeply into economics, biology, religious studies, or philosophy.

What are the advantages of delving into these disciplines? As we study crime, what do the various disciplines teach that prepares students for the "real world"? Are students prepared for the opposing viewpoints of crime that they must eventually encounter? Nineteenth-century Russian novelist Fyodor Dostoevsky offers a view of the complexity of crime that suggests that while courtroom adjudications may resolve cases legally, they nevertheless leave open compelling questions about the human condition.

Box 1.4 • Crime and Punishment—Fyodor Dostoevsky

Do we always know how to judge good and evil, right and wrong, whom to blame and whom to excuse? What punishment should have been imposed on homemaking guru Martha Stewart for lying to federal investigators? Or on a juvenile who kills his abuser? Are criminals calculating opportunists, or poor and culturally disadvantaged people who end up behind bars because they perceive few options?

In Dostoevsky's famous novel *Crime and Punishment*, a young man named Raskolnikov confesses to robbing two elderly women and then murdering them with an ax. The evidence at the crime scene was muddled, and there was no proof against Raskolnikov other than his confession. He did not permit his attorney to argue that he was temporarily insane, although such a case could have been made. His character, prior to the killings, offered much to be admired. While Raskolnikov was a university student, he had financially supported a dying student and later the student's dying father, leaving himself penniless. He had also rescued two little children from a house on fire and suffered burns in doing so. At the trial for the murders, he did not try to defend himself. When asked about his motive, he cited his poverty and helplessness, and his hope to redirect his life with the stolen money. He noted his shallow and cowardly nature, which was pushed to the limit by deprivation and failure. When asked what led him to confess, Raskolnikov answered that it was his heartfelt repentance. Legally, his case was resolved with a shortened sentence of eight years in prison. Morally, Dostoevsky's novel shows us the loose ends that remain even after such a sentence is imposed.

One compelling reason for the interdisciplinary study of crime is its complexity. Crime is as intricate a phenomenon as the array of human motivations for crime. Moreover, the subject of crime includes considering the punishment response, so crime is further complicated by matters involving authority, organizations, and cultures. Consider what we might call the oversimplified view of crime, the one you might overhear in a bar. Two patrons are arguing furiously. One is convinced that crime is the result of free choice, and that people are responsible for their own actions, while the other attributes criminal acts to circumstances outside of the offender's control, such as one-parent families. If you unpack these assumptions, you may learn that the first person has armed robbers in mind, while the other is talking about juvenile joyriders. But even now the arguments break down. Considering the armed robber, one might demonstrate how "choice occurs within a cage," as Karl Marx put it. Perhaps he is desperate—hungry, drug-addicted, socially or psychologically troubled. And the joyrider, although young and impressionable, nevertheless was not physically forced to take the car.

Criminologist Stanley Cohen (1988) discusses the determinism/free will debate in the context of the infamous My Lai massacre during the Vietnam War, in which most of the U.S. military troops were exonerated despite their deliberate murder of 100 Vietnamese villagers—old men, women, and children. The response of many Americans was to shift the accountability for the soldiers' acts to their superiors in the army. Even though Lt. William Calley gave the order and was prosecuted for his offense, many argued that he was made a scapegoat by the army. His Captain, Ernest Medina, who was not convicted of any crime, was also viewed with sympathy by citizens back home. Rather than blame the individuals who ordered and carried out the killings, many people preferred to blame the war itself, the U.S. culture, or the army's corrupt system. Thirty-six years later, in 2004, the human rights violations of My Lai were on many people's minds when they first saw the photographs of American soldiers humiliating and abusing Iraqi prisoners at Abu Ghraib prison in Iraq. How institutionally widespread was the practice? Were soldiers too untrained for such assignments? Or did those individuals simply choose to behave sadistically because they were in a position to do so? In this instance, criminal charges against the soldiers were swiftly filed by the army and illustrate an increased emphasis in our nation's thinking about individual responsibility.

Criminologists as professionals have been studying crime for more than a century. However, not every scholar who studies crime or takes an interest in crime is a criminologist. Scholarly disciplines give us a way of examining many parts of the human story by training our minds to be versatile as well as disciplined. Each discipline offers a systematic way of seeing the world, its human inhabitants, and imagining its future. Each discipline has its own history, assumptions, methodologies, and criteria for verifying assertions about the subjects that are studied. Moreover, every discipline creates a particular reality and emphasizes particular values. The uniqueness of each field of scholarship, its strengths as well as limitations, becomes more evident as we compare disciplines to one another. The common theme of "crime" allows the reader of this book to do that sort of comparison. How does each discipline contribute to our understanding of the criminal and of the society that punishes the criminal? How are crimes influenced by genetics, personality, socialization, government and laws, religious beliefs, morality, and rational choice? If the "universe" is a place where all things come together, the model of the "university" is an evolving mirror of the universe. When we place crime at the center of six academic disciplines, juxtaposed against one another and each dissecting the "real world," what new questions and understandings can we create?

Organization of the Text: A Multidisciplinary Approach

The purpose of this book is twofold. The primary objective is to examine six disciplines—sociology, economics, psychology, biology, philosophy, and religious studies—and how they deal with the topic of understanding crime. This multidisciplinary point of view is not the standard one used in most criminology texts, which present the assumptions, theories, and research of, say, sociology, psychology, and biology *as criminologists have come to know them and use them.* Rather, this book consists of a series of original chapters, written by experts within each discipline, who describe the current thinking *within the discipline* as it relates to crime. The disciplinary areas were chosen based on their frequency in the primary literature that criminologists read, as defined by the number of entries found in *Criminal Justice Abstracts,* a quarterly journal summarizing all such literature. Although our relative count of the frequency of each discipline in the existing literature provides an indication of criminology's current incorporation of each discipline, this does not necessarily indicate the actual potential of these disciplines in a multidisciplinary approach.

This book offers a secondary purpose as well, which is to develop an awareness of important strengths and limitations of academic disciplines. With the disciplines laid out "sideways," so to speak, in their focus on crime, the reader can begin to recognize the boundaries of the disciplines and appreciate the features that make them unique. By "holding constant" the subject matter, one can compare how various forms of academic endeavor contribute to the building of knowledge. The cross-section of disciplines offers an opportunity to examine such fundamental matters collectively as disciplinary assumptions, theories, and methods that hold true regardless of the subject matter.

There are advantages and disadvantages to this multidisciplinary approach. The main advantage is that the information provided about each discipline has not been "filtered" through the perspective of a criminologist. The "filter" has a tendency to condense information, leave out important details, and weigh the historic relevance of the discipline more so than the present or future possibilities. As a result, criminologists have become accustomed to reading what other criminologists say about economics, for example, rather than what modern-day economists themselves have to say about crime.

Box 1.5 • "Looking Sideways"

Besides looking forward, there are great dividends for those who will also look sideways. . . . Many of the most important discoveries of the future will come from those wise enough to explore the unknown territories between different disciplines. . . .

Professor Harold A. Zahl, Massachusetts Institute of Technology, inscribed on the main wall of the Stata Center for the interdisciplinary study of "intelligence sciences"—computer sciences, artificial intelligence, decision and information systems, linguistics, and philosophy.

The disadvantage of this approach is that each disciplinary chapter is written by one scholar from their field. Had we asked six other experts to write the chapters, they may indeed have come out quite differently (whereas if we asked six criminologists to write those chapters, they would have come out looking unremarkably similar). Recognizing this dilemma, each discipline is given similar treatment throughout the book so that we incorporate the same basic types of information about each discipline's approach to crime. Each of the following six chapters gives you a sense of that discipline's importance in understanding crime; offers a brief history of the discipline, including major assumptions as they relate to the study of crime as well as primary methodologies; discusses recent scholarly literature from the discipline that bears on understanding crime; ventures to speculate on future directions for the study of crime within the discipline; provides a case study, in a shaded box, that illustrates an important aspect of their disciplinary approach to understanding crime; and, finally, offers a list of recommendations for further reading.

Each discipline is complex and sheds light on a slightly different angle of crime. In the next chapter, on sociological perspectives, readers will come to understand how and why crime and incarceration are patterned by social demographics and other societal factors. In Chapter Three, on economics and crime, readers will learn how economists develop understandings and responses to crime when they assume that crime is the result of a rational thought process. Chapter Four, which looks at psychological perspectives, provides an understanding of individual differences among criminal offenders and how such differences permit explanation and "profiling" of criminal behavior. Chapter Five's biological approach considers sociobiological explanations of crime based, in part, on theories of genetics and evolution. In Chapter Six, on philosophy and crime, readers will examine how philosophers argue what the limits of law should be, based on their understanding of crime and its control. Chapter Seven's focus on religious studies provides an understanding of ways in which issues arising from religion and morality intersect with concerns about crime.

In addition, Chapters Two through Seven are each followed by a "commentary" written by a prominent criminologist with a particular interest in the discipline that is discussed in each preceding chapter. The commentaries offer the reader further insight into how criminologists might understand crime through the perspective of each discipline. In much the same way as other criminologists have stood at the edge of each discipline, these criminologists will discuss the assets that the disciplines have offered, and continue to offer, to the field of criminology, as well as the limitations of each discipline for understanding crime. At the conclusion of this volume, Chapter Eight has been prepared by a criminologist, Bruce A. Arrigo, who takes a critical and interdisciplinary perspective on the study of crime that draws on the six chapters before it. Arrigo constructs an exploratory model for a true interdisciplinary understanding of crime by assessing each discipline's contribution to understanding the intersecting themes of responsibility versus freedom; logic versus emotion; objectivity versus subjectivity; truth versus meaning; and the values of scientism versus humanism.

As they make progress through the book, astute readers may begin to discern the gaps between disciplines as areas where future discovery is most likely. Even though the chapters do not necessarily discuss how the disciplines do (or could) interact with one another, the parallel presentations can be examined for potential areas of intersection among two or more disciplines, areas that can support interdisciplinary study. This type of creative knowledge-building might appeal to certain readers in particular. As we consider the relatively young history of the academic discipline of criminology, perhaps the future direction for understanding crime will call for breadth of knowledge as well as depth, intellectual versatility, and responsiveness to new ideas.

References

Allen, S. (2004). "Shaking Up Life Sciences by Crossing Disciplines." *The Boston Globe*, (June 9):D1-5.

Cohen, S. (1988). *Against Criminology.* New Brunswick, NJ: Transaction.

Faiola, A. (2004). "Youth Violence Has Japan Struggling for Answers." *The Washington Post,* (August 9):A.01.

Feyerabend, P. (1993). *Against Method.* New York: Verso.

Foakes, R.A. (2003). *Shakespeare and Violence.* Cambridge, UK: Cambridge University Press.

Foucault, Michel (1980). "Prison Talk." In M. Foucault, *Power/Knowledge: Selected Interviews and Other Writings, 1972-1977*, pp. 37-54. Brighton, UK: Harvester Press.

Girard, R. (1989). *The Scapegoat.* Baltimore: Johns Hopkins University Press.

Girard, R., and J. Williams (1996). *The Girard Reader.* New York: Crossroad.

Keirsey, D. (1998). *Please Understand Me II: Temperament, Character, Intelligence.* Del Mar, CA: Prometheus Nemesis Books.

Kuhn, T. (1962). *The Structure of Scientific Revolutions.* Chicago: University of Chicago Press.

Lesser, W. (1994). *Pictures at an Execution: An Inquiry into the Subject of Murder.* Boston: Harvard University Press.

Morris, A. (1975). "The American Society of Criminology: A History, 1941-1974." *Criminology* (August):123-167.

Osofsky, J. (ed., 1997). *Children in a Violent Society.* New York: Guilford.

Quinney, R. (1991). "The Way of Peace: On Crime, Suffering, and Service." In H.E. Pepinsky and R. Quinney (eds.), *Criminology as Peacemaking*, pp. 3-13. Bloomington, IN: Indiana University Press.

Rosenfeld, S. (2002). "Reagan, Hoover and the UC Red Scare." *San Francisco Chronicle*, (June 9).

Schwendinger, H., and J. Schwendinger (n.d.). "Who Killed the Berkeley School of Criminology: Round Up the Usual Suspects." Unpublished manuscript.

Young, J. (1981). "Thinking Seriously About Crime." In M. Fitzgerald, G. McLennan, and J. Pawson (eds.), *Crime and Society*, pp. 248-309. London: Routledge and Kegan Paul.

Chapter Two

Sociological Perspectives on Crime

A. Javier Treviño

At the beginning of the semester, when teaching my course in criminology, I tell my students that while there are about 22 universities around the country that grant the Ph.D. in criminology, most professional criminologists have their doctoral degrees in other academic fields. I then ask my students in what field they believe most American criminologists have received their training. Inevitably someone will mention "law." They seem surprised when I tell them that very few lawyers, including criminal lawyers, know anything about the *study* of crime. Another student will then guess "law enforcement." I inform the class that while police officers may know a great deal about, say, types of crimes, surveillance techniques, and arresting procedures, they know very little about what *causes* criminal behavior. (I tell them that I have first-hand experience of this, having taught criminology to people in various branches of law enforcement.) I then ask the students to think about the criminology course they are currently taking. Why is it offered in the Sociology Department, and taught by me, a sociologist? The fact of the matter is that while some American criminologists are trained in biology, psychology, psychiatry, economics, political science, or criminal justice—and indeed, a few may even be lawyers and police officers—a disproportionate number of them have degrees in *sociology*.

There are two reasons for having this short discussion with my criminology students early in the course. First, it is to get them to realize that if they want to understand criminal behavior, it is a good idea to also study social behavior; that if they want to explain the crime problem, they had better know something about social problems. Given that the study of social behavior and social problems has historically been the purview of sociology, it seems only logical that the behavior of criminals and the problem of crime should also be the concern of sociology. Second, it is to inform the students that, while we certainly pay attention to biological and psychological influences, the field of criminology is currently dominated by theories that principally consider sociological factors in attempting to explain the causes of crime. For most of its hundred-year existence, theoretical criminology has followed in the footsteps of sociological criminology.

The Emergence of Sociological Criminology

For all intents and purposes we can say that sociological criminology began with the renowned French sociologist, Emile Durkheim (1858-1917). Durkheim believed that *sociology*—the scientific study of human society and social behavior—could explain much of the phenomenon of crime. While Durkheim's theories are complex, they laid the foundation for a significant portion of sociological criminology and influenced the theorizing of others. In this section I will not discuss all of Durkheim's sociological ideas that relate to crime, only his concepts of "social facts" and "normal" crime.

Durkheim began his sociological analysis of crime from two premises. To begin with, he recognized that crime is a *social fact*—a patterned force in society that influences an individual's thinking, feelings, and behavior, on the one hand, and is influenced by social characteristics that he called "currents," on the other. To take a contemporary example, in high-crime urban neighborhoods, residents may believe that they are potential victims of robbery (thinking), experience a sense of vulnerability to their surroundings (feelings), and, as a consequence, may purchase a handgun and spend much of their time indoors (behavior). Although the academic discipline of sociology did not yet exist, Durkheim insisted that social facts should be systematically analyzed because they explain variation in behavior across segments of society and over time. Durkheim, whose nineteenth-century work was later translated into English during the twentieth century (1951), conducted an extensive study of suicide, an act normally believed to result from a private and personal decision, in part to refute the assumption that behavior was motivated only by individual psychology. In the case of suicide, he found that social factors including religious affiliation, societal politics, and characteristics of occupational groups could predict the frequency of individuals taking their own lives in a given society.

Durkheim's second premise is that there has never existed a society without crime. Imagine a society of saints, he says, "a prefect cloister of exemplary individuals" (1966:68). Even in such a situation the slightest infraction against the rules will be punished and regarded as a "crime." Crime, then, is not only *normal*; it is also a *necessary* part of all societies. Let us take in turn Durkheim's two ideas about crime, that it is normal and that it is necessary.

First of all, crime is normal because it is found everywhere. A society without crime is impossible. Indeed, if we were to ever find a society without crime, Durkheim contends, it would be characterized as an abnormal or "pathological" condition. He infers from an absence of crime that such a society would have to impose very harsh measures to keep its citizens from breaking the laws. For example, while there are no societies without crime, there have existed, and currently do exist, societies with very low rates of such crimes as prostitution, murder, robbery, gang delinquency, and so on. The former Nazi Germany was such a society. Durkheim believed that the price to be paid for very low crime rates is twofold: (1) the citizens of these totalitarian or authoritarian regimes have very little freedom in expressing individual originality, through their words or actions, and, as such, (2) the possibility for progressive social change in these societies is minimal. Moreover, because progressive social change is desirable, both crime and the criminal are necessary; that is to say, they provide a useful role in this progression.

Durkheim gives as an example of the social-change utility of crime the case of Socrates, the noted Greek philosopher. According to ancient Athenian culture, Socrates was considered a criminal for simply espousing his philosophical beliefs. In 399 B.C.E., he was arrested, tried, and convicted of a crime, namely, "the independence of his thought" (Durkheim, 1966:71). Socrates was subsequently executed by means of a poisoned cup of hemlock, but, according to Durkheim, his death was not in vain. In Durkheim's view, Socrates' crime stimulated progressive change rather than stifled new ideas. Durkheim observed that Socrates' case aroused the public and "served to prepare a new morality and faith which the Athenians needed, since the traditions by which they had lived until then were no longer in harmony with the current conditions of life" (Durkheim, 1966:71). The case of Socrates—of the criminal as agent of progressive social change—is not unique. Periodically, throughout history, there have been criminals who have, through their crimes, brought about social reforms. Consider, for example, that in 1963, Martin Luther King Jr. was arrested and held in the Birmingham, Alabama, city jail for engaging in illegal demonstrations—sit-ins, marches, and so forth—against the state's racial segregation laws and practices. King's involvement in these illegal activities of civil disobedience, in these "crimes," served to progress the Civil Rights movement and end the Jim Crow laws of segregation. These two cases, that of Socrates and King, illustrate that there are some laws that need to be broken if society is to progress.

Durkheim's "crime as normal" concept and his other ideas about crime and deviance did much to further the development of sociological theorizing about crime. It is to a general discussion of sociological theories of crime that we now turn.

Box 2.1 • On the Duty of Civil Disobedience

Unjust laws exist: shall we be content to obey them, or shall we endeavor to amend them, and obey them until we have succeeded, or shall we transgress them at once? . . . If the injustice is part of the necessary friction of the machine of government, let it go, let it go: perchance it will wear smooth—certainly the machine will wear out. If the injustice has a spring, or a pulley, or a rope, or a crank, exclusively for itself, then perhaps you may consider whether the remedy will not be worse than the evil; but if it is of such a nature that it requires you to be the agent of injustice to another, then I say, break the law. Let your life be a counter-friction to stop the machine.

Henry David Thoreau, "On the Duty of Civil Disobedience" (1849).

Sociological Theories of Crime

In their attempts at understanding crime, sociologists have generally asked, and tried to answer, two basic questions. The first one is: Why do individuals commit crime? And the second, related question is: Why do some communities and certain populations have higher rates of crime than others? Simply put, the broader question is: What are those social factors that *cause* crime? In order to *explain* the causes of crime, sociologists have developed theories that examine the factors that produce criminal behavior and high crime rates.

A *theory* is a scientific explanation for a *causal relationship* between two (or more) measurable phenomena (a change in *X* causes a change in *Y*). For example, an increase in poverty leads to an increase in crime. Theorists might first observe an increase in the poverty rate that is followed by an increase in the crime rate. Then the theorist would develop an explanation demonstrating the sociological connections between poverty and crime to rule out the possibility that the poverty-crime correlation is merely a coincidence. Any phenomenon that can be measured is called a variable. A *variable*, then, is a phenomenon that can be measured either mathematically (e.g., the degree of poverty) or by categories, as this or that type (e.g., sex: male or female). Sociological theories of crime look at variables that have to do with social structure, social process, or social conflict.

Social structure is a vague term, but it generally refers to a society's (or group's) "framework." This framework controls various aspects of social life, thus making everyday activities fairly regular and predictable. As such, social structure gives *order* and *stability* to society. For example, even before you walk into your criminology class for the first time, you already have a good sense as to what type of behavior you can expect from the other students (e.g., sitting at their desks, taking notes, raising their hands to ask a question) and from your professor (e.g., lecturing in front of class, writing on the chalkboard). The reason for this predictability is because the social structure of the classroom consists of, among other things, *norms,* or rules on how to behave, and *roles,* or patterns of behavior followed by the students and professor. In addition to norms and roles, those factors that make up the social structure of the larger society (let's say the United States as a whole) include *statuses,* or the social positions that correspond to the different roles; *values,* or standards of desirability and goodness; and *culture,* or style of life; as well as *social institutions* such as the family, education, and the economy. Social structural explanations of juvenile crime might include neighborhood resources, teenage unemployment rates, and number of parents per household.

Social process refers to the dynamic aspect of social *interactions* through which individuals define their everyday reality. People understand their social lives through ongoing *communication* with others. Sociologists who examine social process, therefore, pay special attention to how people give *meaning* to the behavior of others as well as to various social situations. For example, students and professors abide by the norms and roles of the classroom—that is, they generally behave as they are expected to behave—because they *define* that situation as a classroom, and not as a party or a funeral. Social process variables measure precursors to crime, such as associations with criminal offenders and weak attachments to family members that contribute to the socialization of the offender.

Social conflict refers to the notion that social life is rife with all sorts of disagreements, frictions, and antagonisms, either between individuals or between social units (e.g., interest groups, social classes, populations). The issue of *power*—the ability to get others to do what you want them to do, even if it is against their will—is at the heart of most social conflicts. Because individuals or groups do not all have the same amount of power (authority, influence, clout), they usually compete against each other for it. In a diverse society such as the United States there are many individuals and groups with different and competing *interests* who will want to have as much power as possible in order to maintain or advance those interests. Those groups with enough political and/or economic power determine what the criminal law should be and use it to protect their interests. Consider, for example, how legislation is influenced by such powerful political interest groups involved on opposite sides of the issue of gun control—those groups, like the National Rifle Association, that oppose a legislative ban on handguns, and those groups, like Handgun Control, Inc., that support such a ban.

In general, then, there are three main sociological *perspectives*, or points of view, from which sociologists have developed theories to explain the causes of crime: (1) the social structure perspective, (2) the social process perspective, and (3) the social conflict perspective. In the sections that follow I briefly describe each of the three perspectives, provide a sketch of the main types of theories that are informed by these perspectives, and give a few select examples of specific theoretical statements on crime belonging to these theories.

The Social Structure Perspective

The social structure perspective is a *macro*, or large-scale, point of view that examines the relationships between such factors as norms, roles, statuses, values, culture, and the various social institutions. Sociologists working from this perspective are interested in understanding why a community's order and stability become disrupted. There are generally three categories of theories that consider social structural factors and their disturbance: (1) social disorganization theories, (2) anomie theories, and (3) subculture theories.

Social Disorganization Theories

The concept of *social disorganization*, which emerged in the writings and research of sociologists at the University of Chicago during the 1920s and 1930s, broadly refers to the social condition in which a community's norms, values, and institutions—such as the family, commercial establishments, schools, and social service agencies—have broken down. As a consequence, individual behavior is not as strictly regulated, and the outcome may be high rates of crime in that community. But what causes a community's social disorganization in the first place? The Chicago School sociologists pointed to several factors, including rapid shift in populations, high unemployment, deteriorated housing, low income levels, and large numbers of single-parent households. Thus, social disorganization theory links high crime rates to neighborhood structure.

In their effort to study various social problems, the Chicago School sociologists developed a model of analysis in which they mapped out the city of Chicago into a ring of five concentric circles, or zones. Each zone possessed within it a unique community of people with a unique social structure, in regard to norms, values, culture, and so on. In Zone II in particular (what the Chicago sociologists called "the zone in transition"), they found different types of people living in various racial and ethnic communities, such as Chinatown, Little Sicily, and the "Black Belt." In other words, Zone II had the largest numbers of foreign-born citizens who had recently settled there, and it was in this transitional zone that the greatest amount of social disorganization was to be found.

The social disorganization theory of crime was popularized by the work of two Chicago sociologists, Clifford R. Shaw and Henry D. McKay (1942), who saw a connection between life in transitional slum areas in the city, such as Zone II, and high rates of juvenile delinquency. In mapping delinquency rates throughout various zones of the city, Shaw and McKay observed that the areas of heaviest concentration of delinquency appeared to be in the transitional inner-city communities of Zones I (the central city) and II (the immigrant slum communities). By contrast, those communities farthest from the city's center, Zones IV and V (the suburbs), had correspondingly lower delinquency rates. Shaw and McKay stated that, in the transitional immigrant neighborhoods of the inner city, many diverse cultures and values competed and conflicted with each other, thus making it hard for people to know which ones to follow. What is more, these communities, even when their ethnic composition changed, were the most susceptible to the forces of rapid social change and persistent poverty. These inner-city neighborhoods had all the earmarks of social disorganization. It was here that social institutions had broken down and could no longer maintain effective control over their inhabitant's behavior. Shaw and McKay concluded that in these disorganized communities delinquency was likely to emerge.

Box 2.2 • Concentric Zones

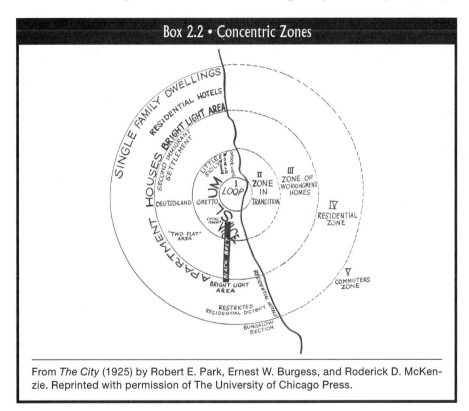

From *The City* (1925) by Robert E. Park, Ernest W. Burgess, and Roderick D. McKenzie. Reprinted with permission of The University of Chicago Press.

Anomie Theories

A second theoretical category of the social structure perspective consists of anomie theories. The classical statement in this tradition was formulated by the sociologist Robert K. Merton (1938) in attempting to explain why the lower classes tend to have the highest rates of crime. Merton uses the term *anomie* to refer to the socially structured *strain* that results when there is a contradiction between a person's aspiration to attain the cultural goal of success, and the lack of legitimate means for attaining that goal.

According to Merton, American culture encourages everyone to strive for success—typically measured in terms of wealth, material goods, and prestige. However, because of their disadvantaged position in the social structure, people in the lower classes may be unable to achieve success through socially approved means such as hard work, formal education, and thrift. As a result, they may feel anger, frustration, and resentment. One alternative available to them is to *innovate*, that is to creatively use illegal means—such as theft, drug dealing, gambling, and prostitution—for obtaining success. In short, Merton explains crime as a negative consequence that stems from poor people's lack of legitimate opportunities in the social structure.

Subculture Theories

Subculture theory is the third variation of the social structural perspective. A *subculture* is simply a culture, or a way of life, with it own unique norms and values, that exists within the dominant culture. In U.S. society, the dominant culture is characterized by middle-class norms and values that stress hard work, delayed gratification (postponement of rewards), formal education, and discipline. However in lower-class neighborhoods, where people experience life as frustrating and dispiriting, a distinct lifestyle, or subculture, develops with its own set of norms and values. Because these lower-class norms and values tend to emphasize such unconventional behaviors as immediate gratification, street smarts, and risk-taking, they are in conflict with those of the dominant culture. As such, they are regarded by the larger society as "deviant" behaviors.

Beginning with the seminal book *Delinquent Boys: The Culture of the Gang* (1955), Albert K. Cohen first proposed a theory that, contrary to Merton's strict focus on social structure, earnestly considered subculture as a context for the expression of juvenile delinquency. Seeing the delinquent gang as a lower-class subculture with its own peculiar values that are in opposition to those of middle-class society, Cohen explained delinquent behavior as a reaction to middle-class values that lower-class youths reject. Engaging in "non-utilitarian, malicious, and negativistic" delinquent behaviors—such as vandalism, petty theft, and gang wars—is a way by which lower-class youths could gain status among their peers.

Elaborating on Cohen's subculture theory Walter B. Miller (1958) identified the unique subculture—with its distinct value orientations, which he called *focal concerns*—that characterizes lower-class society. In Miller's view, the expression of these focal concerns by lower-class youths promotes delinquency. The lower-class focal concerns that Miller noted include trouble, toughness, smartness, excitement, fate, and autonomy.

"Trouble," which refers to being in trouble with the law or staying out of trouble, is a dominant concern of lower-class people. "Toughness," which includes such traits as masculinity, bravery, and physical strength, may be defined by displays of fighting prowess. "Smartness," which is equated with cunning, conning, and "street sense" rather than with level of education or high IQ, may be demonstrated in hustling, con artistry, and gambling. The focal concern of "excitement," which has to do with the constant search for thrills, may result in risky behavior involving drinking, drug abuse, or "scoring" with women. "Fate," which includes the view that most things that happen to people are beyond their control and that nothing can be done about them, is based on the observation in lower-class communities that in order to be successful, one needs to get the right breaks or be in the right place at the right time. Finally, a concern for "autonomy" is based on the characteristic of self-reliance, which is admired in lower-class communities. Autonomy also may be perceived as a resentment of authority and rules.

In addition to these focal concerns, Miller identified other social conditions typically found in poor areas that produce a distinctive lower-class subculture that may promote illegal or violent behavior. He observed that lower-class families are frequently headed by females, so that boys do not have a masculine role model and therefore acquire an exaggerated sense of masculinity, or "toughness." What is more, crowded conditions in lower-class homes mean that the boys tend to hang out on the street, where they can form gangs. When the focal concerns interact with these and other such social conditions of the lower-class culture, the outcome, says Miller, is the creation of a "generating milieu" for gang delinquency.

The Social Process Perspective

The social process perspective is a *micro*, or small-scale, viewpoint that looks at such factors as interactions, communication, and the various meanings and definitions that people give to social situations. Sociologists who employ this perspective are interested in understanding how behavior patterns are communicated and how those communications define social settings, as well as how such processes of society as schooling, work life, family life, and peer relations affect people's behavior. There are generally three categories of theories that consider social process factors and their influence on behavior: (1) social learning theories, (2) social control theories, and (3) social labeling theories.

Social Learning Theories

According to social learning theories people learn the techniques and attitudes of crime from close intimate relations with criminal peers. The most prominent of the social learning theories that endeavors to explain why people become criminal is Edwin H. Sutherland's (1947) theory of *differential association*.

The theory of differential association states that learning criminal behavior involves learning three things on the part of the individual. First, it means mastering certain specific techniques for successfully committing a crime. For example, in becoming a professional "torch," an arsonist, a person has to know about the techniques of effectively setting fire to a building without leaving tell-tale signs of intentional arson. It means that the arsonist needs to know to use a cigarette lighter rather than a match, to use solid fuels available at the scene if possible, and if a liquid fuel is brought to the scene, it means to know to put it in a container (made from, for example, waxed paper) that disintegrates thoroughly and will be undetectable in the postfire debris. Second, the learning of criminal behavior involves acquiring the appropriate motives, drives, rationalizations, and attitudes that justify violations of criminal laws. For instance, people must have sufficient and compelling reasons to engage in the crime. Finally, people must learn general "definitions favorable to violation of law." This means that how people define the social conditions they experience will determine whether they partake in criminal behavior. For example, if someone sees an opportunity (and has mastered the required skills) to counterfeit $20 bills as a way of getting rich quick, he or she may engage in that behavior.

According to Sutherland, people learn these ideas principally in the process of communicative interaction with their most intimate social companions—family, friends, peers—who have the greatest influence on their criminal behavior and attitude development. In Sutherland's theory, crime is caused by associating with people who transmit "definitions" that favor violations of the law. This, he says, is the principle of differential association.

Social Control Theories

Social control theories examine how certain social processes of individual relationships—particularly those involving relationships within families, peer groups, schools, churches, and so on—control people's activities so that they are largely involved in conventional behavior. This helps to explain why most people follow most of the rules most of the time. It also explains the opposite: why some people, who are not constrained by these social processes, break the rules and deviate.

The most popular version of social control theory is Travis Hirschi's (1969) theory of *social bonds*. According to Hirschi, most people are controlled by their bonds, or ties, to conventional society and to conventional others (such as friends, parents, neighbors, teachers, and employers). Crime occurs when the processes that bind people to society are weakened or broken. This means that social control is lessened, and people are free to engage in crimes and other uncontrolled behaviors. Hirschi maintains that a social bond consists of four main elements: attachment, commitment, involvement, and belief.

"Attachment" refers to the strength of a person's affectionate ties to conventional others such as parents, peers, coworkers, and so on. Simply put, if a person's associates are oriented toward law-abiding behavior, then the greater the attachment to these associates, the less likely that person is to engage in criminal behavior.

A second element is "commitment," which refers to the degree to which a person's time, energy, and effort are invested in conventional ways of behaving. The more people gain by being involved in conventional activities, like getting an education and saving money for the future, the less likely that they will want to jeopardize these gains by being involved in crime. On the other hand, people who lack a commitment to conformity, and thus have relatively little to lose, are more likely to be involved in risk-taking behavior, such as shoplifting, auto theft, and drug dealing.

The third element, "involvement," has to do with the proportion of a person's time engaged in the pursuit of conventional activities. Heavy involvement in socially acceptable activities, having to do with school, work, family, recreation, and so on, leaves little time for getting into trouble with the law. This element is based on the commonsense observation that being busy restricts opportunities for criminality. The idea of involving high-risk inner-city youths with conventional late-night recreational sports was the impetus behind the "midnight basketball" programs that developed in Harlem, Philadelphia, Chicago, and other cities. As an intervention and outreach program, midnight basketball is intended as a form of crime prevention by keeping youths busy in conventional activities (in this case with playing basketball), so that they don't have the time, energy, or opportunity to engage in delinquency.

The final element of the social bond has to do with the degree of "belief" that a person has regarding the conventional norms, values, and laws of society. For example, the more people believe they should obey the rules of society, the less likely they are to violate those rules. Conversely, the less they believe in the rules, the more likely that they will participate in illegal acts. In sum, the four elements of the social bonds have a controlling effect on delinquency.

Social Labeling Theories

The third branch of the social process perspective, social labeling theories, explain how behavior becomes *defined* as criminal. Sociologists who employ social labeling theories maintain that no behavior is intrinsically criminal. A behavior is bad or evil only when society defines it as such. This means that people are criminal only because they have been so *labeled*. For example, during the Middle Ages in Europe, scores of people (some scholars estimate close to one million) were put to death (frequently in very torturous ways) for the crime of witchcraft. While there are still peo-

---

Box 2.3 • Shooting for the Basket, and in the Process, for a Better Life

The stampeding sounds of sneakers echoed through the second-floor gymnasium at the YMCA on Riverdale Avenue here, as Randy's Bus and Van team squared off against the team from Saturn of White Plains in a ferocious basketball game.

The Yonkers program is part of New York Midnight Basketball, which has leagues currently in Manhattan, the Bronx and Brooklyn as well as a women's league. A sister program exists in Albany. The program targets an inner-city population ages 17 to 26. New York Midnight Basketball, founded by Gov. Mario M. Cuomo in 1994, serves about 500 people a year.

The games, which begin at 10 and 11:30 P.M., are held two nights a week. In order to play, participants have to attend pre-game workshops on topics like résumé writing and interviewing techniques; AIDS awareness and health-related issues like alcohol and drug abuse; preparation for the high school equivalency diploma and applying for college financial aid, and conflict-resolution skills. Some coming workshops will even include job-recruiting sessions from local employers. From the 1994 New York Midnight Basketball program in New York City, about 40 percent of the participants moved on to college or full-time jobs. Each participant is scheduled for one game and one workshop each week.

Merri Rosenberg, *New York Times*, August 6, 1995. p. 13WC.1

---

ple today who identify themselves as witches, and while some may consider these witches, along with their beliefs and practices, as odd, they are not generally regarded as criminals deserving of punishment. What has changed is society's *reaction* to the identity of "witch" and the practice of witchcraft. We no longer regard witches as criminals or consider witchcraft a felony.

Frank Tannenbaum (1938), an early pioneer in labeling theory, stated that if relatively harmless acts of youths—such as minor vandalism, joyriding, and sexual exploration—are interpreted unfavorably by the community, the juvenile becomes viewed as bad and evil not only by others, but by himself or herself. In other words, the negative labels—"delinquent," "incorrigible" "hooligan," "menace," and so on—given to the adolescent by law enforcement agencies, parents, teachers, and other authority figures, become the basis of his or her personal identity. Once this negative, or stigmatized, self-image is accepted by the teen, he or she may seek the company of others similarly labeled. As Tannenbaum puts it, "the person becomes the thing he is described as being." Tannenbaum refers to this example of *symbolic interaction,* or communication of powerful symbols from one individual to another, as the *dramatization of evil*.

The Social Conflict Perspective

In analyzing social phenomena, sociologists operating from the social conflict perspective focus on the problems of dissensus, conflict, and coercion. Accordingly, conflict theorists operate from two premises: that every society experiences social conflict, and that every society involves the coercion of some of its members by others. Conflict in society is typically seen as resulting either from the inequalities of *political power*, or from the inequalities of *economics*. In the case of political inequalities, it is said that there is a *conflict of group interests*; in the case of economic inequalities, it is said that there is *class conflict*. In general, there are two main categories of theories that consider these two types of conflicts: (1) group conflict theories, and (2) Marxist theories.

Group Conflict Theories

Group conflict theorists assume an ongoing struggle between a variety of organized "interest groups" that are either competing for *resources*—those things that people want and attempt to acquire, such as land, wealth, power, or status—or are involved in a conflict of *values*—traditional beliefs based on religion, politics, or morality. The winner in this struggle over resources or values gains the power, through legislation, to decide which behaviors are legal and illegal.

The classic statement on crime from this position is provided in George B. Vold's (1958) *theory of group conflict*. Vold saw society as a collection of different interest groups involved in an ongoing series of moves and countermoves through which they vie for power. Those groups that gain an advantage by political power are able to influence the passage of criminal law, and thus define as criminal those behaviors that threaten their interests, that is, their resources and values. Consequently, Vold saw those persons who are most likely to be officially defined and processed as criminals—gang members, mafiosi, saboteurs—as losers in a social struggle for control of the police power of the state.

Vold did not presume that criminal behavior was inherently harmful to society. Consider Vold's example of conscientious objectors, who, during wartime, refuse to participate in war activity for political or moral reasons. Conscientious objectors are considered criminals because they are members of a minority group whose beliefs and behaviors (pacifism at all times) are legally opposed by the more politically powerful majority group supporting the war effort. For Vold, criminal behavior is minority group behavior, and its development is a political process.

Marxist Theories

Marxist theorists see a wide variety of social ills—from poverty to racism, suicide to drug abuse—as ultimately stemming from *capitalism*, the economic system that is characterized by the private ownership of economic goods and that allows individuals to freely pursue monetary profit through the exchange of those economic goods. Capitalism makes for the *unequal* distribution of economic goods, thus giving rise to various *social classes*, or groupings of people based on their economic standing in society. Poverty, for example, is one consequence of capitalism because the upper classes, who possess the most wealth and political power, take advantage of the lower classes (by making a profit off their labor, for instance) and thus keep them at the bottom of the class system. A conflict for economic resources exists between the different social classes in a capitalist society. The consequence is that those with economic and political power control the legal definition of crime and the way in which the criminal justice system enforces the law.

Marxist sociologist Richard Quinney (1977) sees predatory street crimes such as robbery and burglary, which are typically committed by members of the lower classes, as an inevitable outcome of inequality in capitalist societies. He describes these street crimes as crimes of "accommodation," meaning that they are the logical behaviors of people who have been brutalized by the dire economic conditions of poverty and unemployment. Quinney argues that almost all crimes engaged in by the poor are necessary for their survival; it is their way of "getting by." Quinney's Marxist analysis also recognizes crimes of "domination and repression" caused by capitalist power structures, although they may not be officially recognized as crimes in legal codes that are influenced by capitalist interests. Such crimes include police corruption, price fixing, environmental pollution, political assassination of foreign leaders, oppression of the poor through the "welfare state," and contributing to the social injustices of sexism, racism, and economic exploitation. As such, Quinney maintains that crime is either directly or indirectly produced by the economic inequalities of capitalism.

In sum then, three general sociological perspectives—focusing on structure, process, and conflict—inform the types of theorizing, that is, the kinds of explanations of crime and criminal behavior, proffered by sociological criminologists. We now look at the types of research methods they employ in carrying out their research studies.

Research Methods and the Sociological Study of Crime

Generally speaking, sociologists utilize several *research methods*, or strategies for obtaining empirical information, in their study of crime and criminals. In this section, I discuss only four of the most commonly applied methods.

The first and most popular research method involves the use of *crime rates* that demonstrate the "prevalence" (percentage of the population) and "incidence" (frequency of occurrence) of crime in a certain region or sector. Crime rates are typically obtained from three main sources: (1) officially reported crime statistics, (2) victim surveys, and (3) self-report surveys.

Government agencies such as the Federal Bureau of Investigation and the U.S. Department of Justice annually make available *official statistics* on crimes and offenders. The largest and most widely used of these data sets is the FBI's Uniform Crime Reports, which present information on crimes reported to police and arrest patterns for particular crimes. *Victim surveys*, such as the National Crime Victimization Survey, sponsored by the Bureau of Justice Statistics of the U.S. Department of Justice, involve asking crime victims specific questions about their encounters with criminals. Finally, *self-report surveys* are given, in the form of a questionnaire, to people who are asked to provide information on the type and frequency of illegal acts they have committed in the recent past. Regardless of which of these three sources, or any combination of them, is used to obtain data on crime, the next step is for researchers to take these crime rates and relate them to various social factors such as the economy, population density, and region. For instance, the FBI's Uniform Crime Reports show that crime rates vary by region. Compared to the other regions of the United States, the South, which consists of states including Georgia, Alabama, and South Carolina, has consistently had higher rates of crime in almost all crime categories, but especially homicide. Sociologist Raymond Gastril (1971) explains the South's persistently high murder rate through a type of subculture theory that he calls the "Southern regional culture of violence."

Another, related research method involves the identification of personal or demographic *traits*—such as social class, race, gender, and age—among persons regarded as criminals. For example, gender-related crime patterns have consistently revealed significant differences in crime and arrest rates and in types of crime involvement. All common sources show that crime has been and still is a predominantly male behavior. However, they also indicate gendered preferences for certain crimes. For example, males are more likely to be involved in "serious" crimes, such as aggravated assault, robbery, and burglary, whereas females have greater involvement in prostitution-type offenses and minor property crimes. Along with gender, the most significant demographic trait to have an impact on criminal involvement is age. It has always and everywhere been the case that the proportion of the population involved in serious crime tends to peak in adolescence or early adulthood and then decline with age. Simply put, young people account for a disproportionate amount of crime is all societies, and young men represent an even greater number.

The third research method, the *life history*, is used in describing the criminal as an individual involved in a life of crime. In this method a previously or currently active offender is interviewed and/or guided to write

Edwin H. Sutherland. *WIth permission of the American Sociological Association*

about his or her personal experiences with crime and criminals and their way of life. Perhaps the most famous of these records is *The Professional Thief* (1937), written by self-defined thief "Chic Conwell," given an alias to protect his identity, and the sociological criminologist Edwin H. Sutherland. In this study, Conwell provides Sutherland with a revealing, first-hand account of the professional lives of pickpockets, shoplifters, and confidence tricksters, and how they learned the techniques of stealing and succeeded (or did not succeed) in the profession of theft. Sutherland explains the origin and development of the professional thief through an early version of his differential association theory. He states that a person becomes a professional thief through the processes of "recognition and tutelage" by other professional thieves.

The last research method used in the sociological study of crime to be discussed here is *participant observation*, or the direct study of criminals in their natural setting. Because of the potential danger to the researcher of working in a criminal setting, to say nothing of the ethical issues that may arise from the study (e.g., should the researcher report a crime that he or she has witnessed?), participant observation is used infrequently. Nevertheless, this technique has produced some penetrating accounts of criminals and their environment. One of the more famous of these participant observer studies is Francis A.J. Ianni's *A Family Business: Kinship and Social Control in Organized Crime* (1972). For two and one-half years, Ianni observed and participated in the various activities of the Lupollo crime family of New York and, as such, gained a rare inside view into the world of Italian-American organized crime.

Current Scholarship in Sociological Criminology

In their effort at conducting empirical research, sociologists of crime continue to rely primarily on the use of crime data derived from official sources such as the U.S. Bureau of the Census, the Bureau of Justice Statistics, and the Federal Bureau of Investigation, as well as on various self-report surveys, such as the National Household Survey of Drug Abuse, which charts trends in drug abuse among the general population. Thus, the bulk of sociological research on crime deals predominantly with statistical data. Indeed, most of the professional journals in which sociologists are likely to publish their crime studies—for example, *American Sociological Review*, *Ameri-*

can Journal of Sociology, Social Forces, Social Problems, Criminology, and *Crime & Delinquency*—tend to be highly statistical. While a few researchers make use of the more qualitative methods, such as the life history and participant observation, it appears likely that the future direction of sociological research on crime will continue to be dominated by the quantitative approach. While this approach tends to focus on measuring crime rates and traits, some of these studies seek to empirically test the validity of existing theories such as anomie, social learning, and social control.

As for current work in the development of sociological theories of crime, there are two general trends. The first is to advance the legacy of a particular theory that has had relatively wide acceptance by considering the more recent empirical research and theorizing what has been added to that tradition. Freda Adler and William Laufer's *Advances in Criminological Theory: The Legacy of Anomie* (1995) is a prime example of such an effort. The second trend is *theory integration,* or the attempt to identify commonalities in several theories in order to produce a new more general theory that explains more than any of the combined theories alone. One of the best examples of theory integration is Michael Gottfredson and Travis Hirchi's *A General Theory of Crime* (1990), in which they integrate concepts from social control theory and other sociological traditions along with concepts from sociobiology and psychology.

It is well beyond the scope of this chapter to discuss all of the various ways in which sociology informs the study of crime. However, even in this brief presentation of sociological criminology, there are two important points we can take away. The first is that, in their effort to better understand the causes of crime, sociologists have formulated a variety of theories focused on structure, process, and conflict. These theories consider how such social facts as culture and institutions, interactions and communications, and power and inequalities are associated with crime. Even if these theories don't always explain the causes of crime, they at least serve to guide us in better understanding crime and criminal behavior.

The second point is that sociologists have relied on several research methods for obtaining data on the relationship between crime and certain populations. By utilizing quantitative data like the FBI's Uniform Crime Reports, researchers have determined which populations have the highest arrest rates; by employing qualitative techniques such as the life-history method, sociologists have derived detailed depictions of the offender's social world.

Keeping these two points about theory and methods in mind, in the remainder of this chapter I will focus on a topic that is informed by many of the sociological approaches just discussed: the disproportionate number of young black men involved in the criminal justice system. However, before I enter into a substantive discussion of this topic, a brief commentary is in order.

To begin with, it is important to acknowledge that sociological criminology is helpful in analyzing—that is, in explaining, interpreting, and evaluating—various concrete issues related to crime (for example, the fairness of the current drug laws as well as the necessity of critiquing the criminal justice system on its patterns of arrest, incarceration, and sentencing). We have already seen how Durkheim's concept of "crime as normal" helps us to understand why it was necessary to challenge the moral convictions of ancient Athens as well as the "Jim Crow" racial segregation laws of the Deep South. Durkheim's sociological ideas about crime, therefore, provide a rationale for the criminal actions of Socrates, Martin Luther King Jr., and many other social reformers. Similarly, the social conflict perspective helps us to understand that the Jim Crow laws were unjust and, as such, needed to be violated. The upshot is that sociological criminology, with its theories and methods, is highly instrumental in understanding many crime issues, including the racial inequality that exists in the U.S. criminal justice system.

Racial Inequality in the Criminal Justice System: The Case of Young African-American Men

While African-American men made up about 4 percent of the general population in 2001, they constituted nearly *one-half*—47 percent—of the prison population. Nationwide, black men were incarcerated at 9.6 times the rate of white men (Human Rights Watch, 2000). In 2000, 38 percent of all adults on probation and 44 percent of all adults on parole, were black (U.S. Department of Justice, 2002a). Prior to the twentieth century, research on crime was dominated by biological views on individual traits and assumed that criminals must be inferior—genetically, intellectually, or psychologically—to nonoffenders. The general idea that social forces, rather than individual weakness, contributed to crime was threatening to the status quo and did not begin to take root until the middle of the last century. The importance of social forces to the understanding of crime is compelling when we examine young African-American men.

It is noteworthy that for almost every measure of social disadvantage—female-headed households, low educational achievement, unemployment, and poverty—the rate for blacks greatly exceeds the rate for whites. According to the U.S. Bureau of the Census, in 2000 more than 80 percent of white families were married-couple families, while less than one-half of all black families were married-couple families. As for educational attainment, the proportion of African Americans aged 25 years and over with at least a high school diploma was 10 percent less than their white counterparts, and bachelor's degrees were earned by 19.7 of white men compared with 11.4 percent of black men.

African-American men also participate in the labor force at a much lower rate than their white counterparts. In 2000, white men had a labor force participation rate of 96.4 percent, compared with 91.9 percent for black men.

Not only was the unemployment rate for black men more than twice that for white men, employed white men were almost twice as likely to be employed in higher-paying managerial and professional jobs. Looking specifically at black adult males, we find that they were far less likely than their white counterparts to have an annual income of $75,000 or more: 5.7 percent compared with 15.3 percent, respectively. Moreover, the poverty rate for black men (20.2%) was three times that of white men (6.8%).

To sociologists, these data are indicators of *social marginality,* or limited access to power structures due to social characteristics, so it is not surprising that arrest and conviction rates for young black men are significantly—indeed, alarmingly—higher than for any other demographic group. What is more, we can reasonably expect that these dismal statistics of young black men are positively correlated with their disproportionate involvement in the criminal justice system, as both offenders and victims. Sociologists have assumed that the explanation lies in the interaction between race and other social variables, and can be explained by understanding theories of social structure, social process, and social conflict.

Box 2.4 • Summary Statistics of African-American Men

Total percentage of U.S. population—4 %[1]

Total percentage of prison population—47%[2]

Total percentage on probation—38%[3]

Total percentage on parole—44%[4]

Total percentage with annual income of $75,000 or more—5.7%[5]

Total percentage living below poverty line—20.2%[6]

---

[1]U.S. Bureau of the Census, 2000.
[2]U.S. Bureau of Justice, 2002a.
[3]U.S. Bureau of Justice, 2002a.
[4]U.S. Bureau of Justice, 2002a.
[5]U.S. Bureau of the Census, 2000.
[6]U.S. Bureau of the Census, 2000.

Racial Crime Statistics

Before examining specific criminal justice statistics, it is important to understand two facts. The first is that the overwhelming numbers of African Americans are *not* offenders, but are law-abiding citizens. Indeed, many blacks serve responsibly and conscientiously as police officers, correctional officers, judges, and jurors. The second, and somewhat paradoxical, fact is that blacks—but in particular young black men—have long been a symbol of the fear of crime in the United States. Fueled by the media and opportunistic "law and order" politicians, the image of the violent perpetrator that comes to mind for many Americans, regardless of race, is that of a young black man. Thus, many are apt to incorrectly conclude that most black men are criminals. Such is the perception (the myth) that has persisted since the Civil War: Crime is violent, black, and male (Russell, 1998). But do the official crime statistics support this perception?

While crime rate data are likely to be interpreted in a variety of ways, and indeed have been criticized by some for being flawed (as we will see later), one fact that almost all researchers agree on is that African Americans, particularly young black men between the ages of 15 and 40, perpetrate a strikingly disproportionate percentage of street crime. Statistics indicate that, when compared to white males, African-American males generally commit a notably large proportion of those crimes that people fear most: aggravated assault, robbery, rape, and homicide. These statistical disparities apply not only to patterns of offending, but at every stage of the criminal justice system. From detention to arrest, from sentencing to incarceration, black men are present in numbers greatly out of proportion compared to their numbers in the general population. This means that, on any given day, 23 percent of black males in their twenties are in some way under the control of the criminal justice system. If trends had continued in the "war on drugs" that began in the 1980s, the United States would have reached the "point where three out of every four Black males [would] be arrested, jailed, and acquire a criminal record by age 35" (Miller, 1996:215). Moreover, black male involvement with the court system begins early, typically during an offender's teenage years. For example, a 1994 study of juvenile detention decisions indicates that African-American juveniles were far more likely than white juveniles to be detained at each decision point in the criminal justice system (Wordes, Bynum, and Corley, 1994, cited in Miller, 1996:76).

Concerning arrest rates for blacks, the data are particularly disconcerting. The Federal Bureau of Investigation's 2003 Uniform Crime Reports indicated that while there were more than 13 million arrests nationally (this number included only those arrests for which race information was given), more than 2.5 million—or 27 percent—of these arrestees were African Americans (Federal Bureau of Investigation, 2004:288), despite the fact that they represented approximately 13 percent of the total U.S. population. Specifically, African Americans made up 37.2 percent of all persons arrested for violent crime and 48.5 percent of all murder offenders (Federal Bureau of Investigation, 2004:288).

Regarding incarceration, one important irony is that even as the proportions of blacks convicted of committing serious violent crimes remained essentially stable since the early 1980s, disproportionate incarceration rates of African Americans grew steadily worse into the 1990s (Tonry, 1995:65). In 1988, the U.S. Department of Justice estimated the chances of incarceration in either a juvenile or adult correctional facility by the age of 64 to be 3 percent for whites and 18 percent for African Americans (Free, 1996:13). A 1995 study found that one in three black males in the 20-29 age group was under some form of criminal justice supervision on any given day—either in prison or jail, or on probation or parole. Further, a black boy born in 1991 stood a 29 percent chance of being imprisoned at some point in his life, compared to a 4 percent chance for a white boy (Mauer, 1999:124-125). More recent data reveal that these differences in incarceration rates between whites and blacks are a continuing trend.

During the early 1990s, when the country was spending at least $75 billion annually in direct costs to apprehend and lock up offenders, black inmates outnumbered white inmates six to one. In 1990, for every 100,000 whites, about 289 were in jail or prison; for every 100,000 blacks, about 1,860 were in jail or prison. Thirteen years later, in 2003, those numbers had skyrocketed: for every 100,000 white males, 465 were in jail or prison; whereas for every 100,000 black males, 3,405 were in jail or prison (U.S. Department of Justice, 2004).

When it comes to race, there is perhaps no more glaring discrepancy in the administration of criminal justice than in sentencing. To be sure, since at least the 1980s, harsher penalties have been imposed on African Americans, as, absolutely and proportionately, more blacks went to prison, and when they got there, they were held for longer periods of time. Indeed, the mean time served in federal prisons, in 2000, was 40.4 months for blacks, compared to 25.1 months for whites. The greatest sentencing disparity between the races was for drug offenses (to be dealt with in more detail later), with whites serving a mean time of 36.4 months and blacks serving a mean time of 52.4 months (U.S. Department of Justice, 2002a).

As for the ultimate punishment—the death penalty—African Americans have been much more likely than whites to be sentenced to death. Between 1930 and 1985, there were 3,909 executions in the United States, with more than one-half of those executed being African-American (Free, 1996:10). Despite recent focus on racial discrimination and the death penalty, blacks continue to be overrepresented in statistics regarding capital punishment. In 2000, 42.7 percent of prisoners under sentence of death were black. Of the 85 prisoners executed that year, 35 (or 41.1%) were black (U.S. Department of Justice, 2002a). And of the 66 prisoners executed in 2001, 17 (or 25.75%) were black. Little wonder that, in 2001, 72 percent of black respondents in a survey said they believed the death penalty was applied unfairly, while only 36 percent of whites shared that opinion (U.S. Department of Justice, 2002a). Owing to a long history of racially discriminatory practices, African Americans understandably tend to be more skeptical than whites about the fairness of the application of the death penalty.

Various studies on capital sentencing strongly suggest that, because of race, defendants who kill whites are more likely to be sentenced to death than defendants who kill blacks. At least two general conclusions may be drawn from these findings: (1) white victims are valued more highly by the criminal justice system, and (2) black offenders who victimize a white person are more likely than offenders in other offender-victim combinations to receive death sentences. In a substantial number of instances, police and prosecutors, judges and jurors, newspaper editors and readers, have tended to react with more fear and moral indignation to the murder of white persons than to the murder of black persons (Kennedy, 1997:311ff).

Statistics show that in addition to perpetrating a disproportionate amount of crime, African-American men are more likely than white men to be victims of violent crime at significantly higher rates. Data for the years 1993 to 2000 show that whereas for every 1,000 white males, 40.8 were victims of violent crime, for every 1,000 black males, 51.2 were victims of violent crime (U.S. Department of Justice, 2002a). Indeed, homicide has now become the leading cause of death among young black men. In 1998, the U.S. Centers for Disease Control and Prevention reported that the life expectancy for blacks was approximately six years shorter than for whites and that, after heart disease and cancer, homicide was the next largest contributor to the six-year discrepancy (Centers for Disease Control and Prevention, 2001:780). Moreover, given the pervasive patterns of residential segregation in American society, most crime (more than 80 percent) is *intraracial*, or a matter of black-on-black crime, which means that young black men have the greatest probability of falling victim to the violence of other young black men.

Social Facts, Disparities, and Discrimination

What, then, are we to make of these grim statistics on young black men that point to their disparate rates of crime, arrest, incarceration, sentencing, and victimization? In addressing this question there are two main considerations. The first is: Can these data—derived from such official sources as the U.S. Department of Justice and the FBI's Uniform Crime Reports—be used to satisfactorily study and explain the causes of the black-vs.-white crime differential? There is no doubt that the Uniform Crime Reports, which give the number and demographic traits (age, rage, and gender) of people who have been arrested, has been heavily criticized as an unreliable source for crime statistics on several grounds. First, many victims, but in particular lower-income African Americans, tend not to report many serious crimes because they either do not trust the police, or do not have confidence in the police's ability to solve crimes. Second, because it is quite common to have a higher police presence in African-American inner-city neighborhoods, this makes it more likely that African Americans will have higher rates of arrest. These and other criticisms serve as a caution to sociologists who work with the research method of crime rate analysis. In other words, while statistical data obtained from official sources and surveys can be helpful in illustrating some important crime patterns, these data are at best incomplete, and at worst, wrong.

The other question that we must consider in understanding young black men's overrepresentation in the criminal justice system can be articulated as follows: Is racism in the criminal justice system the main reason that proportionately so many more blacks than whites are subject to the administration of criminal justice, or is it simply that blacks are more prone to commit a greater amount violent crime? The first part of the question compels us to acknowledge the social fact of racism (in its personal and institutional forms) and the disorganized inner-city communities and negative labeling that such racism tends to perpetrate against African Americans. In the second part, which deals with criminal behavior, we must consider such social facts as differential associations, lower-class focal concerns, and political and economic inequalities. Thus, there are two points to be made here. The first is that the above-mentioned questions of data accuracy and racism revolve around a variety of social facts that sociologists must consider. The second is that the two questions also bear on the crucial issue of disparity versus discrimination.

Sociologists agree that the criminal justice system is marked by stark racial *disparities*, or differences in the black/white rates of involvement in criminal offending. They do not, however, generally agree on whether these disparities are the result of racial *discrimination*, or unequal treatment on the basis of race.

Relying on the official crime statistics, most sociologists believe that a substantial part, but certainly not all, of racial disparity in the administration of justice is attributable to blacks committing more serious crimes than whites. To be sure, many scholars concede that most studies fail to demonstrate that a substantial racial bias pervades the system of criminal justice. This is not to say that there is no racism in the system, that no discrimination occurs in individual cases, or that there are no prejudiced police officers, prosecutors, and judges—only that "the overwhelming weight of evidence . . . is that invidious bias explains much less of racial disparities than does offending by Black offenders" (Tonry, 1995:50). These scholars therefore maintain that the disparate rates of crime, arrests, and sentencing can be taken as reasonable reflections of African Americans' disproportionately greater involvement in serious crime.

Other researchers—particularly and most significantly African-American scholars—reject as inconclusive those studies that indicate blacks' greater involvement in offending. University of Florida law professor and criminologist Katheryn K. Russell (1998) contends that because many of these studies focus on only one specific stage of the criminal justice system (e.g., sentencing), they therefore cannot detect the racial discrimination that may permeate other stages of the system (e.g., prosecutorial charging, plea bargaining). One answer, she says, is to conduct multistage research of the criminal justice process, which will not only better assess the extent to which young black men are propelled through the system as a whole in relation to white men, it will also help in determining whether there is more or less discrimination at the "front end" (e.g., arrest) than at subsequent points in the system (e.g., adjudication or disposition). Some sociologists maintain that there is sufficient compelling evidence to demonstrate that the criminal justice system is characterized by *institutional racism*, or the perpetuation of circumstances that oppress blacks even in the absence of overt racial discrimination.

Regardless of whether one leans toward disparity (blacks commit disproportionately more serious crime than whites) or discrimination (blacks are overly represented in the courts and prisons because of racism), or accepts them both as explanations of blacks' disproportionate involvement in the system of criminal justice, it is undoubtedly the case that the *root causes* of criminality among blacks have to do with the long-standing and disastrous social and economic disadvantages of the African- American community. Moreover, it is also the case that all databases, including the official sources commonly utilized by researchers in ascertaining the relationship between race and crime, have their shortcomings, and that the disparity and discrimination studies on race and crime that employ these data are also limited.

Toward an African-American Sociology of Crime?

Setting aside for the moment the inherent shortcomings that plague disparity and discrimination studies on race and crime, the question still remains: How do we explain why violent crime is much more prevalent among African-American youths than among white youths? In an attempt to answer this question, in all its ramifications, it is necessary to consider the state of sociological criminology.

Helen Taylor Greene. *With permission of Helen Taylor Greene*

Many African-American sociologists and criminologists, like Katheryn K. Russell, advocate for the creation of a race-conscious approach to the study of crime that explores concepts and variables that depart from the traditional domain of crime research. To be sure, since the 1960s, there have been several African-American scholars, both sociologists and criminologists, who have taken a sociological approach in developing a black perspective on crime and justice; these include Coramae Richey Mann, Darnell F. Hawkins, and Lee E. Ross. Criminologists Helen Taylor Greene and Shaun L. Gabbidon, in their books *African American Criminological Thought* (2000) and *African American Classics in Criminology and Criminal Justice* (2001), have highlighted the theoretical and policy contribution that African Americans have made in historical and contemporary criminological thought.

Sociologist Marvin D. Free's (1996:57-58) irritation with sociological criminology's attempt to explain racial disparity in crime is based on the inadequacy of its theories. Accordingly, he attacks sociological-criminological theory on several grounds. First, these theories, he contends, tend to disregard the possibility that the laws themselves may be racially biased as evident, for example, in the punitive differential made between crack and powder cocaine (see the case study below). Second, they frequently ignore the possibility that some of the differences in the black/white rates of offending may be due to differences in patrolling by the police. Because many lower-class African Americans live in heavily patrolled areas of the city, any lawbreaking is more likely to result in a police contact than similar lawbreaking that occurs in suburban or rural areas, which are predominantly white. Third, many of the variables contained in these theories (e.g., opportunity, median family income, educational attainment, female-headed households), may differentially impact criminal behavior by race. Finally, and more pointedly perhaps, Free maintains that sociological-criminological theory is tacitly premised on two faulty and contradictory assumptions: (1) that African Americans are culturally inferior, and (2) that there is no such thing as a distinct African-American culture. One regrettable consequence of these assumptions is that sociological-criminological theories do not incorporate elements of the black experience in their explanations of black crime.

Shaun L. Gabbidon. *With permission of Shawn L. Gabbidon*

What is needed, says Free, is a black perspective on crime that seriously considers the thoughts and experiences of African Americans as well as their history of discrimination. A black sociology of crime should focus, not on personal or demographic traits, but on social problems such as poverty, illiteracy, unemployment, selective law enforcement, discrimination, segregation, inadequate housing, and nutrition. Finally, a minority view on crime changes the focus of analysis from the individual who has committed a crime to the exploitative structural system in which the individual has resided. In sum, Free contends that a black criminology will raise such questions as: "(1) To what extent do laws (e.g., drug legislation) differentially impact the African American population? (2) Under what structural conditions are African Americans more (or less) likely than Whites to be officially processed by the criminal justice system and receive stiffer sentences?, and (3) What effect does institutional racism have on the distribution of crime in America?" (Free, 1996:71).

Given the frequent contact of black inner-city youths with the criminal justice system, it is high time that sociological criminology—in its theory, methods, and research—take seriously an African-American perspective on crime and punishment.

Box 2.5 • Case Study: Federal Sentencing for Crack versus Cocaine

Of all the issues relating to the problem of black crime, none is more controversial and contentious than the "war on drugs." Succinctly put, the war on drugs refers to a policy, first proposed by President Richard M. Nixon in 1970, that attempts to reduce the supply, distribution, and use of illicit narcotics by increasingly punitive criminal measures. The war on drugs took a dramatic turn in 1986, immediately following the death, from a cocaine overdose, of college basketball star, Len Bias, when the U.S. Congress enacted the federal Anti-Drug Abuse Act.

It is no exaggeration to say that, for the last three decades, no national policy has done more to expand the numbers of young African-American men subjected to the administration of criminal justice than the war on drugs and the Anti-Drug Abuse Act. This is the case for two reasons: (1) law enforcement has purposely targeted low-income African-American communities for arresting drug offenders, and (2) in considering the mandatory minimum penalties for cocaine offenses, the 1986 Act distinguished between powder cocaine and crack cocaine and *established significantly higher penalties for crack cocaine offenses*.

If the war on drugs is the most contentious issue relating to the problem of black crime, the punishment distinction between crack cocaine and powder cocaine is the most controversial issue in the war on drugs. The controversy stems from the charge, made by some critics, that the U.S. Congress engaged in racial discrimination when it enacted the federal Anti-Drug Abuse Act of 1986 that punishes crack cocaine offenders much more harshly than powder cocaine offenders. Under the 1986 Act, a person convicted of possession with intent to distribute *five grams* or more of crack cocaine is subject to a mandatory minimum sentence of five years in federal prison. By contrast, only if a person is convicted of possession with intent to distribute at least *500 grams* of powder cocaine is he or she subject to a five-year mandatory minimum sentence. This is a 100-to-1 drug quantity ratio, meaning that the penalty for possession of crack cocaine is 100 times harsher than the penalty for possession of powder cocaine

A problem with distinguishing between crack and powder cocaine in this way is that crack cocaine tends to be used and sold largely by blacks and powder cocaine largely by whites, which means that the harshest penalties are mostly experienced by blacks. According to the U.S. Sentencing Commission's 2002 report on crack/powder sentences, the overwhelming majority—about 85 percent—of crack cocaine offenders consistently had been black, while only 5.6 were white. In 2002, African Americans comprised the vast major-

Box 2.5, *continued*

ity of those found guilty of crack cocaine crimes, but only 30.5 percent of those found guilty of powder cocaine crimes (U.S. Sentencing Commission, 2002:62-63).

The upshot is that, as a result of the 100-to-1 crack/powder cocaine punishment differential, blacks are sent to prison in unprecedented numbers and are kept there longer than whites. In great part because of the difference in quantity-based penalties, in 2000, the average sentence for crack cocaine offenses (118 months) was 44 months, or almost 60 percent longer than the average sentence for powder cocaine offenses (74 months) (U.S. Sentencing Commission, 2002:90). Controlling for like amounts of cocaine, in 2000, crack defendants convicted of trafficking in less than 25 grams of cocaine received an average sentence that was 4.8 times longer than the sentence received by an equivalent powder defendant (U. S. Department of Justice, 2002b:29).

Federal prosecutors contend that disparities in black/white sentences result not from unequal racial treatment but from the proportions of large-scale traffickers in crack who qualify for federal prosecution because of their substantial role in the drug trade. Data analyzed by the U.S. Sentencing Commission, however, casts doubt on this contention. In the Commission's analysis of crack defendants in 2000, only 5.9 percent of the defendants were classified as high-level dealers (e.g., managers, supervisors), while fully *two-thirds* were street-level dealers or couriers. Thus, because of this high concentration of street-level dealers, the mandatory minimum penalties apply most often to them (64.2 percent)—most of whom are inner-city African-American men—and not to serious major traffickers (U.S. Sentencing Commission, 2002:99).

The war on drugs and the issue of the crack/powder cocaine punishment differential can be adequately understood from a social conflict perspective. Group conflict theorists argue that since African Americans as a racial group possess little political clout, they therefore had little or no say about the enactment of the 1986 Anti-Drug Abuse legislation. The Act basically serves to protect the resource (the supply of powder cocaine) of drug-using, influential white Americans by focusing law-enforcement efforts away from powder cocaine and toward crack cocaine. Marxist theorists, on the other hand, explain the use of the cheaper drug, crack cocaine, by African Americans—who are more likely than whites to be poor and unemployed—either as a way of making money fast (through street-level crack dealing) and survive their dire economic conditions, or as a way of escaping their economic woes (through crack use).

Conclusion and Future Directions

We have seen that the vast majority of theorizing in criminology—that is, the efforts at explaining the causes of crime—have been largely influenced by the fundamental sociological concepts of social structure, social process, and social conflict. The three major sociological perspectives premised on these concepts have spawned some of the most important theories in all of criminology. What is more, sociology as a discipline has disproportionately determined the research methods (such as the use of crime rates, the life history, and participant observation) that sociological criminologists have employed in obtaining empirical data. In conclusion to this chapter I propose three future directions that I believe the discipline of sociology (and, by implication, criminology) should take in further advancing its endeavors in theorizing and conducting research.

For starters, a considerable number of theories in criminology are either explicitly or implicitly premised on the notion that offenders are rational—that is, calculating and logical—in their thinking and actions. For example, the rationality premise is at the heart of Sutherland's explanation that on the basis of learning criminal techniques as well as their assessment of the situation in regard to the availability of opportunity and the probability of detection, offenders deliberately choose whether to implement these techniques in carrying out a crime. Although the rationality premise is not at the forefront of Sutherland's theory of differential association, is it implied and crucial to his explanation of why people commit crime. The same applies to Merton's idea that because lower-class people want to achieve success, they devise, through conscious effort, innovative—that is, deviant—forms for doing so. The fact of the matter is that there is much about criminal behavior that is not based on rational calculation, but rather on *irrational responses* stemming from fear, shame, fight or flight impulses, or acute stress. By the same token, *resiliency,* the power to resist negative social environments and experiences, can neutralize social factors that encourage criminal behavior. I contend that theories attempting to explain criminal behavior must consider the intervening effects of such emotional influences, and that criminologists need to examine the sociological roots of offenders' irrational responses through the use of interviews, questionnaires, and life histories.

Second, much theorizing in sociology has relied on the old scientific postulate of looking for causal relationships between variables. While this approach has served criminology well in accounting for some of the causes of crime—for example, that labeling a youth as "delinquent" leads him or her to become delinquent—it has become increasingly the case in the natural sciences and mathematics that cause-and-effect explanations cannot adequately capture the infinite complexity of the physical and social worlds. There are far too many paradoxes and contradictions—there is too much randomness—in social reality for sociologists and criminologists to attempt an understanding of crime and criminal behavior through mere cause-and-effect theorizing. While it may be true that labeling can lead to the "dramatization of evil" in some youths, it is also the case that negative labeling has no detrimental effect on many other youths, that a child labeled "delinquent" may engage in vandalism and also voluntarily engage in community clean-up projects, that the only way a young man knows to prevent his best friend from robbing a liquor store and getting into trouble is by beating him up. I argue that future theorizing in sociological criminology must abandon the simplistic causal approach and take seriously the problem of *societal complexity*.

Finally, the demographics of crime need to be brought into clearer focus as a subject of sociological study. Because the majority of crime around the world and throughout history has been a problem of male involvement, it is necessary that criminological theory and research give adherence to *male-conscious perspectives* on crime—that is to say, criminology must examine male cultural viewpoints. A focus on males, as feminist activist Gloria Steinem recently observed, is needed to understand the "white male factor" as a cause of "supremacy crimes," including serial murder and random school shootings (Steinem, 2004). We have also seen that several noted U.S. African-American scholars have called for a black perspective that considers African Americans' thoughts, and experiences about crime and justice; the same may be said about other "minority" populations as well—Latino, Native American, and (especially in the particular case of terrorism) "Arab"—as of men at different stages of the life cycle and in different socioeconomic positions.

I believe that these three proposals for the discipline of sociology to inform criminological theory and research—to recognize offender's irrational responses as an outcome of sociological forces and a predictor of subsequent behavior, to take into account the societal complexity of crime, and to develop male-conscious and race-conscious perspectives on crime and justice—should lead to future trajectories for sociological criminologists in better understanding crime.

Suggested Further Reading

Akers, R. (1998). *Social Learning and Social Structure: A General Theory of Crime and Deviance*. Boston: Northeastern University Press.

Chesney-Lind, M. (1997). *The Female Offender: Girls, Women, and Crime*. Thousand Oaks, CA: Sage.

Cloward, R. & L. Ohlin (1960). *Delinquency and Opportunity*. Glencoe, IL: Free Press.

Gibbons, D. C. (1994). *Talking About Crime and Criminals: Problems and Issues in Theory Development in Criminology*. Englewood Cliffs, NJ: Prentice Hall.

Hall, J. (1952). *Law, Theft, and Society*. Revised edition. Indianapolis: Bobbs-Merrill.

Lemert, E.M. (1951). *Social Pathology*. New York: McGraw-Hill.

Matza, D. *Delinquency and Drift*. New York: Wiley.

Pepinsky, H.E. & R. Quinney (eds., 1991). *Criminology as Peacemaking*. Bloomington, IN: Indiana University Press.

Platt, A.M. (1969). *The Child Savers: The Invention of Delinquency*. Chicago: University of Chicago Press.

Quinney, R. (1970). *The Social Reality of Crime*. Boston: Little, Brown.

Schur, E.M. (1973). *Radical Non-Intervention: Rethinking the Delinquency Problem*. Englewood Cliffs, NJ: Prentice Hall.

Taylor, I., P. Walton & J. Young (1973). *The New Criminology*. New York: Harper & Row.

Turk, A.T. (1969). *Criminality and the Legal Order*. Chicago: Rand-McNally.

Wolfgang, M.E. & F. Ferracutti (1982). *The Subculture of Violence*. Beverly Hills, CA: Sage.

References

Adler, F., and W. Laufer, eds. (1995). *Advances in Criminological Theory, Vol. 6, The Legacy of Anomie*. New Brunswick, NJ: Transaction.

Centers for Disease Control and Prevention (2001). "Influence of Homicide on Racial Disparity in Life Expectancy—United States, 1998." *Morbidity and Mortality Weekly Report*, 50:777-795.

Cohen, A.K. (1955). *Delinquent Boys*. Glencoe, IL: Free Press.

Durkheim, E. (1951). *Suicide: A Study in Sociology*. New York: Free Press.

Durkheim, E. (1966). *The Rules of Sociological Method*. New York: Free Press.

Federal Bureau of Investigation (2004). *Crime in the United States—2003. Uniform Crime Reports*. Washington, DC: U.S. Government Printing Office.

Free, M.D. (1996). *African Americans and the Criminal Justice System*. New York: Garland.

Gabbidon, S. L., H.T. Greene, and V.D. Young (2001). *African American Classics in Criminology and Criminal Justice*. Thousand Oaks, CA: Sage.

Gastril, R.D. (1971). "Homicide and a Regional Culture of Violence." *American Sociological Review,* 36:412-427.

Gottfredson, M., and T. Hirschi (1990). *A General Theory of Crime*. Stanford, CA: Stanford University Press.

Hirschi, T. (1969). *Causes of Delinquency*. Los Angeles: University of California Press.

Human Rights Watch (2000). *Punishment and Prejudice: Racial Disparities in the War on Drugs*. Online http://www.hrw.org/reports/2000/usa/index.htm. New York: Human Rights Watch.

Ianni, F.A.J. (1972). *A Family Business: Kinship and Social Control in Organized Crime*. New York: Russell Sage Foundation.

Kennedy, R. (1997). *Race, Crime, and the Law*. New York: Pantheon Books.

Knepper, P. (2000). "The Alchemy of Race and Crime Research." In M.W. Markowitz and D.D. Jones-Brown (eds.), *The System in Black and White: Exploring the Connections Between Race, Crime, and Justice*, pp. 15-29. Westport, CT.: Praeger.

Mauer, M. (1999). *Race to Incarcerate*. New York: The New Press.

Merton, R.K. (1938). "Social Structure and Anomie." *American Sociological Review*, 3:672-682.

Miller, J.G. (1996). *Search and Destroy: African American Males in the Criminal Justice System*. Cambridge, UK: Cambridge University Press.

Miller, W.B. (1958). "Lower Class Culture as a Generating Milieu of Gang Delinquency." *Journal of Social Issues*, 14(3):5-19.

Quinney, R. (1977). *Class, State, and Crime*. New York: Longman.

Quinney, R. (1991). "The Way of Peace: On Crime, Suffering, and Service." In H. Pepinsky and R. Quinney, eds., *Criminology as Peacemaking*. Bloomington, IN: Indiana University Press, pp. 3-13.

Russell, K.K. (1998). *The Color of Crime: Racial Hoaxes, White Fear, Black Protectionism, Police Harassment, and Other Macroaggressions*. New York: New York University Press.

Shaw, C.R. & D.D. McKay (1942). *Juvenile Delinquency and Urban Areas*. Chicago: University of Chicago Press.

Steinem, G. (2004). "Supremacy Crimes." In S.M. Shaw and J. Lee (eds.), *Women's Voices, Feminist Visions*, pp. 241-243. Boston: McGraw-Hill.

Sutherland, E.H. (1937). *The Professional Thief*. Chicago: The University of Chicago Press.

Sutherland, E.H. (1947). *Principles of Criminology*. Philadelphia: J.B. Lippincott.

Tannenbaum, F. (1938). *Crime and the Community*. New York: Columbia University Press.

Taylor, G.H., and S.L. Gabbidon (2000). *African American Criminological Thought*. New York: State University of New York Press.

Thoreau, H.D. (1849). "On the Duty of Civil Disobedience." http://www.constitution.org/civildis.htm

Tonry, M. (1995). *Malign Neglect: Race, Crime, and Punishment in America*. New York: Oxford University Press.

U.S. Bureau of the Census (2000). *Census 2000 Summary File*. Washington, DC: U.S. Government Printing Office. http://www.census.gov/

U.S. Department of Justice, Bureau of Justice Statistics (2004). *Prisoners in 2003*. Online http://www.ojp.usdoj.gov/bjs/prisons.htm. Washington, DC: U.S. Government Printing Office.

U.S. Department of Justice, Bureau of Justice Statistics (2002a). *Sourcebook of Criminal Justice Statistics—2002*. Online http://www.albany.edu/sourcebook. Washington, DC: U.S. Government Printing Office.

U.S. Department of Justice, Bureau of Justice Statistics (2002b). *Federal Cocaine Offenses: An Analysis of Crack and Powder Penalties*. Washington, DC: U.S. Government Printing Office.

U.S. Sentencing Commission (2002). *Report to Congress: Cocaine and Federal Sentencing Policy*. Washington, DC: U.S. Government Printing Office.

Vold, G.B. (1958). *Theoretical Criminology*. New York: Oxford University Press.

Wordes, A., T. Bynum, and C. Corley (1994). "Locking Up Youth: The Impact of Race on Detention Decisions." *Journal of Research in Crime and Delinquency,* 31(2):140-165.

Commentary

Francis T. Cullen

In this chapter, A. Javier Treviño provides a clear and informative tour through past and more contemporary sociological thinking about the causes of criminal behavior. Readers should now be well-grounded both in how sociologists approach the study of crime and in what is distinctive about the kinds of theories they formulate. I will raise four issues that build upon and hopefully enrich the discussions offered by Treviño.

Challenging Individualistic Theories of Crime

Within American society, early sociological theories took on importance not simply for what they said but also for what kind of thinking they challenged. Two of the more important sociological traditions—the Chicago School's social disorganization theory and Robert K. Merton's anomie or strain theory—were first published in the 1930s. At this time, it was commonplace to attribute crime and deviance to *individual pathology*, such as biological inferiority (criminals were not as "evolved" as upstanding citizens) or psychological illness (criminals lacked a superego or were "acting out" unconscious and unresolved impulses). For scholars in the new field of sociology, however, these explanations ignored the social nature of human beings and implicitly suggested that how American society was arranged had nothing to do with crime.

Indeed, for these sociologists, the organization of communities and the social structure had important *consequences*. Thus, the Chicago School theorists cautioned that if youths were raised in disorganized communities—neighborhoods characterized by poverty, people moving in and out, densely populated tenements, and racial/ethnic conflict—they would be exposed to values and life experiences (e.g., contact with local gangs) that would place them at risk for crime. Similarly, Merton warned that crime and deviance were rooted in the inconsistency inherent in teaching that *everyone* can be financially successful—the so-called "American dream"—in a society in which opportunities for success were not equally available across the class structure. This contradiction meant that many Americans, especially impoverished citizens, would be exposed to the frustration of not reaching the goals they were taught to cherish. The resulting strains, warned Merton, would push many of them to break the law.

The enduring message of these early sociological theorists is that it is intellectually indefensible to blame crime exclusively on people being "bad" or pathological. To be sure, some individuals may become involved in crime because their biology makes them overly impulsive or because they have weak consciences. But the larger reality is that the life paths that people take, whether into or away from crime, are shaped by the circumstances they encounter—by the families they are born into, the schools they attend, the neighborhoods that surround them, the jobs available, and the society in which they are enmeshed. By contrast, theories that focus only on individual traits risk acquitting the social order of any involvement in crime. In so doing, they implicitly advance the notion that crime can be prevented by concentrating on removing "bad apples" from the community rather than exploring how the "barrel" itself—that is, society—may have "bad" or criminogenic features in need of correction.

Sociological Ideas in Context

Treviño acquaints the reader with a variety of sociological theories. As might be anticipated (and as has been suggested), these theories did not all arise at the same time. Rather, they have tended to accumulate over the course of the better part of a century, waxing and waning in popularity. Why has this occurred?

One possible explanation for the status of any given theory is that perspectives become popular because they have considerable empirical support. In this scenario, researchers take the key concepts from a theory (e.g., strain or social disorganization) and then study whether these variables are able to explain why some people but not others commit crime or why some communities but not others have a high crime rate. If theories receive empirical support, then they are endorsed by criminologists and survive; those without empirical support are dismissed as incorrect.

In reality, however, sociological theories—as with nonsociological theories of crime—have tended to flourish or decline almost independently of what the scientific research has shown. There are many reasons for this: the theories are complex and often the available data are able to test only part of the theory; the research yields conflicting results, with different tests reaching different conclusions; criminologists have not yet decided how much negative evidence must exist before we can safely say a theory is falsified. But the larger truth is that many criminologists do not endorse or reject theories strictly on *scientific grounds*. Rather, like other people in society, their allegiance to a theory is also shaped by what ideas *make sense to them*.

What we believe about crime (and other social issues) is often influenced by the social experiences we have had. For example, I grew up in Boston and attended an integrated, inner-city high school where I witnessed the consequences of inequality first hand. My parents also were sensitive to social exclusion because, as Irish Catholics, this was part of our ethnic group's heritage. For these and similar reasons, theories that emphasized denial of opportunity always struck me as being "true." (I also had a chance to study with Robert K. Merton, who developed strain theory, at Columbia University.)

In a like vein, different theories have been more or less popular because of "what was going on" in society and the experiences to which people were exposed. Thus, in the 1930s, the rapid and seemingly chaotic expansion of cities made theories of "disorganization" sensible. In the 1980s, the decline and turmoil that characterized many cities again made disorganization a popular explanatory concept. Theories emphasizing denial of opportunity earned many supporters in the early 1960s at a time when Presidents John F. Kennedy and Lyndon B. Johnson promised to eliminate the barriers to equality and to build a "Great Society." By the latter years of the 1960s and into the 1970s, this optimism waned as America was marked by urban riots, war protests put down by state officials using physical and sometimes lethal force, and revelations of government corruption in the Watergate scandal and similar affairs. In these times, theories emphasizing conflict and inequality in power won many adherents.

There are two lessons to be drawn from this discussion. First, for criminologists, the challenge is to move beyond embracing theories that are personally comforting and to assess ideas based on the scientific evidence. If criminologists fail to take this step, then they almost certainly will continue to trumpet theories that assuage their biases, even though such perspectives may be empirically incorrect. Second, for readers, this is an occasion to inspect why you believe what you do about crime. Why do some theories "make sense" to you, whereas others strike you as "ridiculous"? How are your beliefs about crime influenced by the life experiences you have had? Are you willing to consult the scientific studies and to let them affect your thinking about crime?

Before and Beyond the Teenage Years: The Life-Course Paradigm

As Treviño has conveyed, it is an empirical regularity across communities and societies that participation in crime reaches a peak during the teenage years. As a result, sociologists have tended to construct theories over the years that focus on what happens to individuals during adolescence and as they make the transition into adulthood. Thus, are they exposed to gangs in disorganized neighborhoods? Do they experience the strain of failing at school and of being denied fruitful employment? Do they lose their attachment to parents as they move into high school, give up on educational advancement, and hang out on street corners with "nothing to do"? Do they exist in a society that marginalizes them and makes no offer of a decent job and way to make a living?

These and similar questions—addressed by leading sociological theories of crime—are important to consider. But they also make a problematic assumption: that youths arrive in adolescence largely as blank slates and then are pushed into or away from crime by what they experience over the next decade or so. In recent years, however, it has become apparent that those who turn to serious delinquency during their juvenile years and who grow up to be "career criminals" start their pathway into crime during *childhood*. The early years of their lives are marked by numerous "risk factors" that undermine their healthy development: mothers who consume drugs while pregnant; exposure to brain-damaging levels of lead in their residences; chaotic, if not abusive, family situations; deep levels of poverty; ineffective schools; and little access to early intervention programs that might have helped them. Not all children consigned to these trying circumstances develop into serious offenders, but nearly all serious offenders can trace the origins of their criminality to childhood.

This empirical reality has profound implications for sociological theories of crime. Most important, they must now extend their focus from the teenage and young-adult years backward to childhood. They must explain not simply why crime climbs as kids enter adolescence, but also why there is a strong connection between conduct problems in childhood and subsequent conduct problems as an older youth (a behavioral phenomenon called "persistence" or "stability"). For a perspective such as social disorganization theory, this might mean focusing not only on how disorganization produces juvenile gangs but also on how disorganized neighborhoods impede the healthy development of infants and expose children to an array of antisocial influences.

It is also the case that youths who are serious or high-rate offenders are at risk for continuing their criminal participation into adulthood. There are, of course, many youths who experiment with delinquency during their juveniles years, a group that Terrie Moffitt (1993) terms "adolescent-limited" offenders. Other youths, notes Moffitt, are "life-course persistent" offenders. For this group, extensive antisocial conduct as a juvenile is a strong predictor of later antisocial conduct. Research is now emerging that tries to explain this continuity in offending. Complementary research examines when and why adult offenders "desist" or stop committing crime. For example, using control theory to guide their research, Robert Sampson and John Laub (1993) show how "adult social bonds"—such as securing a good job and having the good fortune of a good marriage—are important factors in diverting adult men from their wayward ways.

Theory and research that focus on this development of criminal careers fall under the increasingly popular *life-course paradigm*. In essence, this approach studies individuals from the womb to their death bed. It tends to be an integrated theory in that it realizes that individuals are biological creatures, have psychological traits, and are shaped by social circumstances. The future of criminology—including sociological criminology—is likely to be explored within the boundaries of this life-course theoretical paradigm.

Sociological Theories and Criminal Justice Policy

Treviño's analysis also shows that sociologists have particular views on what might be done to control crime. Importantly, a sociological understanding of crime causation would lead us to question whether the dominant strategies used to suppress crime today will have the desired effect. In this regard, for three decades, state and federal governments have tried to punish America out of its crime problem. Since the early 1970s, state and federal prison populations have increased sevenfold. Counting those in local jails, the population of offenders behind bars on any given day exceeds *two million* Americans. Another 4.75 million residents are on probation or parole. Altogether, more than 6.7 million are under some type of correctional supervision. As Treviño points out, this use of the correctional system to control crime falls disproportionately on young African-American males.

Beyond the sheer *quantity* of control, a key concern is the *quality* of the control to which offenders are subjected. In many places, the penalties given to offenders have become increasingly punitive. The goal has been to inflict more and more pain on offenders: mandatory imprisonment rather than community-based sanctions; long rather than short sentences; making life in prison harsher through crowding, poor food, inadequate medical services, reinstituting chain gangs, and eliminating key rehabilitation services (e.g., access to college education); and sending youths to boot camps and other "get tough" programs. Todd Clear (1994) has called this the "penal harm movement."

Why would we expect this punishment-oriented approach to reduce crime? To be sure, the criminality of some offenders is curtailed simply because they are behind bars and not in the community (this is called an "incapacitation effect"). But the research generally shows that prison sentences do not deter more than community sanctions; that longer prison sentences produce more recidivism, or relapse into criminal behavior, than shorter sentences; and that efforts to "get tough" (such as through boot camps) tend to be ineffective or backfire. Again, why is this so?

Sociological criminology provides a ready answer: For a policy intervention to reduce crime, it must *target for change what actually is causing crime*. Sociological theorists have identified an array of factors that are likely implicated in the cause of crime, including, for example, social disorganization, structurally induced strain, a breakdown of social bonds, close contact with a criminal subcultural values, being labeled and reacted to as a criminal, and enduring class and racial inequality. It is sobering to pause for a moment and to realize that "get tough" criminal justice policies do virtually nothing to alter these root causes of crime or to change the people who have ended up in crime because of their exposure to these criminogenic conditions.

The message to convey, then, is that policymakers ignore the wisdom produced by sociological theories at a high cost. By pursuing policies based on limited, if not faulty, understandings of crime (e.g., crime is simply a "rational" choice), they subject offenders to punitive measures that may impose discomfort but do little to reduce the chances of recidivism. This failure to reform offenders while in the grasp of the criminal justice system has two disquieting consequences: first, offenders who might have been saved from a dismal life in crime are not; and second, the well-being of innocent citizens who later are victimized by these "punished" but unchanged offenders is needlessly sacrificed at the altar of criminological ignorance.

References

Clear, T. (1994). *Harm in American Penology: Offenders, Victims, and Their Communities.* Albany: State University of New York Press.

Moffitt, T. (1993). "Adolescent-limited and Life-course-persistent Antisocial Behavior: A Developmental Taxonomy." *Psychological Review*, 100:674-701.

Sampson, R., and J. Laub (1993). *Crime in the Making: Pathways and Turning Points Through Life.* Boston: Harvard University Press.

Chapter Three

Economics and Crime

Robert A. Rosenthal

At a party, upon learning that I am an economist, it is not uncommon for someone to ask me, "What's going on in the stock market?" or "Do you think this recession is over?" No one has ever asked me if I think capital punishment is a deterrent to crime, if drugs should be legalized, or whether crime rates are likely to rise in response to higher unemployment rates—yet many economists, including me, spend as much, if not more, time studying, thinking, and lecturing about these issues than about recent movements in the Dow Jones Industrial Index or the growth rate of Gross Domestic Product.

The discipline of economics is generally divided into two major areas of study: *macroeconomics* and *microeconomics*. While macroeconomics deals with issues pertaining to the big picture, such as unemployment, economic growth, and inflationary forces, microeconomics focuses on the behavior of the individual decisionmakers, who influence not only the economy, but the larger society as well. Simply stated, these decisionmakers fall into two categories—consumers and producers, or more simply, buyers and sellers. Most introductory economics textbooks define economics as the study of the scarcity of resources and the process of how limitations of land, labor, and capital are allocated among competing wants. A clearer depiction of what economics is about is best described by pointing out that like other social sciences, it studies the behavior of individuals.

Economic analysis is usually linked to the study of how people respond to an array of economic-related variables, and the early theorists did indeed focus on those matters. One of the most celebrated contributions to economic thought revolves around eighteenth-century Scottish economist Adam Smith (1776/1937) describing a pin factory and the economic advantages of division of labor. Here, Smith, like many of the classical writers of his time, focuses exclusively on the application of economics to the objective functions of production and efficiency.

Division of labor meant specialization and greater productivity. In a pin factory, for example, the unspecialized worker could make one pin per day, but certainly not twenty. On the other hand, in a small 'manufactory' with ten men each specializing in a part of the pin-making operation, the output would be upward of 48,000 pins a day, or 4,800 per worker instead of one of even twenty. (Burtt, 1972:55)

Adam Smith. *With permission of The Warren J. Samuels Portrait Collection at Duke University*

However, the fundamentals of microeconomics,[1] while certainly concerned with matters of production, efficiency, and division of labor, extend well beyond variables that might involve profit or production levels. Most noneconomists incorrectly assume that the discipline of economics is limited to prices, production, costs, and the like. The reality, however, is something else entirely, for in the latter part of the nineteenth century, a more qualitative methodology to economics was introduced by way of **utility theory** into the study of decisionmaking. Utility theory, simply stated, offered that people act in a manner that allows them to maximize their utility or "well-being." Clearly, there is a sense that what people do, they do to make themselves as happy as they can possibly be—perhaps suggesting a psychological as well as economic element in their behavior. Regardless, this theory simply allowed for the notion that different people may have different means of attaining maximum utility; and given such variations in goals, each might pursue them in a different way.

Many individuals seek fortune, power, and fame in various combinations and to various degrees. But what, one might ask, of the anonymous benefactor? The example of charitable giving provides evidence of alternative routes to happiness. If one were only concerned with the accumulation of wealth and income as a goal, it would be difficult to explain why people give money away. *Utilitarians* could easily explain this in their own terms: giving makes people feel better about themselves and hence adds to their overall level of well-being or "utility." Thus, if people attempt to maximize this thing we call utility, they could do so by pursuing a number of seemingly contradictory courses of action. This is known as the "law of maximum utility," which economists believe is fundamental to human nature.

Rational Behavior

Economic analysis has infiltrated and, in some cases, rewritten disciplines as diverse as sociology, biology, and law. Regarding sociology, the pioneering work of Gary Becker (1968) covers such issues as marriage, divorce, and child rearing. The essence of Becker's work is that when individuals make life-altering decisions such as these, they are as likely to use the economic principle of "optimizing" as they do when buying a television or engaging in a job search. The principle of optimizing means that whenever individuals find themselves at a decision point, they intuitively measure any relevant costs and benefits to help them reach an optimal decision—one that will maximize their utility. Before acting, consciously or not, people simply ask themselves, "Is it worth it?"

An example can be drawn from the everyday life of a college student facing those dreadful 8:00 A.M. classes. Consider you are on your way to class and you are running just a bit late. You know that most professors frown upon tardiness, but you also know how important that cup of coffee is before you begin your day. Upon arriving at the cafeteria, you see a line much longer than usual and you know that if you wait, you will definitely have to walk into class at least five minutes late. It's early in the semester when first impressions matter the most. What to do? Without having ever heard of cost-benefit analysis, and all of its intricacies, your mind instantaneously shifts into high gear and processes a great deal of information. You weigh the costs of going in late against the benefits of having your caffeine fix. Some may opt to forego the coffee while others will risk the dirty look from the professor, or worse yet, a possible reprimand in front of your peers. The fact that there is no single correct response to this dilemma is why everyone will not decide to take the same course of action. First, caffeine cravings differ among different people. Second, a student's need for approval in the eyes of their professors will also vary. These two factors (there are others as well) may be sufficient for the balance of costs and benefits to differ among people, thus leading to two different, seemingly rational decisions.

Economists' assumptions about individuals' decisionmaking show that economists, first and foremost, assume that individuals are *rational*. More important to the understanding of crime, economists believe that it is possible for an individual to make the *wrong* decision based on rational thought. For example, because it is still early in the semester, the student may not have known that the professor is often 10 minutes late to each class and, therefore, wrongly, as it turned out, decided to forgo the coffee. That information might have changed the costs and benefits sufficiently to convince the student to wait for the coffee. Despite the student making what turned out to be the wrong choice, he acted "as if" he were making the right choice. A wrong choice may not be evidence of irrational behavior. Insufficient information, not irrational decisionmaking, prevented him from making a utility-maximizing choice.

What all this leads to is the basis for the economic approach to crime. If human actions are calculated so as to maximize utility, then people are behaving as if they are rational decisionmakers. By weighing the costs and benefits of their actions, humans are capable of deciding what course to follow. This approach offers a crucial extension to baseball legend/amateur philosopher Yogi Berra's rule, "When you come to the fork in the road, take it." In this case, when you come to the fork in the road, you take the route that yields the maximum of net benefits over costs, or simply, the one that will facilitate maximizing utility. It's not as catchy as Yogi's advice, but as a model of human behavior, it has far greater predictive ability.

As I indicated above, the operative question that economists typically assume about decisionmaking is, "Is it worth it?" How did this approach to human behavior—the maximizing of one's welfare by carefully (even if subconsciously) weighing costs and benefits, or this rational thought process—ultimately find its way to the study of crime and criminal behavior? How could the criminal mind, deviant and far beyond the norm as some psychologists believe, be analyzed in the context of rational choice theory? Close examination will show that this is not a stretch at all, at least not in the theoretical thoughts of many economists as well as in their empirical findings.

Crime and Marginal Analysis

To proceed, it is necessary to distinguish between the different types of criminal behavior as classified by the U.S. Department of Justice's household survey data to determine the rate of criminal victimization (U.S. Department of Justice, 2002). Data for 2002, for example, reveal that there were a total of 22,880,630 violent and property offenses committed in the United States. Of that total, 17,539,220 involved property crimes such as household burglary and motor vehicle theft. The violent crime category, including rape, robbery, simple assault, and aggravated assault, accounted for 5,341,410 offenses—about one-third the number of property offenses. Represented another way, we observe that the rates at which persons age 12 and older are victimized by violent and property crimes are, respectively, 23.1 and 159 per 1,000 households. This suggests that a person has a far greater probability of being a victim of a crime against his or her property than against his or her person.

These are important facts surrounding the extent and depth of crime affecting the United States, which might surprise those who typically get most of their information from the popular press. Journalists simply give disproportionate attention to extraordinary, bizarre, and brutal acts, such as celebrity athletes accused of rape or homicide, disenfranchised teenagers going on a shooting spree, or painfully disturbed mothers drowning their children. This distorts the public's perception as to the reality surrounding most of the criminal offenses inflicted on our society today. Because the data show that most crimes are related to monetary incentives, I will initially apply the economic model to crimes such as larceny and burglary and momentarily postpone a discussion of nonpecuniary crimes. In addition, because some disciplines theorize that lawbreakers are biologically, psychologically, or culturally different from conformists to the law, it is compelling to restrict the analysis to one involving financial rewards where economists argue that the same theories explain criminal and noncriminal behavior alike.

The model economists use to explain criminal behavior is similar to the "being late vs. stopping for coffee" scenario described above. Only, here, we need to add another important component of the economic approach to behavior—*marginal analysis.* Economists suggest that when decision-makers ask, "Is it worth it?," they think in terms of the additional costs that will be incurred compared with the potential for additional benefits to be derived. In other words, we hypothesize that rational people ignore "sunk costs" when optimizing. An example would be akin to someone who subscribed to a magazine by taking out a one-year subscription for $37.50 per year. The subscription department notifies the subscriber that a two-year subscription would cost only $50.00. Here, the additional or marginal cost of the second year is only $12.50. The rational consumer would probably decide to take the two-year subscription, reasoning that the second year is only one-third the cost of the first. The point is that once the initial year's subscription is a given, what dominates the decision for the second year is the marginal cost of $12.50, and not the total of $50.00. Economists believe that this type of reasoning is common and explains consumer behavior.[2] That's why retail stores often advertise a second pair of shoes at 50 percent off instead of simply 25 percent off all shoes. That incentive is more likely to get buyers to purchase two pairs instead of just one, or possibly none at all.

How might this add to the understanding of criminal behavior? It is important to emphasize that economic analysis does not try to explain or predict the behavior of any one individual's likelihood of committing crimes, but rather it tends to look at an *aggregate,* or large collection, of behaviors and policy decisions, their impact on crime rates, and the responses by criminals to those policies. In this context, it is perhaps easier to understand the manner in which this approach can be applied to criminology and related public policy.

Again we look at Becker's well-known economic model of crime, based in part on the *principle of deterrence,* which assumes that our awareness of potential rewards and punishments affects our decision to commit crimes. In particular, it is assumed that criminals change their behavior in response to changing incentives. Thus, crime might increase in response to greater benefits associated with committing the crimes, or by a reduction in costs associated with criminal behavior. Regarding the latter, social policy might be associated with the number of police officers in a particular city. This, in turn, might increase the likelihood of detection, arrest, and conviction, thereby raising the costs of criminal behavior. Or, suppose that the price of marijuana suddenly spikes upward due to a drought in marijuana-growing regions. This implies that for each sale of a given quantity of marijuana, the profits are higher, thus inducing more drug trafficking.

More specifically, we can demonstrate how analysis of marginal costs might work in relation to a set of options facing the burglar anticipating breaking into a house to make off with the maximum economic reward possible. We have all heard of examples either in television shows or in the news reflecting the "real life" of thieves who have been known to "case a joint" prior to the commitment of a break-in to someone's home. What exactly is the purpose of "casing" the potential crime scene? Simply stated, casing increases the level and accuracy of information a burglar possesses prior to committing the crime so as to "optimize" the net benefits of the theft. This example requires us to introduce the use of a simple diagram that illustrates economic theory's contribution to understanding criminal behavior (see Box 3.1 below).

Let's assume that a potential burglar had stolen cars in his youth but was never detected and maintains a clean arrest record. He has recently taken a job for $8.00/hour working as a carpet shampoo assistant. Such a job allows an individual to gain entry to many private homes in the course of doing his or her job, providing access to information about the potential "take" one might be able to score from any number of homes in the community. First we consider the benefits. The object of the burglary is economic gain, especially because an hourly rate of $8.00 is not a lot of money. The potential burglar quickly notices that all homes, despite their exteriors looking so similar, are not the same. He observes that some have jewelry in full view, expensive artwork, and high-end electronics throughout the house, while others are relatively devoid of items that have market value on the street. He then considers which of these would make the most sense to burglarize first, and then ranks the others sequentially.

This produces what economists call a marginal benefits curve, which looks as follows:

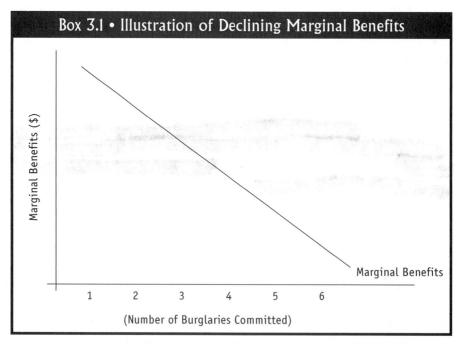

What this tells us is the first break-in committed by the criminal is going to be—other things equal—at the home where the largest stock of easily liquidated items can be found. The next home targeted would yield a lesser "take" and so on. Economists like to use the term "other things equal," which in this case suggests that factors other than the expected "loot," such as the risk of detection, is the same in all homes. It is standard for police to consider those who had the most recent information about a particular residence as suspects because they were in a good position to estimate the rewards of the efforts.

Just as in every other activity, there are costs associated with committing crimes. The costs associated with burglary might include tools to facilitate a break-in as well as some training that allows one to break-in to a home in the shortest amount of time, minimizing the chances of being detected, arrested, and convicted. Once again, the "casing out" of the homes would be relevant here. Some houses may have silent alarm systems, vicious dogs, bars on the window, and a private security force, while others may have simply a sticker on their front door suggesting that the home is alarmed but in fact it is not. Only an insider (or in this case the "shampoo man") is likely to have access to this information. Once obtained, we can see why the costs—or, more specifically, the marginal costs associated with this activity—would increase with each break-in, as shown in Box 3.2.

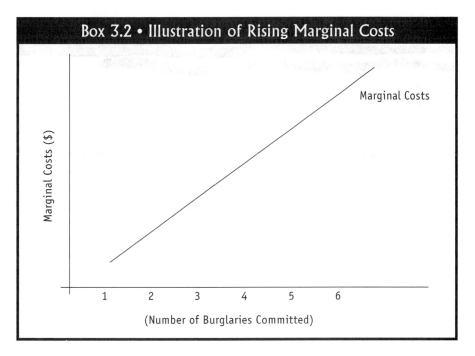

Box 3.2 • Illustration of Rising Marginal Costs

In seeking to minimize detection, the rational criminal would (other things being the same) first select the house with the least number of devices that might thwart his efforts. It is better to avoid the pit bull and the security force and go for the "mock" security system. The costs associated with this "job" would be lowest. But as the criminal is forced to continue burglarizing houses, he must eventually find homes that in fact are more challenging, thus incurring higher marginal costs. In addition to the factors mentioned above that cause the marginal cost curve to rise, there is another consideration that also explains the rising marginal cost curve.

Even if each home were comparably equipped with the same anti-theft devices, the marginal cost to the criminal would still increase as more homes are burglarized. The reason is that as additional break-ins occur, even the most skilled thief is likely to leave a trail of clues that police can piece together. As those clues accumulate with each additional act of burglary, the likelihood of arrest and conviction increases, thereby increasing the cost of "doing business." So just how many burglaries is this criminal likely to commit in a relatively short period of time, in the same neighborhood, prior to his having to find another rug shampoo job in some other town? We consider that in the next section.

Optimizing Behavior

Just as the student late for class had to weigh the costs and benefits of each action and decide whether to stop for the coffee, economists theorize that offenders will, consciously or not, act as if they are rational, and thereby commit only four break-ins in order to optimize their net benefits, or the benefits that remain after factoring out the costs (see Box 3.3). After this point, the marginal costs begin to exceed the marginal benefits, and the rational criminal will choose another method or target, or perhaps stop breaking the law altogether.

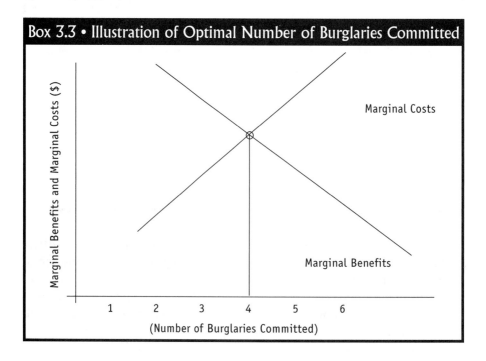

Box 3.3 • Illustration of Optimal Number of Burglaries Committed

Marginal Benefits and Marginal Costs ($)

Marginal Costs

Marginal Benefits

1   2   3   4   5   6

(Number of Burglaries Committed)

Optimization, in economic terms, occurs when the marginal benefits of certain actions no longer exceed the marginal costs, or more precisely, when marginal benefits that are downward-sloping equal the marginal costs. Any further activity beyond four attempts at burglary will yield a loss, with the marginal cost exceeding the marginal benefit of that last attempted burglary.

[handwritten: optimization => benefits = costs.]

Opportunity Costs: An Implicit Cost of Crime with Significant Implications

[handwritten: opportunity cost - the next best alternative that will be sacrificed when choosing an action (to engage in a certain behavior)]

Another important concept in understanding the rational approach to crime is that of *opportunity cost*, which basically stipulates that any time one decides on one course of action (sleeping late the night after a party) there may be associated costs such as missing a class, not playing tennis, or perhaps not seeing Katie and Matt on the *Today* show. The opportunity cost of sleeping late would be the value of the next best alternative not chosen. That is, we tend to choose that activity or make a choice based on that choice providing the most satisfaction or utility. The opportunity cost, therefore, unlike many other more obvious accounting costs, is not necessarily measured in dollars, but in utility or satisfaction. In our example, if the "partied-out" late sleeper would have chosen to attend her early morning class instead of sleeping in, then we can say that her opportunity cost of sleeping may have been missing her professor's explanation of supply and demand. If we can assume that her skipping class was not due to a malfunction of her alarm clock or forgetting to set the clock, but rather a deliberate action, then it would be reasonable to state that she acted as if she was rational when deciding that she was incapable of absorbing economic theory that early after a late and wild night of partying. More formally, opportunity cost is defined as the next best alternative that must be sacrificed when choosing a particular course of action to satisfy a want.

Economists have made significant efforts to support their model with statistical analysis covering all types of crimes committed by all subgroups of the population.[3] Despite their breadth and range, I will initially discuss criminal behavior within a particular demographic group—young adult men. I chose this younger cohort as a counterargument to the belief that wisdom and rational behavior only happens in "older" subgroups. Professor Richard Freeman (1996) of Harvard University analyzed patterns of crime among this subgroup by highlighting the opportunity cost concept. He argues that the depressed labor market during the 1980s and 1990s contributed to the rise of criminal activity among less-skilled men.

Freeman shows how the disproportionate rate of criminal behavior associated with young males can be explained by examining two additional demographic characteristics: race and education. He points out that in

1993, one-third of 25-to-34-year-old black men who were high school dropouts were incarcerated. Moreover, the numbers incarcerated or under supervision of the criminal justice system (incarcerated, paroled, or on probation) do not accurately measure the actual rate of participation in criminal activity because not every criminal is caught, arrested, or (especially) imprisoned. Noting the limited labor market opportunities of young black men without a high school diploma, Freeman calculates a trend that demonstrates a rising rate of criminal activity among nonincarcerated men over the period 1977–1992. What's important is that when looking at the earnings potential associated with criminal behavior compared with legal alternatives over this same time period, Freeman (1996:33) concludes that his "bottom line assessment of the pecuniary side of the calculus is that earnings from crime increased relative to earnings from legal work in the 1980's, and that the hourly rewards to crime exceeded the hourly rewards from legal work." Young men with an opportunity cost or legal earning capacity of $5.00 per hour to $6.00 per hour of after-tax wages earned approximately $10.00 per hour in criminal activity. This and other studies demonstrate that young men do in fact respond to economic incentives associated with criminal activity. It is consistent with the notion that their opportunity cost of committing crime, that is, expected earnings in the legal labor market, is woefully low, often too low to motivate them toward legal means of support. Most importantly, we observe that due to the combination of a decline in legal earnings and the increased opportunities for criminal activity, perhaps associated with the increase in drug dealing, the behavior of young black men falls neatly into the expectations and inferences of the economic model.

There is another aspect of the equation relevant to this group that must be considered. Besides the relative earnings capacity as an incentive to commit crime, there is another cost component of participating in illegal activities. As indicated earlier in the chapter, as costs associated with crime increase, we would expect that the perceived "optimal," and therefore actual, level of crime would decline. One important group of costs consists of the *expected punishment* associated with criminal activity. By expected punishment, we mean the likelihood of being arrested and convicted, and the severity of the incarceration that may follow such convictions. For example, if there is a 10 percent probability of being convicted of a crime for which there is an average sentence imposed of 10 years, then the expected cost of punishment in committing that crime would be one year of imprisonment. Even though no one might ever serve that length of time for that crime, it might be easier to understand if you think in terms of the following. If one commits a given crime 10 times with a 10 percent likelihood of getting caught each time, then there is a certainty that he would be caught at some point and would serve 10 years. That averages out to one year for each crime committed and hence an *expected* punishment of one year.

A basic and significant premise of the economic model is that changes in expected punishment should produce changes in criminal behavior.

Until now, we have centered our attention on crimes primarily involving property or economic gain. But the economic approach to understanding crime is not limited to studying crimes involving financial motivation. There is a wide body of literature that examines the impact of deterrence on adults' violent and nonviolent crimes (DiIulio and Piehl, 1991; Ehrlich 1973, 1981; Levitt 1996, 1997). Returning to the focus on youth, however, Steven D. Levitt (1998) observed that there had been minimal previous work testing the responsiveness of juvenile crime to changes in punishment. His work focuses on the fact that from 1978 to 1993, the rate at which juveniles were arrested for violent crime rose approximately three times the increase for adults. The contrast in growth rates involving murder are even more compelling. Arrests of juveniles committing murder rose 177 percent during this time period, while the rates for adults actually fell slightly. Why should there be such a variance in these rates of growth between minors and adults? Levitt hypothesized that changes in relative punishments, that is, declining penalties for juveniles, relative to adults, accounts for more than one-half of the differential in these startling growth rate disparities. The declining costs to juveniles rendered it more "profitable" to commit their crimes than if those same offenses had been committed by adults.

The point here is simple. Even as boys become young men, they appear to behave in a manner consistent with the economic model. Levitt's findings suggest that a sudden increase in the cost side of the equation (being punished more harshly as an adult compared to a minor) will modify behavior in a positive way—to reduce criminal activity among those leaving minor status. More specifically, Levitt reports that "in states in which the juvenile courts are most lenient vis-à-vis the adult courts, violent crimes committed by a cohort fall by an average 3.8 percent on average when the age of majority is reached. In contrast, violent crimes rise 23.1 percent with passage to the adult criminal justice system in those states in which the juvenile courts are relatively harsh compared to the adult court" (Levitt, 1998:1159).

Skeptics ask how such young and reckless youths can engage in such sophisticated calculation. Are young people capable of acquiring the information necessary to act rationally, and do they have the capacity to modify their behavior in response to that information? Levitt's evidence suggests that a deterrent effect is present. Even moving beyond scientific empiricism, one can find evidence of "rational" thinking in anecdotal form. For example, a revealing collection of interviews with adolescent offenders (Glassner, Ksander, and Berg, 1983:220, quoted in Levitt, 1998) suggests a dramatic drop in criminal activity as the offenders reach the age of maturity. Interviewee comments, such as, "When you are a boy, you can be put into detention home. But you can go to jail now. Jail ain't no place to go," speak to the fact that individuals are more capable of rational behavior than many give them credit for.

Opportunity Cost from a Broader Perspective

There is more evidence that economic trends have an effect on crime. One study of men without a college education (Gould, Weinberg, and Mustard, 2002) showed that when their wages, adjusted for inflation, fell by more than 20 percent, property and violent crimes increased by 21 percent and 35 percent, respectively, during that period. What is most interesting was that the strongest link in declining wages and rising crime rates was found to exist between wages and property crimes, such as burglary, and certain specific violent crimes, including assault and robbery, often associated with monetary incentive. What this demonstrates once again is how decisions may be based on comparing the relative benefits of different courses of action. Perhaps most compelling is that even after excluding the effects of individual and family characteristics and deterrence variables such as arrest rates and police expenditures, declining wage trends explained more than 50 percent of the increase in property and violent crime indices over the period studied.

Another gauge of economic conditions is unemployment rates. Many economists and sociologists agree that unemployment rates move in tandem with crime rates—higher unemployment breeds additional crime—but they disagree on the reasons. Some sociologists believe that poverty, caused by unemployment, breeds a subculture of "different" individuals. The theory behind the economists' view is quite different. The economic model predicts that as opportunities—jobs—become scarce, the relative attraction of illegal activities is enhanced. The economic model states that the opportunity cost of engaging in illegal market activities decreases during periods of rising unemployment, making criminal acts somewhat more profitable and therefore more enticing. A sociologist colleague of mine, who places a great deal of weight on the impact of socialization, subcultural norms, and individual morality, challenges the economic model by asking if I would switch to crime if I found myself unemployed. Clearly, he believes that an upstanding citizen such as myself would never turn to criminal behavior. Because it is a hypothetical question anyway, my instinct is to agree and say, "Of course not." However, there are two problems with this response. First, if I think of myself as the primary "breadwinner" of my family, I wonder how desperate I would have to be to consider stealing a loaf of bread. Is there no point where I or anyone would turn to some criminal act to feed myself and my family? At some point, wouldn't the benefits justify crime in one's own mind? In the play *Les Miserables*, revolutionary leader Jean Valjean demonstrates that even noble and righteous men may break the law when faced with certain untenable choices. So, despite my having a record of no arrests and having never previously committed burglary, it is possible that under certain conditions, I might just be compelled to do so. The contribution of economic theory, however, is not, once again, to predict what I or any one individual may or may not do when confronted with the need to choose between two alternatives. Therein lies the second problem: As job conditions worsen, as the relative costs and benefits shift, some—not all, maybe not even most—but a sufficient number of souls will alter their behavior in ways significant enough to change the level of criminal activity.

What happens when we move from *anecdotal evidence*, based on hearsay, to *empirical research*, based on systematic and scientific observation? In the matter of the relationship between unemployment and crime rates, while there is no shortage of research, the evidence is mixed. Box (1987) in a review of the literature found that 20 out of 35 published studies suggested that unemployment and crime were positively related. The remaining 15 were unable to find any statistical significance between these two variables. However, it should be noted that there is a theoretical twist that might contribute to the difficulty of establishing the statistical reliability of this relationship.

While we understand that during adverse economic conditions, some individuals with lesser skills and limited employment experience may be attracted to an alternative to legal wage-earning opportunities, we would expect this to be consistently demonstrated throughout the literature. However, when more people are out of work, it may become increasingly difficult to engage in criminal activity, because the potential victims, or targets, change as well. For example, the fact that more people are likely to be home throughout the day thus reduces the chances of the perpetrator going undetected in the course of committing the crime. In addition, during recessionary periods, there may be fewer potential victims with less cash on hand. These possibilities have suggested to some that during economic downturns, one sees effects that at least partially offset each other. In other words, the relative benefits from crime have induced more criminal behavior, while the costs of committing those crimes may have also risen, thus reducing the optimal number. Because both of these factors may be operating, the net effect becomes a question not easily answered by theory alone. Hence, it may not be surprising that the statistical studies are divided as to the impact of unemployment on crime. Despite these inconsistencies, there is fairly compelling evidence that at least with regard to the most recent period of economic growth, the full employment that we experienced in the last half of the 1990s clearly contributed to the decline in crime rates.

White-Collar Crime and Adult Behavior

While some types of crime are related to unemployment, white-collar crime generally requires employment and is not a crime committed by the poor or disadvantaged. That is, white-collar criminals, or those who engage in crimes such as tax fraud, insider trading, and corporate corruption, without the violent acts that often accompany other crimes motivated by economic gain, probably operate under a different set of behavioral assumptions than street criminals. The sociological approaches that focus on one's limited socioeconomic status cannot explain the behavior of those engaging in such white-collar crimes. While some have tried, it would be an oversimplification to attribute white-collar crime simply to greed.

Interestingly, Alan Greenspan, Chairman of the Federal Reserve, has recently commented on the current problem of white-collar crime, which has increased in recent years despite declines in violent and property crimes. His comments, while recognizing that greed is never in short supply, assert that it is not a change in human behavior toward even greater greed, but rather that "avenues to express greed had grown enormously" (Norris, 2002). The proliferation of stock options as a means of executive compensation, for example, introduced a novel and yet dreadful incentive structure that could easily be used as a means toward enhancing one's wealth if corporate profits could be artificially inflated. So, having discovered a low-cost approach to accumulating "paper" wealth in their accounting ledgers, corporate leaders did indeed fake whatever they needed in order to drive stock prices—and their own salaries and reputations—skyward. The point is that as the incentives or potential benefits changed, so did the behavior of seemingly law-abiding citizens. Despite their affluence, their behavior turned toward illegal activity in conjunction with their already lucrative "day" jobs. Their rational choices operated in much the same way as the high school dropout who turns toward dealing drugs to supplement the cashier position at Wal-Mart.

The educational level of society has increased in the past 20 years and in the minds of some of the more educated public, if you want to commit a crime, *fraud*—the taking of money or property through deception or cheating—would seem to be the most rational choice. Why? Simple: The benefits in terms of financial gain tend to be greater than robbery, for example, while the costs in terms of punishment are generally less. Financial pressures clearly contribute to the incentives to create fraud. Given a downturn in the economy, the perception that the opportunity to commit fraud is there for the taking, coupled with financial pressures, provide the incentives for a rising level of white-collar crime. Opportunities that were not available in the past might include financial crimes associated with the proliferation of the Internet: software privacy, e-mail pyramid schemes, identity theft, and the like.

One final word about taking advantage of opportunities, even those that cross the line of legality: How many respectable, seemingly law-abiding citizens do we know who might cheat a little on their taxes, pirate the occasional software program, exceed speed limits, or hack their way into DirecTV? A very good friend of mine commits all of these crimes. He is, by these legal standards, a criminal, but at the same time he is a senior vice president of a consulting firm, very active in his church, charitable to those less fortunate, and most generous to his employees. He justifies this seemingly contradictory behavioral pattern on the basis that he cares about others and if mega-corporations are ripping off people, he doesn't mind "breaking the law." While I do not judge his behavior, I do maintain that his behavior would be different if the likelihood of arrest, conviction, and sentencing for his transgressions were different. In fact, he admits that he perceives the costs associated with breaking those laws as zero, or something close to that. Consequently, I offer that beyond his moral character, his disdain for corporate monopolies, and his concern for "the little guy," his decisions are most influenced by the costs and benefits of those actions rather than by predetermined notions of right and wrong.

decisions => influenced by costs & benefits rather than right & wrong

Public Policy Alternatives

The contribution of the economics discipline extends beyond understanding how costs and benefits, utility theory, and opportunity cost might explain criminal behavior. In fact, much of the research in the discipline involves applying economic theory to public policy alternatives. Knowing that criminals may act rationally has profound implications for seeking and implementing policies or governmental regulations that most efficiently will lessen criminal behavior. This requires us to recall Box 3.3 introduced earlier in the chapter. Recall that the optimal number of burglaries committed (from the criminal's perspective) would occur at Level 4. That is the point after which the marginal cost of committing a crime would begin to exceed the marginal benefits. Public policy can influence that optimal number in one of two ways. One approach might be to increase the marginal costs through law enforcement or punishment, which would theoretically increase the deterrent effect. For example, cities can increase their police forces, which should increase the costs of illegal activity to the criminal by raising the probability of being apprehended. That would shift the MC curve upward to MC' (it actually shifts to the left), thereby reducing the optimal level of criminal activity (see Box 3.4). Alternatively, one could consider imposing longer prison sentences, increasing the certainty of serving time if convicted ("three strikes and you're out" laws), or making a greater investment in the technology that facilitates forensic science and the apprehension of criminals. The impact of each of these, at least in theory, would be as indicated in Box 3.4.

Interestingly, each of the above policy options tends to be associated with a somewhat conservative perspective toward crime reduction. Because of that, economists are often labeled as such when it comes to public policy options. However, this need not be, and in fact, is not necessarily so. Still focusing on Box 3.4, we can introduce another policy alternative, representing a different and more liberal political and philosophical approach toward crime reduction. Recall that one of the factors that influences the cost of criminal behavior is the opportunity cost of wages that could be earned in various legal jobs. We previously indicated that the decline in wage rates for low-skilled youths (Freeman, 1996), relative to accessible criminal

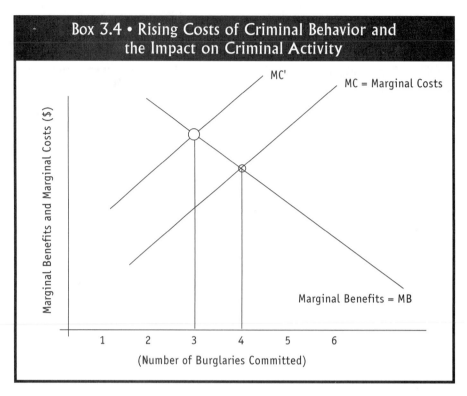

Box 3.4 • Rising Costs of Criminal Behavior and the Impact on Criminal Activity

activities, contributed significantly to rising crime rates. Clearly, another policy option would be to promote programs that are designed to increase wage rates for those members of society that are most prone to committing crimes. Thus, any program that enhances the employability and wage-earning capacity of young adults—higher wages, more liberal minimum-wage laws, more human capital investment, more intensive on-the-job training opportunities, or improved inner-city educational opportunities—would contribute to raising the "opportunity" costs of criminal activity. Attractive job opportunities cause a shift of the MC to the left, thereby reducing the equilibrium level of crime. While economists often support this approach, conservative politicians and talk-show pundits are more apt to emphasize the punishment side of costs and cite those studies as the appropriate and expedient route to crime reduction.

Before attempting to summarize the overwhelming amount of research that has been directed toward this issue, it might be useful to understand exactly what it is that economists are trying to unravel and why. There are many ways to reduce crime. Some jurisdictions might spend more on their police departments by hiring more police per capita. Alternatively, others might depend on their prison systems and decide to minimize parole opportunities. In the former situation, the probability of arrest may be greater, while in the latter, the average time served by a convict increases. Either way, the costs of criminal behavior go up and consistent with our model, the equilibrium level of crime should go down. In applying various statistical techniques to test for the validity of these relationships, we are concerned with what economists call the *elasticity,* or sensitivity between the variables. So first, our investigation seeks information on whether the sign or direction is consistent with our theory (does a greater probability of arrest reduce criminal activity in a particular area?) and second, by how much.

The importance of this can be framed in another way using economic principles. Any community has limited resources. If we can determine that the last dollar spent by increasing a police presence reduces crime by some level, compared with adding dollars to build more prisons to accommodate longer prison terms, then we have a better means of allocating those scarce crime-fighting resources. If, on the other hand, it can be shown that dollar for dollar, job training programs that enhance the wage-earning capacity of the high crime–risk population are even more effective toward reducing crime, we would suggest that such programs have a greater *marginal productivity* of crime reduction. This means that in addition to the myriad known factors that encourage or discourage crime, when job training joins the mix, the crime reduction effect is greater than when more police join the mix. The challenge for the economist is to identify which policy tends to be the most productive toward the process of crime reduction. This would allow economists whose mantra is often to promote maximizing society's output (in this case the output is crime reduction) to advocate for one type of policy over another, assuming that such sensitivities between the relevant variables could be ascertained. Such efforts can be daunting. The obstacles in unraveling these relationships and elasticities are due in part to matters such as: (1) acquiring reliable data, or data that consistently measure a particular phenomenon; (2) applying the correct statistical model; (3) identifying which crime-reducing activity is responsible for any progress toward crime reduction; (4) ruling out the effects of intervening factors such as the demographics of area populations; and (5) a host of other statistical nuances far beyond the scope of this chapter (Cornwell and Trumbull, 1994; DiIulio, 1996; Niskanen, 1994).

The findings of studies on deterrence need to be considered with caution. They all examine existing policies to see if there is evidence to support the notion that programs centered on deterrence can reduce crime. Although many studies fail to demonstrate a relationship between crime, on the one hand, and on the other hand, intervention programs that increase the certainty and/or severity of punishment, the failure may be the result of careless implementation of the program rather than the underlying theory of rational behavior. Failing to find a relationship between crime and punishment cannot be interpreted as evidence that criminals are not rational beings, as examples below will illustrate.

As is true of most scholarly research, studies of deterrence are reported in professional journals that are often of a technical nature and essentially speak to a limited audience, in this case other social scientists. For example, one comprehensive work (Cameron, 1988) summarizes more than

125 studies on the deterrent effect and crime. In this work, Cameron begins by reiterating Becker's position that criminals are rational and that several studies seem to support the notion that by increasing the certainty and severity of punishment we can deter crime. He warns, however, that oversimplified analyses may be misleading. To challenge the deterrence model, nine economic explanations are offered that are designed to counter the basic proposition that punishment deters crime. Cameron, himself an economist, suggests that due to *spillover* or *displacement* effects, greater deterrence efforts such as increased police forces in a given neighborhood may simply shift criminal activity to an alternative location, time of day, or type of offense. Thus, he maintains that in the short run, these efforts of deterrence simply "export" crime and the long run impact will depend on other communities' ability to react to an increase in crime in their jurisdiction.

While Cameron may be perfectly correct that in this situation, overall crime may not be reduced but only relocated, this argument, perhaps paradoxically, adds support to the notion that criminals are rational. When criminals seek to commit their crimes in locations with comparatively low costs (lower probability of arrest, for example), they are exhibiting precisely the behavior economists predict. The problem is not the economist's faith in the model, but rather the policy that induces the crime to be exported to another locale. In this case, all one can establish is that deterrent efforts are too localized. Just like mosquito control is a difficult task if towns work independently, so too can crime control be evasive under those conditions.

The concept of *substitutability*, or replacing one method with another, provides yet another example of rational behavior, accompanied by the appearance of ineffective deterrent effects. When mandatory prison sentences for robbery with a firearm were introduced in Arizona in 1984, the results suggested that "rational offenders, viewing armed robbery as more costly than in the pre-intervention period, were compelled to reduce the number of robberies perpetrated with a firearm." (McPheters, Mann, and Schlagenhauf, 1984:562; quoted in Cameron, 1988:314) In fact, while this reduction occurred, there was an increase in robberies *without* a firearm. One might view this as a failure to reduce crime rates, particularly robbery. However, if the goal of the policy was to lessen the likelihood of homicide during robbery by reducing the use of guns, then one would have to consider this a success. In either case, as the robbers shifted away from the more harshly punished act of armed robbery to the lesser act of robbery without a firearm, one can see clearly that rational thought entered into the decision-making process of the criminal.

Another measure of the deterrence model has to do with the availability of legitimate income opportunities. Cornwell and Trumbull (1994) demonstrate that while most measures of the criminal justice system's deterrent effect are weaker than previously believed, high wages (particularly in the manufacturing sector) appear to be very effective in deterring crime. While this important result is not a consequence of any particular public program, it most definitely suggests that public policies along the lines of increasing employment and training opportunities could be effective toward crime reduction. In addition, once again, it speaks to the "rational behavior–utility maximizing model" from a more liberal perspective—one that gets relatively little attention given current political leanings of Congress and the general population. If one's wage is enhanced due to the acquisition of a new skill, the cost of committing crime goes up, theoretically resulting in a lower number of crimes committed. Increasingly, the research evidence seems to support this.

Imprisonment: An Economic Approach

To refine the discussion of deterrence, we can look at a single component of deterrence: incarceration. Whereas deterrence in general is likely to be classified as a conservative approach to crime, longer prison sentences have different ramifications than, for example, increasing policing resources. Just as in other matters in which statistical analysis is relied upon to clear things up, there is a critical ambiguity that surfaces with this question.

Additional prison space permits longer sentencing and greater rates of incarceration. If this is accompanied by reduced crime rates, it is difficult to know whether it is the deterrent effect associated with a greater probability of incarceration, or simply a reduction in the number of criminals roaming free, that contributes to such findings. Does it matter? Well, it does and it doesn't. It does to the extent that it might be nice to know that deterrence works. This would provide credibility for the rational choice model and thereby lend further support for other programs that focus on deterrence. On the other hand, even without that knowledge, economists are also concerned with allocating dollars in the most optimal way to reduce crime. If we know that building more prisons and increasing sentencing is cost-effective, then more dollars for more prisons would make a great deal of economic sense, regardless of which effect is responsible.

This introduces a broader consideration regarding imprisonment and its cost-effectiveness. Thus far, our analysis has primarily been focused on the *private* benefits and costs of decisionmaking—those that accrue to the offender. Those decisions impact on the overall level of criminal activity. There is, however, another application of cost-benefit analysis with inclusion of what economists call *social costs*—costs that are imposed on "third parties," or those not involved in a particular transaction. In a work entitled, "Does Prison Pay?," DiIulio and Piehl (1991) recount a provocative debate based on a report by economist Edwin Zedlewski (1987). His analysis concluded (as it turns out, falsely) that if 1,000 felons were imprisoned, it would save society approximately $430 million a year in property losses, physical injuries, and human suffering—these items collectively representing the social costs of crime.[4] Measuring this against the $25 million ($25,000 annual cost per year to imprison one felon) produces a benefit-cost ratio of almost 17. By locking up those felons, society reaps a benefit of $430 million (by avoiding the social costs those felons would impose) at a cost of only $25 million. The net benefit is more than $400 million.

Of course, the reaction to Zedlewski's study was quick and not very friendly. Most significantly, critics charged that Zedlewski overestimated the number of crimes committed per criminal per year because he used the mean to represent the "average" criminal. The mean, unlike the median, which critics said he should have used, was distorted upward by a small group of exceedingly high-risk offenders, while the vast majority of offenders committed fewer than 20 offenses each. While the mean number of offenses measured was 187, the median was closer to 15 per year. That is, one-half of those incarcerated would be committing less than 15 crimes per year, and the other half more than 15. Therefore, using 15 in the numerator, rather than 187, generates a benefit cost ratio of incarceration of just over 1, grossly below the benefit cost ratio of 17 reported by Zedlewski. Using this estimate, locking up those 1,000 felons may not be all that cost-effective. Once again, we see how a statistical quirk can lead to enormously wide-ranging results with dramatically divergent policy implications. The debate raged on with statistical and anecdotal arguments on both sides, often biased in both directions. DiIulio and Piehl (1991:31) suggest that "extremists on either side of the Zedlewski debate are bound to be disappointed . . . [T]he net benefits of imprisonment are neither as large as Zedlewski's analysis would predict nor as miniscule as Zedlewski's strongest critics would assert." The point here is rather simple. Zedlewski, using cost-benefit analysis, touched off a debate with far-reaching implications in the public policy arena. The fact that a particular aspect of his work was highly criticized and erroneous is not as important to the discipline of economics as his overall methodology, which continues to draw attention and have an impact on policy implementation.

There are other considerations in this cost-benefit framework. Most importantly, one needs to know whether prisons confine the most active criminals, or if less dangerous criminals will be caught in the dragnet instead. Once again, this has a significant effect on determining benefits of additional incarceration. If we remove the most active, then the numerator in the benefit-cost ratio rises (more savings to society from reduced crimes committed) and the call for additional prisons makes sense. However, if the criminal justice system is already doing its job well, meaning that they have already incarcerated the most active criminals, then there is a strong likelihood that additional prisons would incarcerate the remaining less active criminals, producing what economists call a *low marginal product*. The savings associated with these felons would probably be too low to be cost-effective.

Alternatively, we can look at another study by Steven D. Levitt (1996), who estimated the impact of the increased incarceration of criminals on specific crime rates. His findings are rather compelling. Specifically, he demonstrated that had the incarceration of criminals not tripled, as it did from 1973 through 1994, property crimes would be almost 50 percent more frequent than they in fact were. Whether this is due to the deterrent effect associated with a greater likelihood of imprisonment, or simply the removal of criminals from society, is neither certain nor is it the primary concern of economists. Rather, the main economic issue is that Levitt finds this to be supremely *efficient*. Noting that the cost of crimes avoided on an annual basis would have amounted to approximately $54,000, compared to the cost of incarceration estimated at nearly $3,000/month, he calculates an annual net benefit of $24,000 for each criminal behind bars. While these results are not as extraordinary as Zedlewski's, the methodology used to reach his findings is both more sophisticated and credible.

Before moving to the next section, it is important to reiterate the main point. Economists, more so than others who study crime, are apt to think in terms of punishment as a deterrent to crime. It fits their model and there is substantial, though not universal, empirical support for this position. It is also consistent that economists look at imprisonment beyond the deterrent effect, as a relatively cost-effective means of reducing felonies. These issues are not yet resolved, and perhaps they never will be. It is probably fair to say that a healthy component of the debate has been a result of the theoretical and empirical work introduced by economists in an area once thought to be largely the principle domain of other disciplines.

Box 3.5 • Case Study: Homicide

Most of our discussion has centered on how rational choice theory can be applied to crimes that involve some form of monetary gain. The calculus is rather straightforward: if the benefits of a certain activity appear to exceed the costs, then action is warranted. We have focused on monetary benefits such as the net economic gains associated with illegal activities when compared to legal options. But can the theory of "maximizing" behavior fit into the world of those who commit violent acts such as murder and rape?

First, a reminder of the theory must be stipulated. It is important to remember that the rational choice or optimizing theory that economists apply to the world at large does not need to involve financial considerations to be relevant. *Maximizing utility* implies taking an action that yields some net benefit that may or may not be of a financial nature. Thus, it is the belief among many economists that under some circumstances, one would commit homicide to accomplish that end. If that is the case, then even homicide rates should be negatively related to factors that increase the punishment associated with these crimes. Is it possible to find evidence that could support the extension of this utility-maximizing approach to such an emotional, evil, and potentially irrational act? Well, economists have done just that.

It was the early work of Isaac Ehrlich (1973, 1975) that perhaps most opened up the firestorm of controversy in this area. Ehrlich theorized that homicides occur due to two distinct motives: one encompassed hate, jealousy, and other emotional conflicts; the other was simply a spillover of

Box 3.5, *continued*

offenses related to property crimes. He stipulated that acts related to love or hate should be equally responsive to expected gains and losses as any others. In other words, people can be very nasty when and if they think certain actions will leave them in a better situation.

Take for example a murder case that made national headlines about 15 years ago. In October, 1989, Carol Stuart, a pregnant, white lawyer was shot in the head in the Mission Hill neighborhood of Boston. Her husband, Charles, a fur store manager, called the police on his cell phone and reported that he had also been shot in the stomach by a black man with a raspy voice. The Boston police aggressively investigated the murder, turning Mission Hill into a war zone. A false arrest was made after the police stopped and searched countless young black men. There was a racial upheaval throughout the city, with calls for reinstating the death penalty and worse. Carol Stuart died, as did her baby after being delivered by Cesarean section. Ultimately, it was discovered that Charles Stuart had planned the entire episode. He stole his employer's gun, increased insurance policies on his wife, cleverly dispensed of the murder weapon, and established an extraordinary web of lies, which included shooting himself, to point the police in the wrong direction. His demise and ultimate suicide was perhaps due to the mistake of his younger brother's inability to continue to live with the knowledge and participation of an act that he could no longer conceal. Why did he do it? Psychologists might say he was a psychopath. Economists would say that he saw this route as a means toward a better life for himself. The evidence showed that despite the impression generated after the shooting that they were the perfect couple, they often fought over Charles' Friday nights out on his own, Charles was not anxiously embracing fatherhood, he was unhappy in his job, and he wanted to start his own restaurant. In sum, this seemingly outrageous and manipulative act was about money and personal freedom. He wanted the insurance money to open a restaurant.

One might ask, "How rational could Stuart have been, given the outcome of the case?" Our response would be to say that Stuart was acting as if he was making a rational decision. What often happens is that despite the appearance of rational behavior, individuals make bad choices due to imperfect information. We do it all the time. We make decisions that we regret, decisions that—had we known all we needed to know—we probably would have made differently. Had Stuart known that his brother would crack under pressure, he might have arranged things differently and gotten away with murder. Had he known that the police would eventually catch up with his charade, he may never have attempted to do it.

There are countless other cases: for example, the Pamela Smart case, in which a high school teacher manipulated her student lover to kill her husband; the O.J. Simpson case, which needs no description; and Rabbi Fred Neulander's life sentence for the murderous plan to terminate his troubled marriage by hiring two hit men. These all point to individuals meticulously planning and calculating the death of someone close to them, simply to help free themselves from some relationship with overtones of financial concern. Were these individuals psychotic? I don't know. But they certainly would fall

Box 3.5, *continued*

into one of Ehrlich's two categories for committing murder and therefore are relevant to the economic theory of choice.

Thus, as in other criminal acts, the punishment for committing a homicide, weighted by the probability of being punished, is the price that must be paid by someone who attempts to increase his or her own utility by killing another person. And as we have hypothesized, an increase in the cost of committing homicide reduces the margin of benefits over costs, thereby decreasing the number of homicides. Ehrlich included three components in the cost of committing homicide: the probability of arrest, the probability of conviction, and the probability of execution once convicted. His results demonstrated a statistically significant inverse relationship between all three factors and the homicide rate; that is, as any one of the factors contributing to the costs of committing homicide went up, rates went down. Most controversial was his finding that capital punishment was shown to have a deterrent effect on homicide. His study is most remembered for one of his simple but compelling conclusions: that one additional execution in a year could reduce the number of homicides annually by eight. Luksetich and White (1982) aptly remind us that it is the more conservative conclusions that tend to get reported and perhaps exploited. In summarizing Ehrlich's findings, they point out that he also found in the same study that declining unemployment has a greater impact on reducing homicide rates than does capital punishment. Recall that this indirectly raises the cost of criminal acts by increasing the opportunity cost of legal activity.

While it might seem surprising to discover this relationship between economic conditions and homicide, one must recall that homicide often results as a by-product of armed robbery or other such criminal offenses. To the extent that a reduction in the latter is more theoretically consistent with falling unemployment rates, we can see the link more clearly. Beyond the theoretical link, however, the outpouring of political controversy that surrounded the capital punishment component of his findings was not surprising. It was the first major work demonstrating empirically that capital punishment deters homicide. Needless to say, Ehrlich was not without his critics, and his was hardly the last word. The earliest critics challenged his findings by attacking methodological problems such as the actual span of time included in his data. In fact, it probably is responsible for much of debate that is still ongoing today.

A reasonable question might be why is it so hard to determine definitely whether capital punishment does in fact deter homicide. The answer lies, once again, in the complexity of the statistical techniques that attempt to sort out the cause and effect of a policy on outcomes. In the case of capital punishment, the issue is confounded by a number of problems. One such statistical limitation that is often discussed is the difficulty of assessing the impact of any policy measure when its use is relatively limited as in the case of capital punishment. Further consideration of the data limitations and statistical modeling is beyond the scope of this chapter.

Twenty years following his initial investigations, Ehrlich (1996) acknowledges that not every single offender might respond to incentives. He does maintain, however, that the self-serving nature of violating legal and moral codes provides ample reason to treat criminals as rational beings.

Political Economy of Crime: A Radical Perspective

Clearly, not all economists think alike. There are various quips regarding economic thinking, such as if you have three economists in a room, you'll wind up with four opinions. While this might be a bit of an exaggeration, there is certainly a grain of truth in its implications. These differences among economists, more often than not, are manifested in the popular press in areas such as tax cuts, a balanced budget, and inflation-unemployment tradeoffs. In most cases, the debates have significant political overtones, thus displaying the inevitable but oftentimes uneasy mix between politics and economics.

The *political economy* of crime is another contentious area between mainstream classical economists and those who take a more radical view of crime. This section is designed to merely introduce this alternative approach, with the understanding that a comprehensive treatment is well beyond the scope of this chapter. The roots of the political economy perspective stem from the writing of Karl Marx. It was Marx who first aroused most of the attention to the idea that many wrongs in society, certainly crime included, could be traced to the workings of the capitalist system. Marx argued that the accumulation of capital goods and advanced technology displaces workers and depresses their wages, thus rendering too many of them redundant. The resulting *surplus labor population*, or pool of available unemployed or semi-employed laborers, was manipulated by employers to suppress the wages of those remaining employed and limit any improvement in their labor status. While this despair by workers was seen as a benefit to employers, it also contributed to a propensity for the oppressed to commit crime. While the Marxian view of capital accumulation has been challenged and faulted for many reasons, this perspective on why crime develops—as an alternative for some to gainful employment—may not be all that different from the rational choice model.

The Marxian perspective argues that in fact, laws were established to treat particular segments of the population as deviants when their actions may be interpreted as being disruptive of capitalist social relations. For example, Humphries and Greenberg (1981:223) contend that nineteenth-century legislation against smoking opium was indicative of the sinister workings of the power structure within the capitalist system. The nineteenth century saw hundreds of thousands of Chinese immigrants arriving in California to work in railroad construction, agriculture, and mining. Their opium-smoking habits were largely ignored or, at most, treated as a cultural nuance while the economy was expanding. However,

Karl Marx. *With permission of The Warren J. Samuels Portrait Collection at Duke University*

when jobs became scarce during the depression of the 1870s, white laborers, joined by small business owners, found themselves in competition with Chinese retail businesses and forced legislation that banned the smoking of opium. Other methods of opium ingestion, which were not part of the Chinese cultural practice, remained legal. The authors conclude that the combination of an economic crisis coupled with weak class consciousness among workers helped to label such cultural practices as criminal acts.

Similarly, Linebaugh (1976) comments on the transformation of forest "common rights" to what he called the "inexorable expropriation of forest rights" in mid-nineteenth century Germany. In essence, the forest served as a safety net against business cycles and natural disasters for peasants who depended upon the free wood for a multitude of reasons: basket-making, tanning, tile-making, and so on. When the law changed to protect business owners, the sudden elimination of their primary source of income turned many peasants into criminals as they continued to do what they had always done—take wood from the forests rather than "starve, emigrate or work in factories." Only now, this was an illegal act, theft, and they were criminals.

While the patterns of crime can be traced to class distinctions, power struggles, and political developments, one cannot dismiss the role of the rational choice model, although political economists are very much at odds with rational choice economists. Part of what disturbs political economists is found within the simplifying assumptions of the rational choice model, particularly as it concerns the policy implications of applying cost-benefit analysis to controlling crime.[5]

First, there is overwhelming skepticism on the matter of whether spending more on crime prevention will in fact increase the probability of apprehension and conviction. Political economists challenge the notion that additional dollars spent will automatically be effective by raising the costs to the criminal. In addition, there is doubt that the actual level of government expenditures on crime prevention accurately reflects society's true preferences. Regarding the latter, political economists contend that the wishes of particular groups with vested interests are more powerful in influencing public expenditures than the society at large. Their vision for a better world would require a reallocation of society's scarce resources, rather than assuming that the best resource distribution should rely on individuals' rational choices. It is this latter point that is so dear to the rational choice model of our economy, and is tied in so closely with market concepts including efficiency and optimization.

In fact, the radical perspective, simply stated, has stipulated that the problem of crime in the United States will not be significantly reduced unless there is a fundamental redistribution of power in our society (Gordon, 1971). The position is predicated once again on the idea that the actions of the State in capitalist societies primarily benefit members of the capitalist class, and if solutions to the problems continue to be evasive, then nothing short of a complete overhaul of the power structure could bring about effective change.

It is important to add that while the Marxian approach is rooted in a totally different theoretical model than the rational choice model, there is oddly some common ground between them. Political economists argue that the system dictates choices that force many individuals to turn to crime for their survival.

> Driven by the fear of some economic insecurity and by a competitive desire to gain some of the goods unequally distributed throughout the society, many individuals will eventually become "criminals." . . . Radicals therefore argue that nearly all crimes in capitalist societies represent perfectly rational responses to the structure of institutions upon which capitalist societies are based (Gordon, 1971, quoted in Andreano and Siegfried, 1980:102)

What is most interesting here is that the radical perspective supports the notion that *given the alternatives and given the foundations and the existing power structure of the economic hierarchy found within the system,* most criminals are merely behaving in an optimizing manner. Where they passionately part ways with the rational choice approach to crime is in solving the problem. While political economists see solutions only associated with restructuring the whole system, the rational choice model seeks to work within the system by altering the costs and benefits of criminal behavior so as to make crime "less profitable." So, even within the Marxian perspective, a view held by a minority of economists, there is an opportunity to comprehend the rational choice model further.

Conclusion and Future Directions

Rational choice economists represent the majority, although not all, of economists who are interested in crime. Economists believe that utility theory—including the concepts of cost-benefit analysis, marginal analysis, deterrence, optimization, and opportunity cost—explains not only most behavior, but most criminal behavior.

Events including and since September 11, 2001, have ushered into the mindset of the U.S. public something that had previously seemed too distant and remote from our consciousness: the suicide bomber. The most devastating suicide bombing in the history of the world happened in the United States and was facilitated by the nation's very own assets—commercial aircraft. The loss of life was unprecedented, as was its impact on many sectors of our economy. Can this act, this homicidal taking of thousands of lives in addition to one's own, be explained within the context of the model of rational choice? As preposterous as it may seem, perhaps it can.

The New York Times (Van Natta, 2003) published a chilling piece concluding that "the suicide bomber is clearly the weapon of choice for international terrorists. Terrorist groups now rely almost exclusively on this tactic to carry out their attacks." This observation begs for an explanation. Interestingly, it is the position of the author that the rationale behind such behavior may be best expressed in economic terms. Reporter Jessica Stern interviewed the prominent Hamas leader, Ismail Abu Shanab. He spoke of the "eye for an eye" policy in Islamic law and the abundant supply of would-be bombers in Gaza. Stern concluded from her interview that suicide bombers are a terrorist organization's "most economically viable way to conduct its bloody business. . . . It's certainly cost effective, both financially and in terms of the number of terrorist lives ultimately put at risk." These considerations all point to cost considerations of terrorist groups. From an organizational perspective attempting to achieve its goal, there are plenty of bombs, but there are even more willing bombers. Thus, the resources required to inflict such damage, while spreading unimaginable terror, are considered cheap and, hence, a bargain.

With so many volunteers willing to take their own lives, one ordinarily might conclude that "they" are crazy, and thus their behavior could hardly be considered rational. However, researchers who have studied this conclude that in fact, terrorists tend not to suffer psychological disorders. They attribute such drastic behavior to "diminishing expectations." When a people fail to achieve through conventional means, radical behavior is not uncommon. More to the point of the rational choice model, though, the recent surge in suicide bombings is simply due to the expected benefits associated with volunteering—it is the fastest and surest way to be honored while simultaneously enhancing your surviving family's financial well-being. In their world, there is ever-lasting glory to be gained. The suicide bomber's family can forever celebrate his or her heroism and martyrdom. Therein lies the benefit side of the model. Organizationally, nothing could be more cost-effective; while to the bomber, no alternative could generate such accomplishment and achievement.

The policy implications in this instance, however, are not so simple. The best political and military strategists have yet to find a workable solution. Ideas, however, do fall into the cost-benefit model and typically call for a transformation of political systems to foster greater freedom and economic opportunity. Accomplishing this would enhance the potential benefits of pursuing a more conventional means of achievement than suicide bombing. In effect, it raises the opportunity costs of suicide to the potential martyr. If successful, it can also raise the costs to extremist groups by reducing the relatively abundant number of would-be bombers. While this is a simplistic treatment of one of the most complex and dangerous crises facing the United States today, it does nevertheless offer a theoretical foundation for reducing terrorist atrocities.

Endnotes

1. The "classical" school of economics—represented by David Ricardo and Adam Smith, for example—dominated economic thinking up until the late nineteenth century and best exemplifies the more conventional emphasis on objective factors such as prices, costs, and income distribution.

2. Closely related to this is the concept of utility theory, which essentially states that as buyers consume successive units of the same commodity, additional units bring lower levels of satisfaction (or utility) to that consumer. An example would be the declining satisfaction one might derive from eating additional slices of pizza.

3. Perhaps no one has contributed more toward this effort than Isaac Ehrlich. See, for example, several of his early works such as, "Participation in Illegitimate Activities: A Theoretical and Empirical Investigation," *Journal of Political Economy*, 1973, 81:3, 521-65; "The Deterrent Effect of Capital Punishment: A Question of Life and Death," *American Economic Review*, June 1975a, 65:3, 397-417; and "Crime, Punishment, and the Market for Offenses," *Journal of Economic Perspectives,* Winter 1996, 10:1, 43-67.

4. This figure is determined by assuming that each felon commits 187 crimes per year at an average cost per crime committed of $2,300: ($2,300 x 187 x 1,000) = $430,100,000.

5. It should be mentioned that other approaches to the study of crime have similar objections to the rational choice model. In economic terms, this limitation to the application of market efficiency is based on the idea that perfect information (necessary for optimal results) is highly unlikely in public-sector decisionmaking and policymaking.

Suggested Further Reading

Bouckaert, B., and G. De Geest (2000) *Encyclopedia of Law and Economics, Volume V. The Economics of Crime and Litigation.* Cheltenham, UK: Edward Elgar.

Welsh, B.C., D.P. Farrington, and L.W. Sherman (2000). *Costs and Benefits of Preventing Crime: Economic Costs and Benefits*. Boulder, CO: Westview Press.

S.D. Levitt (2004). "Understanding Why Crime Fell in the 1990s: Four Factors that Explain the Decline and Six that Do Not." *The Journal of Economic Perspectives*, 18(1):163-190.

Ludwig, J., and P. Cook (2003). *Evaluating Gun Policy: Effects on Crime and Violence*. Washington, DC: Brookings Institution.

References

Andreano, R., and J.J. Siegfried (1980). *The Economics of Crime*. New York: John Wiley and Sons.

Becker, G.S. (1968). "Crime and Punishment: An Economic Approach." *Journal of Political Economy*, 76 (March/April):169-217.

Box, S. (1987). *Recession, Crime and Punishment*. London: Macmillan.

Burtt, E.J., Jr. (1972). *Social Perspectives in the History of Economic Theory*. New York: St. Martin's Press.

Cameron, S. (1988). "The Economics of Crime Deterrence: A Survey of Theory and Evidence." *Kyklos*, 41(2):301-23.

Cornwell, C., and W.N. Trumbull (1994). "Estimating the Economic Model of Crime with Panel Data." *The Review of Economics and Statistics*, 76(2):360-366.

DiIulio, J., Jr. (1996). "Help Wanted: Economists, Crime and Public Policy." *Journal of Economic Perspectives*, 10(1):3-24.

DiIulio, J., Jr., and A.M. Piehl. (1991). "Does Prison Pay?: The Stormy National Debate Over the Cost-Effectiveness of Imprisonment." *The Brookings Review*, 9(4):28-35.

Ehrlich, I. (1996). "Crime, Punishment, and the Market for Offenses." *Journal of Economic Perspectives*, 10(1):43-67.

Ehrlich, I. (1981). "On the Usefulness of Controlling Individuals: An Economic Analysis of Rehabilitation, Incapacitation and Deterrence." *American Economic Review*, 71(3):307-322.

Ehrlich, I. (1975). "The Deterrent Effect of Capital Punishment: A Question of Life and Death." *American Economic Review*, 65(3):397-417.

Ehrlich, I. (1973). "Participation in Illegitimate Activities: A Theoretical and Empirical Investigation." *Journal of Political Economy*, 81(3):521-565.

Freeman, R.B. (1996). "Why Do So Many Young American Men Commit Crimes and What Might We Do About It?" *Journal of Economic Perspectives*, 10(1):25-42.

Glassner, B., M. Ksander, and B. Berg (1983). "A Note on the Deterrent Effect of Juvenile vs. Adult Jurisdiction," *Social Problems*, 31(2):219-221.

Gordon, D. (1971). "Capitalism, Class, and Crime in America." *Review of Radical Political Economy*, 3(3):51-75.

Gould, E.D., B.A. Weinberg, and D.B. Mustard (2002). "Crime Rates and Local Labor Market Opportunities in the United States: 1979-1997." *The Review of Economics and Statistics*, 84(1):45-61.

Humphries, D., and D.F. Greenberg (1981). "The Dialectics of Crime Control." In D. Greenberg (ed.), *Crime and Capitalism*, pp. 209-254. Palo Alto: Mayfield.

Labaton, S. (2002). "Downturn and Shift in Population Feed Boom in White-Collar Crime." *The New York Times*, Section 1 (June 2):1

Levitt, S.D. (1998). "Juvenile Crime and Punishment." *Journal of Political Economy*, 106(6):1156-1185.

Levitt, S.D. (1997). "Using Electoral Cycles in Police Hiring to Estimate the Effect of Police on Crime." *American Economic Review*, 87(3):270-290.

Levitt, S.D. (1996). "The Effect of Prison Population Size on Crime Rates: Evidence from Prison Overcrowding Litigation." *Quarterly Journal of Economics*, 111:319-351.

Linebaugh, P. (1976). " Karl Marx, the Theft of Wood, and Working Class Composition: A Contribution to the Continuing Debate," *Crime and Social Justice: Issues in Criminology*, 6:5-16, reprinted in D. Greenberg (ed.) *Crime and Capitalism*, pp. 76-97. Palo Alto: Mayfield.

Luksetich, W.A., and M.D. White (1982). *Crime and Public Policy: An Economic Approach*. Boston: Little Brown.

Marx, K. (1867). *Capital, vol. 1*. Tr. S. Moore and E. Aveling. New York: International Publishers. Reprinted 1967.

McPheters, L.R., R. Mann, and D. Schlagenhauf (1984). "Economic Response to a Crime Deterrence Program Mandatory Sentencing for Robbery with a Firearm." *Economic Inquiry,* 22:550-570.

Niskanen, W.A. (1994). "Crime, Police, and Root Causes." *Policy Analysis,* 218:1-23.

Norris, F. (2002). "The Markets: Market Place; Yes, He Can Top That." *The New York Times* (July 17): A1.

Smith, A. (1776/1937). *The Wealth of Nations.* New York: Modern Library.

U.S. Department of Justice, Bureau of Justice Statistics (2003). *Criminal Victimization, 2002,* NCJ 199994. Washington, D.C.: U.S. Department of Justice (August).

Van Natta, D., Jr. (2003). "The Terror Industry Fields Its Ultimate Weapon." *The New York Times,* The Week in Review, Section 4, (August 24):1.

Zedlewski, E.W. (1987). *Making Confinement Decisions.* Washington, DC: U.S. Department of Justice, National Institute of Justice.

Commentary

Kimberly Kempf-Leonard

There is a bit of a love-hate relationship between criminologists and economists—I should know, as a criminologist who associates professionally with a number of economists, both those who adhere strictly to rational choice theory and those whose axioms differ. Some criminologists have integrated their work with that of economists, but that integration chiefly has been among scholars with a Marxist perspective. It is really rational choice theory, dominant in economics and rooted in the eighteenth-century belief that behavior results from conscious efforts to maximize pleasure and minimize pain, that has attracted economists to study crime. During the past decade, criminologists have achieved some success integrating principles of rational choice into their studies. But how much do rational-choice economists, using theories and methods developed to study consumer behavior, for instance, contribute to our understanding of crime?

Generally, criminologists will disagree with economists in two main areas: (1) measurement and data, and (2) theories of human behavior. As far as measurement, criminologists believe that economists use secondary data (collected by other researchers) or archival data from criminal justice agencies without appreciating the flaws, idiosyncrasies, or other measurement problems in the data. Crime is not directly observable in most cases. In relying exclusively on such data as official records, criminologists would be concerned that the data represent only a partial reality of crime and might compensate by expanding their sources or using methods borrowed from sociology, such as in-depth interviewing, to create a more complete understanding. As concerns theoretical disagreements, criminologists contend that economists' belief in rational choice or free will is exaggerated, causing them to gloss over important social factors that influence crime and put forth explanations that are based on untested and questionable assumptions of free will. Privately, criminologists complain that economists tend to act far too self-important as experts on crime, particularly considering their relatively recent and limited participation in the study of crime. On the other hand, economists can, and many do, apply their techniques to refine statistical models that use large quantities of aggregated data, representing large groups of people, to predict or explain crime and what happens as a result of criminal justice procedures.

Criminologists work to understand patterns of criminality—who gets involved, why, and how; strategies that might prevent such involvement among others; and policy responses that reduce recidivism, enhance public safety, and are consistent with the humanity of society. Criminologists have varied backgrounds in sociology, psychology, biology, political science, anthropology, and economics. *Science* is what unifies criminologists, as well as what sets us apart from other professions, such as law, that focus on crime and justice. An important difference between a scholar who is identified as a criminologist and one who is identified as an economist who studies crime, among other subjects, is the criminologist's specialized focus on crime, criminals, and society's reaction to both.

Measurement and Data Issues

Although our views vary on which theories, methods, or policies are ideal, criminologists generally *do* agree on the fundamentals of science. Most importantly, we share the belief that crime, criminals, and justice systems, as well as other mechanisms of social control, *are* subjects for scientific inquiry. This means that ideas about connections between society and crime can be tested and found either true or false. Given the shared view on criminology as a science, there is also general consensus on five scientific standards to which we hold one another accountable within the discipline of criminology. While some economists share these principles, it is not clear that they are their highest priority.

First, the scope and purpose of research should be clear. For example, we cannot assert cause-and-effect relationships from research designed to be descriptive. Second, assurances must be in place for the ethical treatment of subjects. Some information we seek is particularly sensitive, and some offenders who "volunteer" information may not provide the reality we hope for, so it is especially important that criminologists conduct themselves ethically. Third, we are aware of potential sources of measurement error associated with study designs, data collection, and techniques of analyses. No single study can be perfect, so it is important to acknowledge pitfalls and try to overcome them. Fourth, we understand the extent to which our research is reliable (can be replicated) and valid (representing what we say it does). Fifth, we recognize limitations on our ability to be objective. Criminologists have personal views on topics, such as the death penalty, racial profiling, and the causes of crime, so they must recognize and communicate how their views affect their research. The collection of data directly from human subjects, as through interviews or surveys, or from institutional records (schools, courts, prisons, etc.), has cultivated a nuanced understanding of the data that we work with, its limitations, and its uses.

Theoretical Issues

As Rosenthal aptly explained in the previous chapter, deterrence, rational choice, or decision theory has guided a lot of the work in criminology by scholars trained in economics. The root of these theories was the classical perspective, which was introduced in eighteenth- century Europe during what has been called the "Age of Enlightenment" or "Classical Era." The "enlightened" view of human nature challenged the prevailing ideology of otherworldly determinism, such as demonic possession, and advanced a notion of born innocence, capacity to reason, and free-will motivation (e.g., Beccaria, 1764; Bentham, 1789, 1791; Smith, 1776/1937). Influence of the classical perspective was evident earlier in Western legal codes and policing strategies, but was not really found in criminology until the 1960s, when economist Gary Becker statistically modeled crime using the "expected utility principle" of individual rational choices. Since then, several efforts have been made to replicate and extend the rational choice approach from economics to criminology (see McCarthy, 2000, for a recent review). Becker (1995:12) claimed that "the essence of the economic approach to crime is amazingly simple." However, it is *too* simple for those criminologists who argue that the assumptions of rationality and free will overstate the case (e.g., Blumstein, 1998; Tunnell, 1992). The economists' need to assume individuals' universal capacity to reason seems particularly exaggerated for the many offenders who have problems with substance abuse, impulse control, and impaired intelligence or cognitive abilities. In my view, there is very little room in science for such untested assumptions.

A related disagreement between criminologists and economists has to do with the inclusion of social variables to predict or explain criminal behavior. Most criminologists would challenge the rational choice economic approach to studying crime, as described by Rosenthal in the preceding chapter, because other important individual, family, and societal influences are omitted. There is a good possibility that these multi-level factors, such as substance abuse, prior victimization, parental supervision, and neighborhood conditions, have a powerful influence on offenders' behavior, but these factors are absent from rational choice economic approaches to modeling crime. Some of us are working to adapt economists' models so that they account for differential decision processes and include additional social factors that contribute to crime, and certain economists have taken the cue and incorporated "noneconomic" social variables into their models. For example, Tsebelis (1990:256) emphasized that the "consequence of choices by rational individuals are socially influenced." Rather than assume that the principle of deterrence applies equally to all individuals, Grogger (1991) studied how punishment affects future criminality based on offenders' ethnicity and crime seriousness. Similarly, Levitt (1997) added race, age, welfare, schools, unemployment, and poverty to the traditional "deterrence" variables to explain a reduction in crime.

There are also new developments within the framework of deterrence, rational choice, or decision theory that respond to some of the earlier criticism that not all decisions are rational. One example is *game theory*, which McCarthy (2002:429) summarizes as follows: "[Game theory models] make explicit the assumptions that people know their actions affect one another and use this knowledge in making choices; that is, game theory models assume people act strategically in their interactions." Game theory models also assume that "decision-makers are rational, have knowable preferences, and . . . *they know the rules of the game*" [emphasis added]. In other words, game theorists acknowledge that their theories collapse in situations in which people are unaware of the rules and potential rewards. There are fewer assumptions in *evolutionary game theory*, which allows for the possibility that people may not know the benefits associated with some choices, but repeat behavior when they encounter unintended rewards (e.g., Vila and Cohen, 1992).

[handwritten margin note: knowing game vs not knowing it -]

Another way in which economists contribute to criminology, but one not explicitly mentioned in Rosenthal's chapter, is in the methodological area of *econometrics*. Econometrics is the name given to mathematical and statistical techniques used to examine relationships in large data sets between key economic indicators, such as labor force participation, interest rates, and spending patterns. It is not surprising, given the emphasis on quantitative analyses of a lot of data, that economists would help to advance some statistical techniques. Rosenthal is probably referring to econometrics when he states, "In fact, today, economic analysis has infiltrated, and in some cases, rewritten, fields as diverse as sociology, biology and the law."

A good example of econometrics that is widely applicable to criminology is James Heckman's (1979, 1980, 2001) correction for *selectivity bias*, a contribution that helped him earn the 2000 Nobel Prize in economics. To understand the problem of selectivity bias, recall what Rosenthal explained earlier about the assumption required in statistical modeling about "other things equal." This is the old concern of wanting to compare apples to apples, rather than apples to oranges. Heckman's contribution was to identify a statistical problem in research on labor force participation, whereby people ineligible for employment were being counted as equal to those who were unemployed but seeking jobs. His correction excludes those subjects who are inappropriate to study and thereby enables a more relevant comparison. One application of Heckman's statistical formula has helped criminologists understand better what happens in the sentencing process. One reason we examine sentencing and incarceration decisions is to assess "equal application of the law," or whether similar sentences are given to offenders convicted of similar crimes. We recognize that not all arrestees are eligible for sentencing and incarceration, so we often use Heckman's correction for selectivity bias to assure we are modeling the experiences for comparable groups of defendants appropriate for judges to sentence.

Scientists work within the traditions of "parent" disciplines and methodological experiences in which they were trained, but most criminologists recognize that understanding crime requires a team approach and multidisciplinary expertise. Unfortunately, some economists who study crime have not fully appreciated multidisciplinary collaboration. An officer of the American Economic Association recently acknowledged, "Economists are imperialists, they invade the turf of other professions, other fields of study and research" (Francis, 2002:21). John DiIulio (1996:3) criticized the analytical skills of criminologists in general and argued that "[criminology] is a field that needs to be conquered by economists." Comments such as these inspired the SUNY-Albany School of Criminal Justice to host a seminar in 2002 called "Economists in Crime: Imperialistic Invaders or Creative Contributors." Elsewhere, McCarthy suggests that work by economists fails to have impact in criminology because mainstream criminologists have been "discouraged by the pomposity of some economists' writings" (2002:417). As an example, he cites Becker's comment (1968:176), "I cannot pause to discuss the many general implications of [the rational choice] approach, except to remark that criminal behavior becomes part of a much more general theory and does not require ad hoc concepts of differential association, anomie and the like." Criminologists Michael K. Gottfredson and Travis Hirschi (1990:72) also retort, "the theoretical contribution of the new economic positivism is not as impressive as it is to its authors." It is somewhat ironic that game theory is a contribution from economics, yet poor gamesmanship by a few economists has apparently led to some professional animosities. There is surely a lesson here for us all: that criminology requires a team effort and everyone gets to play.

In the previous chapter, Rosenthal called Adam Smith's (1776) discussion of the utilitarian advantages that accompany division of labor "one of the most celebrated contributions to economic thought," so it is even more curious why many contemporary economists go it alone. Economists are often experts in sophisticated statistical techniques that are critical to many studies, but so are many other social scientists. Moreover, techniques for analysis are of limited value if they are applied to data that are inadequate to the task, and often economists aggregate, or combine, data they had no part in collecting. Despite the obvious savings of time and expense, if the data collection procedures are not fully described, the purpose of the original effort differed, or important concepts were not measured, there is little to be gained by new analysis. Efforts to establish the accuracy and consistency of previously compiled data are even more difficult if the analysis requires aggregation to represent a single large unit or comparison across different locations or time periods.

Two recent controversies in the economics of crime suggest problems that are connected to secondary analysis by scholars whose first area of expertise is economics, not crime. The first is the assertion advanced by Steven Levitt and John Donohue (2001; Donohue and Levitt, 2004) that effective abortion rates explain the decline in crime during the late 1990s. Beyond the ethical issues generated by their controversial notion that aborted fetuses were disproportionately those with procriminal traits, critics of Levitt and Donahue's work contend that the data at the source of the study were inadequate (Joyce, 2004) and note the problem of poorly specified or missing variables (Lott and Whitley, 2001). The second debate is raging over the quality of the data in economist John Lott's influential book, *More Guns, Less Crime* (1998). Lott reports that gun ownership reduces crime, which is contrary to the consensus among many criminologists (Ayres and Donohue, 2003a; 2003b; Donohue and Ayres, 1999; Hemenway, 1998; Plassman and Whitley, 2003).

While my criticism here has targeted economists in criminology, there is ample evidence that criminology, overall, would improve its explanatory and predictive capacities with more cooperative endeavors from scholars interested in understanding crime. Not long ago, criminologist Elliott Currie (1999) denounced as "triumphalism—even smugness" many crime and justice research and policy developments in the United States today. Smugness is unwarranted because, while some types of crime have been on the decline for the past decade, there are continuing problems of high rates of serious crime, imprisonment, and execution as well as new or increasing problems of white-collar crime, fraud, and terrorism. We need to learn how *risk factors*, such as weak parental attachment or rapidly changing norms, contribute to criminal behavior. We also need to understand factors that affect *desistance*, when offenders end their involvement in criminal activity, which undoubtedly includes an element of choice. Finally, we must build knowledge about effective interventions to enhance public safety and assist offenders with their desistance. Budget constraints mean limited funding for research and administration of crime policies, so criminologists need to work efficiently and in a wider arena that recognizes the global connections of U.S. society. Let us hope that in the future there will be no need to question the valuable contributions of economists to criminology.

References

Ayres, I., and J. Donohue, III (2003a). "Shooting Down the 'More Guns, Less Crime' Hypothesis." *Stanford Law Review,* 55(4):1193-1312.

Ayres, I., and J. Donohue, III (2003b). "The Latest Misfires in Support of the 'More Guns, Less Crime' Hypothesis." *Stanford Law Review,* 55(4):1371-1398.

Beccaria, C. (1764/1963). *On Crimes and Punishments,* trans. H. Paolucci. Indianapolis, IN: Bobbs-Merrill.

Becker, G. (1995). "The Economics of Crime," *Cross Sections* (Federal Reserve Bank of Richmond), p. 12.

Becker, G. (1968). "Crime and Punishment: An Economic Approach." *Journal of Political Economy,* 76:169-217.

Bentham, J. (1791). *Panoptican Prison, 2 volumes.* London: T. Payne.

Bentham, J. (1789). *An Introduction to the Principles of Morals and Legislation*, ed. by H.L.A. Hart and J.H. Burns. London: T. Payne (reprinted 1970).

Blumstein, A. (1998). "U.S. Criminal Justice Conundrum: Rising Prison Populations and State Crime Rates." *Crime & Delinquency,* 44:127-135.

Currie, E. (1999). "Reflections on Crime and Criminology at the Millennium." *Western Criminology Review,* 2(1):1-12. http://wcr.sonoma.edu/v2n1/currie.html

DiIulio, J.J., Jr. (1996). "Help Wanted: Economists, Crime and Public Policy." *Journal of Economic Perspectives,* 10(1):3-24.

Donohue, J. III, and I. Ayres (1999). "Nondiscretionary Concealed Weapons Law: A Case Study of Statistics, Standards of Proof, and Public Policy." *American Law and Economics Review,* 1:436-470.

Donohue, J. III, and S. Levitt (2004). "Further Evidence that Legalized Abortion Lowered Crime: A Reply to Joyce." *Journal of Human Resources,* 39(1):29-41.

Francis, D.R. (2002). "Economists Go Afield to Crunch Data on Social Issues." *The Christian Science Monitor*, (June 10), 21.

Gottfredson, M.R., and T. Hirschi (1990). *A General Theory of Crime.* Stanford, CA: Stanford University Press.

Grogger, J. (1991). "Certainty vs. Severity of Punishment." *Economic Inquiry,* 29:297-310.

Heckman, J. (1979). "Sample Selection Bias as a Specification Error." *Econometrica,* 47:153-161.

Heckman, J. (1980). "Addendum to Sample Selection Bias as a Specification Error." In E. Strumsdorfer and G. Farkas, eds., *Evaluation in Studies Review Annual,* 5, pp. 69-74. San Francisco: Sage.

Heckman, J. (2001). "Micro Data Heterogenity and the Evaluation of Public Policy: Nobel Lecture." *Journal of Political Economy,* 109:673-748.

Hemenway, D. (1998). "Book Reviews." *New England Journal of Medicine,* 339:2029-2030.

Joyce, T. (2004). "Did Legalized Abortion Lower Crime?" *Journal of Human Resources,* 39(1):1-28.

Levitt, S., and J. Donahue (2001). "The Impact of Legalized Abortion on Crime." *Quarterly Journal of Economics,* 116(2):379-420.

Levitt, S.D. (1997). "Why Do Increased Arrest Rates Appear to Reduce Crime: Evidence from Prison Overcrowding Litigation." *Quarterly Journal of Economics,* 111:319-351.

Lott, J. (1998). *More Guns, Less Crime.* Chicago: University of Chicago Press.

Lott, J.R., and J.E. Whitley (2001). "Abortion and Crime: Unwanted Children and Out-of-Wedlock Births." *Yale Law & Economics Research Paper,* (April 30), No. 254.

McCarthy, B. (2002). "New Economics of Sociological Criminology." *Annual Review of Sociology,* 28:417-442.

Plassmann, F., and J. Whitley (2003). "Confirming 'More Guns, Less Crime.'" *Stanford Law Review,* 55(4):1313-1370.

Smith, A. (1776/1937). *The Wealth of Nations.* New York: Modern Library.

Tsebelis, G. (1990). "Penalty Has No Impact on Crime: A Game Theoretic Analysis." *Rational Sociology,* 2:255-286.

Tunnell, K.D. (1992). *Choosing Crime: The Criminal Calculus of Property Offenders.* Chicago: Burnham.

Vila, B.J., and L.E. Cohen (1993). "Crime as Strategy: Testing an Evolutionary Ecological Theory of Expropriative Crime." *American Journal of Sociology,* 98:873-912.

Chapter Four

Psychological Perspectives on Crime

C. Gabrielle Salfati and L. Thomas Kucharski

If you were to ask a layperson, someone with no formal training in psychology, "What do psychologists do?" or "What is psychology?," they would probably say that psychologists treat people with emotional problems. They would define psychology as an endeavor that deals with the mind. While one function of psychologists is to provide therapy, less than one-half of those who hold a Ph.D. in psychology work mainly as clinicians or counselors, that is, as providers of therapy to people with mental and emotional difficulties. The belief that psychologists are primarily interested in the "mind" is also incorrect. Such an interest is more the focus of those involved in *parapsychology* the study of psychic, or supernatural, phenomena. An example from parapsychology is the presumed ability of psychics to locate the body of a homicide victim by mentally connecting with them and visualizing the crime scene. While this is interesting, it is more a matter for mystics than for psychologists. Psychology is a scientific discipline, while parapsychology deals with phenomena that are not subject to scientific scrutiny. Although some topics in psychology, such as emotions or feelings, are difficult to study scientifically, psychology nevertheless attempts to use scientific methods and principles to explain these phenomena.

What then is psychology, and what do psychologists do? What contributions has the discipline of psychology made to our understanding of crime, and what theories have psychologists developed to explain the causes of crime or the motivations and behaviors of criminals in the commission of their crimes? In this chapter we will address these questions to the extent that the current knowledge in psychology and crime allows.

An Overview of Psychology as a Discipline

Psychology is best described as the systematic and scientific study of human and animal behavior. Its goals are to describe, predict, control, influence, and/or change behavior. *Behavior* is an overt act that can be directly observed. Physical movements, verbal statements, and social actions that can be measured are all considered behaviors. We can't see memory, thoughts, intelligence, anxiety, prejudice, stress, or someone's beliefs, values, or attitudes. These are all *mental constructs*, or internal states of mind, that are of tremendous importance to psychologists. One way to understand how psychology helps us understand mental constructs is by taking a simple example. Let's say that we go to the store to do the weekly shopping and fail to bring back a number of items requested by our partner who is cooking a big dinner for all our friends that night. We cannot see our partner's dissatisfaction with our shopping failure, but their comments and statements, what they say to us, and how they look at us, are all too easy to perceive. We could categorize the specific words said, measure the volume and tone of their voice, take note of their facial gestures, and so on. From this we might infer that they are disappointed, frustrated, or maybe even concerned about our memory.

In a similar vein, we can't see prejudice but we can hear the prejudicial statements and observe the actions of a person who holds biased beliefs. Similarly, beliefs and attitudes about the death penalty cannot be observed directly but can be measured by asking someone to respond to a questionnaire about their views on capital punishment.

Psychology has evolved from its early beginnings more than 100 years ago, and as described above, is now considered a scientific discipline. Early psychologists were interested in studying basic processes such as physical sensation, perception, and reaction time to stimuli. These processes were considered to be foundational to people's experience and amenable to scientific scrutiny. By *scientific* study we mean a systematic inquiry of measurable phenomena and rigorous testing of the effects of these phenomena on a person. It is a way of understanding how we "know" certain things to be reasonably true. Scientific understanding is sometimes contrasted with "faith," where knowing is prescribed by a religious or philosophical belief system. Faith-based beliefs are accepted because they are what we believe to be the true or ultimate meaning of our experience or existence. They are not something that was shown to be true because of an experiment we conducted.

Knowing in science comes from formulating and testing hypotheses. *Hypotheses* are typically if/then statements that emerge from a theory. A simplified theory might state that violence on television leads to viewers exhibiting violent behavior. The theory would explain why this relationship is thought to be true by incorporating all the relevant scientific principles of psychology. The logical extension of this theory would be the hypothesis: If viewers are exposed to violence on television, then they will behave more violently than those who are not so exposed. Here is where the psychological study of human behavior becomes difficult and complex. What do we mean by television violence? How much TV viewing constitutes significant exposure? How do we define and measure violent behavior? Is it an act that physically harms someone, a slap on the face, or does a physical threat also constitute violence? It is the confidence that we have in these definitions that eventually determines if we believe the results of our scientific analysis of this psychological theory. It all has to do with how we *define and measure* the physical manifestation of a mental phenomenon.

Psychology, as an expansive and expanding discipline, encompasses many subfields that focus on different aspects of the individual and employ various measures of behavior to explain different psychological phenomena. These subfields include social psychology (understanding how a person's social environment influences his or her behavior), developmental psychology (how children develop and mature into adults), cognitive psychology (how an individual thinks about and understands the world around them), biological psychology (how biological predeterminants, genetics, and functions affect an individual's behavior and thought processes), and abnormal psychology (the study of psychological difficulties, maladjustments, and mental disorders). In addition, there are a number of specialties within these subfields, including clinical psychology (assessment, treatment, and therapy), organizational psychology (how individuals function within organizations), and many others. Later in this chapter, we will closely examine the branch of forensic psychology, a subfield that applies theories in psychology to practical considerations in legal proceedings and criminal investigations. We will also consider some of the key differences among the interests and foci of various specialty areas of psychology.

It is important, however, to keep in mind that the aforementioned list is by no means exhaustive; it is only representative of the subfields of psychology that are most often called upon by theorists attempting to explain an individual's criminal behavior. It is also important to remember that although each subfield is concerned with a limited number of psychological issues, most psychologists acknowledge the complexity of the whole person, in terms of their biological heritage and functions, their life history and current social influences, their current behaviors, and their future development.

Understanding Different Aspects of Human Behavior

We said before that psychologists are interested in behavior and the mental constructs or psychological tendencies that underlie it. How do these tendencies to behave come to be? Are they inherited? Are they a result of our biology and genetics? Are they learned from experiences with others? Do biology and social experience combine to create our personalities, our tendencies to behave in criminal or noncriminal ways? These questions all center on the key debate that has been around in psychology since its beginning. The *nature-versus-nurture* debate is about whether individuals are the product of predetermined and uncontrollable biological impulses, or whether they are the product of social experiences, particularly learning through interaction with significant others, such as parents, siblings, and teachers. In a great deal of research that bears on the nature/nurture discussion, scientific psychology has demonstrated that both "nature" and "nurture" factors are relevant. Our physiology, particularly the brain, is dramatically altered as a result of social experience, or "nurture," and our physiology influences the way we behave. Most psychologists believe that nature and nurture interact and influence each other to affect behavior. In this regard, psychology is different from other disciplines such as sociology, where the focus is more on the social environment as a whole—on social structure and culture.

Personality

Some psychologists want to know how elements of personality—such as attitudes, beliefs, abilities, and motivations—arise in the individual, how they are maintained, and how they are related to each other. For example, psychologists who study domestic violence are interested in how certain beliefs about women influence sexual aggression and violence between partners. These elements of personality are believed to be important in criminal behavior.

Physiological Psychology

Physiological psychologists endeavor to understand how physiology influences behavior. They are interested in identifying the brain functions responsible for specific types of conduct. For example, they might ask: Are there brain abnormalities or deficits that are associated with violence and crime? What are the brain mechanisms for aggression? Those physiological psychologists who take an evolutionary perspective might study how genes influence behavior as well as the evolutionary success of certain inherited abilities or characteristics. They might ask: How did these brain mechanisms and their behavioral characteristics evolve?

It is now widely accepted that many psychological characteristics are influenced by our genes. For example, studies of identical twins who share the same genetic makeup have shown that if one twin becomes involved in criminal behavior, the likelihood that the other twin will behave similarly is much higher that that of two biologically unrelated individuals. However, the likelihood that both identical twins will be criminally involved is less than 50 percent. If genes were totally responsible for criminal behavior, then both twins would be involved in criminality 100 percent of the time. This suggests that while genes are important and make some contribution in determining who will engage in criminal conduct, psychological factors also play an important role.

Developmental Psychology

Developmental psychologists are interested in the changes in psychological functions (for example, thinking, emotions, and abilities) that occur as the individual goes through the various stages of life: from birth through childhood, adolescence, adulthood, and late life. Developmental psychologists study the effects of aging on psychological abilities, skills, deficits, difficulties, and tendencies to behave. They look at what causes people to change and develop. Developmental psychologists want to know what changes are typical as the child grows into an adult and beyond. They also want to understand those factors having to do with the development of *attachment*, or the ability to form a close, trusting, and secure relationship with others, as well as how we develop or fail to develop moral principles (see Box 4.1). Later in this chapter, when we discuss some of the key psychological theorists, we will return to these factors and their relationship to criminal behavior.

Box 4.1 • Attachment Theory: The Ultimate Experiment

On a bright, cold day in February, at a clinic in the mountains outside Denver, a mother sits with her arms folded across her chest and a polite, bewildered smile on her face. She is talking about her adopted son, the boy whose troubles have brought her here to the Attachment Center at Evergreen, where she hopes he can be taught to love her. It's just that the boy is so "strange," she says, his emotions so "artificial." When she and her husband brought him home from Romania in June 1991, the boy was 4 and his sister, whom they also adopted, was 8. Their mother was dead, the Romanian adoption broker had said, and their father was an alcoholic and nearly blind. When he wasn't forcing them to beg in the streets or looking for ways to fob them off on childless foreigners, he neglected them.

While the girl seemed to settle in and find some comfort in the ordinary routines of domestic life, the boy could neither accept his new family nor control his overwhelming anxiety. He was clumsy and awkward and subject to night terrors and at the same time oddly reckless. He would deliberately ride his bike in front of cars, darting into traffic at high speed. He lied—instinctively, it seemed, and extravagantly. He couldn't stand it when his mother touched him, but he sought creature comfort in more oblique ways—sneaking into the refrigerator in the middle of the night to "steal" food, for instance. He was rarely invited twice to a schoolmate's house, and the boys he called his best friends never seemed to think they were friends at all.

Margaret Talbot, *New York Times*, May 24, 1998, Section 6, p. 24.

Social Psychology

Social psychologists examine the ways that groups influence a group member's behavior. How do group beliefs impact an individual? What social influences form our attitudes, beliefs, and tendencies to behave? How do social influences lead to criminal behavior? For example, many have asked whether Timothy McVeigh, who in 1995 bombed the federal office building in downtown Oklahoma City, killing more than 100 people, acted alone. Social psychologists would be more interested in how the extremist groups McVeigh might have belonged to could have influenced his thinking, beliefs, and ultimately his devastating actions. Social psychologists usually study group behavior that is directly related to crime and the criminal justice system. As such, they might examine the factors that influence juror's decisions in a criminal trial, or the forces that compel young people to join gangs.

Cognitive Psychology

Cognitive psychologists study the way thinking develops, how it is maintained, and how it influences behavior. The capacities to think rationally and to comprehend abstract ideas are cognitive abilities that may affect individual's decisions to commit crime. Thinking errors or distortions are believed to be crucial elements in several psychological theories that explain criminal behavior. The belief that women who dress provocatively are "asking to be raped," or that a friendly smile from a child is flirtatious or seductive, are examples of thinking errors or distortions of some sex offenders. Failure to think through the consequences of behavior and making a faulty choice to act illegally are other examples of cognitive processes that are relevant to understanding crime.

Clinical Psychology

Another subfield of psychology is clinical psychology. While many *clinical psychologists* are involved in treating people with emotional problems and mental disorders, many others are involved in conducting research. A clinical psychologist, for example, might be interested in studying the relationship of mental disorders to aggressive behavior or the effectiveness of a specific treatment on released sex offenders. Some clinical psychologists specialize in *clinical forensic psychology*, which involves examining the relationship between psychology and law. Using their assessment skills to help inform legal proceedings, forensic psychologists, for example, might assist the court in determining whether a defendant has a mental disorder that impairs his or her ability to stand trial. Or, they might identify particular psychological strengths or weaknesses that would favor one parent over the other in a child custody determination.

An area that has received much attention from clinical forensic psychologists is *risk assessment*, or the prediction of future violence. Many governmental and private organizations have an interest in knowing the level of danger that someone poses. These include parole boards, judges deciding whether to place a defendant on bail or probation, law enforcement officials, threat assessment groups (such as law enforcement departments concerned with whether a stalker might be more than just an annoyance), and the U.S. Secret Service (which is responsible for evaluating personal risk to the president).

Recent events have brought the issue of risk assessment to the public's attention. The numerous instances of school and workplace mass murder that have occurred in the United States and elsewhere have made us all wonder if these horrific events could have been prevented, had we known more about the perpetrators. That is, had we been able to identify those at risk of acting violently, could we have intervened? Making decisions about who does and does not pose a serious threat is a difficult task that has serious ethical, moral, and social implications. Hospitalizing or imprisoning someone because we think they might resort to violence can be a severe deprivation of individual freedom. Conversely, releasing someone into society who will reoffend is irresponsible and dangerous. Given that the methods for determining the risk of dangerousness are limited and less than accurate, psychologists are very conscientious in conducting risk assessments and trying to balance the individual's rights against the community's safety. Ultimately, it is judges and parole boards and other officials that make the decisions, but the opinions of psychologists in risk determinations can have powerful influences on the decision-making process.

More recently, forensic psychologists have been involved in assisting law enforcement by creating an offender profile of the perpetrator of a crime. By examining how the perpetrator acted during the commission of the crime, psychologists interested in profiling can try to identify the type of person who committed the crime. Profilers endeavor to identify the behavioral characteristics of the perpetrator. Who might have committed the offense? What specifically did he or she do at the crime scene? Was it an impulsive or highly planned act? We will have a great deal more to say about offender profiling later in this chapter.

While psychologists differ in their orientations and interests, depending on their subfields, all are primarily concerned with behavior—with how and why an individual acts as he or she does. Almost all psychologists believe that the brain's physiology, our psychological development, and our social experiences are important in understanding behavior in general, and criminal behavior in particular. Psychology is too complex a discipline for any one to be an expert in all subfields. While most psychologists specialize in one or two subfields, they all have a general understanding of the discipline, which results in a common language.

Theoretical Contributions of Psychology to Understanding Crime

There is no comprehensive, generally accepted psychological theory of criminal behavior. Psychologists draw on a wide variety of theories. The contributions of psychological theories to our understanding of crime can be put into three main categories.

1. *General psychological theories that attempt to explain all human behavior, which are applied to the area of crime.* These include personality theory, developmental theory, learning theory, social psychology, and physiological psychological theory.

2. *Psychological theories specifically developed to explain criminal conduct.* These theories are often extensions of one or more general theories of behavior and are typically more narrow in scope. They frequently reflect the theorist's particular orientation and do not attempt to integrate what is known generally about behavior and criminal conduct.

3. *Psychological theories that focus on specific types of crimes*, such as stalking, rape, or domestic violence. Here there is an even narrower focus. Theories that endeavor to explain or understand a particular criminal act may or may not be applicable to other types of criminal conduct. This is the case even with general categories or types of criminal conduct such as sexual offending. For example, the personality characteristics that lead men to rape women might be quite different from the personality characteristics of men who molest children.

Some theories focus more generally on violence and aggression, and not specifically on crime. While some forms of aggression such as assault and murder are illegal, others, such as defending oneself, are not. Psychological theories are frequently interwoven with theories of violence, requiring that we deduce from the latter what is relevant to the study of crime. In order to understand criminal behavior, psychologists must move back and forth between the three aforementioned categories of psychological theory, extracting relevant information from each category.

The varieties of crime are so numerous that one overarching theory is unlikely to explain all criminal conduct adequately. While shoplifting and murder are both crimes, the psychology of the shoplifter is nonetheless apt to be very different from that of the murderer. General psychological theories that explain the conduct of both types of offenders run the risk of being too broad to be useful, while specific theories that explain only one type of offense lack a comprehensive perspective useful in informing public policy and psychological treatment.

General Psychological Theories and Crime

Psychoanalysis   *Psychoanalytic theory ①*

General psychological theories attempt to explain all human behavior. As such, they endeavor to account for the general forces, factors, and influences that govern the way we act. One such grand theoretical approach, *psychoanalysis,* which became prominent during the early 1900s, views human behavior as basically compelled by primitive drives. Sigmund Freud (1856-1939), the father of psychoanalysis, believed that *sexual* and *aggressive* drives motivate all behavior and that these drives need to be managed. Freud called these basic drives *id impulses.* Managing the id impulses so that they manifest themselves as socially acceptable behavior are the functions of the *ego* and the *superego,* two psychological constructs that develop as we change and grow older. The superego is the part of the personality that represents the conscience as it dictates our moral beliefs of right and wrong. Violation of the superego's restraints on our behavior commonly results in feelings of guilt (see Box 4.2).

Box 4.2 • Criminals from a Sense of Guilt

In telling me about their early youth, particularly before puberty, people who have afterwards often become very respectable have informed me of forbidden actions which they committed at the time—such as thefts, frauds and even arson. . . . [S]uch deeds were done principally because they were forbidden, and because their execution was accompanied by mental relief for their doer. He was suffering from an oppressive feeling of guilt, . . . and after he had committed a misdeed this oppression was mitigated.

Paradoxical as it may sound, I must maintain that the sense of guilt was present before the misdeed, that it did not arise from it, but conversely—the misdeed arose from the sense of guilt. These people might justly be described as criminals from a sense of guilt.

Sigmund Freud, "Criminals From a Sense of Guilt" (1916).

Ego and superego development result from socialization—in particular, the way our parents treat us, the kind of role models they present, and the guidance they provide throughout childhood and adolescence. The function of the ego is to adapt id impulses into socially acceptable behavior, while superego development incorporates moral beliefs. Simply put, the ego asks "How can I satisfy my primitive impulses (of sex and aggression) without getting into trouble with society?" at the same time the superego asks: "Are my impulses consistent with my moral convictions?" Attempts to satisfy the needs of the id, and also take into account moral beliefs and rules of society, are not always satisfactory.

Adaptations to unresolved conflicts, losses, and traumas, such as the death of a parent or being the victim of abuse, result in personality characteristics that may hinder the individual from negotiating the challenges of adult life. Freud called these adaptations unconscious *defense mechanisms* that shape behavior. From a psychoanalytic perspective, criminal behavior is explained as a complex process that not only involves a failure to fully develop the ego and superego, it also involves faulty unconscious defense mechanisms. For example, psychoanalysts would view the sexually sadistic killer who is gratified by inflicting pain on his or her victim as someone whose primitive aggressive and sexual impulses result from faulty superego development. Neglect, abuse, witnessing violence and aggression, or any combination of negative influences that disrupt normal development are believed to result in poor adaptation to the reality and morality of adult sexuality. Psychoanalysts argue that failure to develop normal ways of mediating aggressive and sexual id impulses manifests itself in behavior that fuses sex and violence. It is said that the violent and sexual impulses from the id are not appropriately mediated because there is a breakdown of ego and superego controls and/or because of severely maladaptive defense mechanisms. (For a more comprehensive overview of psychoanalytic contributions to criminal conduct, see Redl and Toch [1979]).

Erikson's Developmental Theory

An early follower of Freud was Erik Erikson (1902-1994), one of the most prominent developmental psychologists, whose impact on the discipline of psychology occurred chiefly during the 1950s and 1960s. Erikson abandoned much of his mentor's ideas about sex and aggression and instead focused on personality development across the life span.

Erikson believed that personality development could best be described as a series of challenges, the first being concerned with *basic trust versus distrust*. The challenge of basic trust is for the child to form a meaningful emotional attachment to someone, presumably a parent or caregiver. This formation of attachment sets the stage for all future relationships with other people and also influences all subsequent developmental challenges. Failure of emotional attachment to others in early childhood results in either the absence of attachment needs at later stages in life or an excessive focus on attachment when the individual should have moved on to new developmental challenges.

Developing a secure attachment in infancy forms the psychological foundation for *autonomy*, or independent functioning. Autonomy has to do with developing the ability to function independently of others. This in turn leads to developing a sense that one has influence and competence, and in the late teenage years, with the formation of *identity*, one's sense of self. Early failures in personality development mean that the challenge is unresolved and remains an influence beyond its age-appropriate life stage. This detracts from efforts to meet the next life-stage challenge. Thus, poor psychological development results in a cumulative process in which the failed challenge decreases the chances that subsequent life challenges will be met successfully.

Poor attachment and identity issues are central to Erikson's theory and are believed to influence much of criminal behavior. *Psychopathy*, to be discussed at greater length later, is believed to involve the absence of attachment needs, presumably because of early disruption in the emotional formation of attachment. The psychopath learns to function without close emotional bonds to others and therefore does not develop feelings of empathy for others. When empathy is lacking, victimizing others becomes more probable.

Exaggerated attachment needs and identity problems are present in some cases of stalking and homicide. Let us say that a teenager's emotional attachment to his girlfriend is so intense and his conception of his self so entangled in his relationship to her, that he cannot tolerate losing her. Because his identity is so interwoven with the relationship, losing her feels like an assault on him and her loss like death. Because she refuses to marry him, he strangles her and attempts to kill himself but is apprehended before he can complete the suicide. Here, an unhealthy emotional attachment and a poorly differentiated self-identity are some of the psychological forces that influence the teenager's criminal behavior.

Erotomania is a severe psychological disorder in which the afflicted person relentlessly pursues the idea that the object of their affection reciprocates their romantic feelings and/or fantasies. This obsession with the desired individual continues long after that individual has asserted that he or she is not interested in pursuing a romantic relationship with the afflicted. Believing (quite wrongly) that one is loved by a celebrity may be one way of helping one manage a damaged identity. A good example of erotomania is the case of John Hinckley, who attempted to assassinate President Ronald Reagan in 1981, believing that he needed to do so in order to get the attention of movie star Jodie Foster. Being romantically connected to Foster would, to Hinckley's way of thinking, resolve his emotional attachment needs and sense of self. In this case, thinking errors or distortions are also important factors. Hinckley's belief that killing the president was likely to enhance his chances for a romantic union with Foster is a serious disturbance in thought processes (see Box 4.3). (See Bowby [1944] for more on attachment and crime.)

Box 4.3 • John Hinckley's March 30, 1981, Letter to Jodie Foster

3/30/81
12:45 P.M.

Dear Jodie,

There is a definite possibility that I will be killed in my attempt to get Reagan. It is for this very reason that I am writing you this letter now.

As you well know by now I love you very much. Over the past seven months I've left you dozens of poems, letters and love messages in the faint hope that you could develop an interest in me. Although we talked on the phone a couple of times I never had the nerve to simply approach you and introduce myself. Besides my shyness, I honestly did not wish to bother you with my constant presence. I know the many messages left at your door and in your mailbox were a nuisance, but I felt that it was the most painless way for me to express my love for you.

I feel very good about the fact that you at least know my name and know how I feel about you. And by hanging around your dormitory, I've come to realize that I'm the topic of more than a little conversation, however full of ridicule it may be. At least you know that I'll always love you.

Jodie, I would abandon this idea of getting Reagan in a second if I could only win your heart and live out the rest of my life with you, whether it be in total obscurity or whatever.

I will admit to you that the reason I'm going ahead with this attempt now is because I just cannot wait any longer to impress you. I've got to do something now to make you understand, in no uncertain terms, that I am doing all of this for your sake! By sacrificing my freedom and possibly my life, I hope to change your mind about me. This letter is being written only an hour before I leave for the Hilton Hotel. Jodie, I'm asking you to please look into your heart and at least give me the chance, with this historical deed, to gain your respect and love.

I love you forever,

John Hinckley

---

http://www.law.umkc.edu/faculty/projects/ftrials/hinckley/LETTER.htm

Social Learning Theory

Another major general psychological explanation of behavior is *social learning theory*, attributed mainly to Albert Bandura (1973). Building on B.F. Skinner's ideas about behavior being controlled by its consequences (reinforcements or punishments), Bandura discovered that people change their behavior not only by direct reinforcement or punishment but by simply observing the behavior of others, such as, for example, fellow students in a classroom. Bandura believed that it is not necessary to reward each child in a classroom in order to modify the class's behavior because seeing other children receive rewards for particular conduct will increase the likelihood that all children will do the same. By the same token, seeing someone get punished for unwanted conduct will decrease the likelihood that the observing child will engage in the same unwanted conduct. According to Bandura, the observer refrains from taking part in the punished behavior because they have learned that the behavior results in punishment. The focus is on the external behavior, not on internal mental constructs like fear or shame.

The influence of Bandura's work in particular and social learning theory in general is seen in the research regarding the effects of viewing violence on television. Social learning theorists maintain that observing others acting violently or engaging in criminal activities influences the behavior of the observer if the observed behavior is not punished. Likewise, seeing someone in the immediate environment profit from crime increases the likelihood that the observer will act similarly. Bandura calls this process *vicarious reinforcement*, which means that one's behavior is influenced by observing others being rewarded.

Social learning theory also considers the concept of *modeling*, or imitating behavior. In modeling, there need not be vicarious reinforcement, only observation of someone else's behavior. We would all generally know how to shoot a gun, even if we never held one and never saw anyone rewarded from doing so, because we have repeatedly seen others shooting guns on television. Viewing violent pornographic videos may cause the observer to imitate the behavior observed. Social learning theory predicts that witnessing such behavior increases the likelihood that the viewer will act out in a sexually violent manner. In these ways, social learning theory is relevant not only to understanding sex crimes but also to policy considerations regarding the legal regulation of certain types of pornographic material.

Biopsychology

We have now briefly surveyed three major general psychological theories that are relevant to understanding crime: psychoanalytic theory, developmental theory, and social learning theory. We have deliberately excluded a detailed discussion of biopsychological, neuropsychological, and evolutionary psychological perspectives, as these will be discussed in Chapter Five. Nevertheless it is important to note that genetic factors, evolutionary forces, and the functions of the brain represent three other interrelated general psychological perspectives of great relevance to understanding crime. Indeed, many of the theories discussed above make conceptual connections to neurobiological factors and functions (see Box 4.4). It is interesting, for example, that while Freud developed psychoanalysis many years before a basic understanding of the brain's functioning was achieved, one of his major concepts—the control over urges and drives—correlates closely with what is now known about the functioning of the brain's frontal lobes. This part of the brain's cortex controls urges and emotionally charged drives, including sexual and aggressive, or id impulses. The ability to form an emotional bond to a caregiver is central to survival. It is not difficult to see that such ability has strong genetic determinants that have been passed down through many generations.

Box 4.4 • Brain Development and the Death Penalty

A recent death penalty case in the state of Missouri has drawn the attention of the American Medical Association, psychiatrists, psychologists, and other health experts. In 1993, Christopher Simmons and Charles Benjamin, then aged 17 and 15, abducted and murdered Shirley Ann Crook, a 46-year-old truck driver. Simmons received the death penalty and Benjamin, life imprisonment. After being overturned by the Missouri Supreme Court, Simmons' case went to the U.S. Supreme Court, charged with determining the constitutionality of the death penalty for a 17-year-old. Included in the evidence submitted to the court is the argument that juveniles should not be executed because their brains are not fully developed. The argument is based on new research on the human brain using MRI technology revealing that frontal lobes, or the prefrontal cortex—the cradle of impulse control, emotional regulation and moral reasoning—is not fully developed until the early or mid-20s.

"Scientists can now demonstrate that adolescents are immature not only to the observer's naked eye but in the very fibers of their brains, says the brief [filed] by the A.M.A. and the psychiatrists. Normal adolescents cannot be expected to operate with the level of maturity, judgment, risk aversion or impulse control of an adult."

Paul Raeburn, "Too Immature for the Death Penalty?" *The New York Times Magazine*, October 17, 2004, p. 26.

By no means has our discussion so far entailed an exhaustive review of all general psychological theories, nor was their coverage intended to be in any way complete. Like a good aperitif, the discussion so far will hopefully stimulate the appetite for more in-depth and comprehensive study of psychological theory. Earlier we noted that while most psychologists specialize in a particular subfield, they nonetheless have a general understanding of the discipline's many subspecialties.

Human behavior in general, and criminal behavior in particular, are much too complex to be explained by any one theory. The general theories already discussed allow for the integration of the specific theories of criminal conduct with what we know about human behavior in general. Most psychologists integrate and modify theories and concepts in their attempts at understanding crime. Psychoanalysis, development theory, social learning theory, and biopsychology provide psychologists with the basis for better comprehending and appreciating the specific theories of criminal behavior to which we now turn.

Specific Psychological Theories of Crime

Eysenck's Theory of Personality and Crime

One of the first relatively comprehensive psychological theories of crime was proposed by Hans Eysenck (1977), who believed that understanding criminal behavior required understanding the interaction between environmental conditions, the socialization of the individual, and the makeup and qualities of the brain and nervous system. Eysenck maintained that while genetic factors as well as general intelligence played an important role in determining criminal conduct, three temperament factors played a primary role. He believed that these temperament factors—which he identified as extroversion, neuroticism, and psychoticism—were controlled by the excitability, sensitivity, and reactivity of the nervous system.

Eysenck argued that criminal conduct was most related to extroversion and neuroticism, with each constituting a continuum. For example *extroversion* ranges from the extreme temperament that characterizes the individual as outgoing, active, sensation-seeking, and socially engaged, to the other extreme temperament that characterizes the individual as reserved, socially tentative, quiet, and wont to keep feelings under control. The *neuroticism* continuum spans feelings that are intense and show a tendency to react dramatically to stressful situations, to more stable feelings exhibited by the individual who is poised, calm, and less reactive. Most people fall somewhere in the middle of both continuums. It was Eysenck's contention that highly neurotic, highly extroverted individuals are most likely to engage in criminal conduct.

While research has largely supported Eysenck's theory as it relates to personality in general, his views on crime have been less well supported by the research. Parts of his theory however have been incorporated into other explanations of criminal conduct. For example, Eysenck's belief in the genetic inheritance of temperamental traits remains one of his most lasting contributions to understanding crime.

The Criminal Personality Theory of Yochelson and Samenow

Another early explanation of crime that was initially heralded as groundbreaking but that later fell out of favor is Samuel Yochelson and Stanton E. Samenow's (1976) theory of *criminal personality*. Yochelson and Samenow believed that criminal behavior resulted from a combination of thinking errors and underlying fears. They postulated a large number of distortions in thinking, including the idea that the criminal feared the *zero state*, or being reduced to nothing. In order to protect himself or herself from sinking into an unbearable sense of worthlessness, the criminal employs many of these thinking distortions for self-protection. For example, *criminal pride* represents the unrealistic belief that one is superior to others. This belief is so rigid that it is not responsive to input from others. One aspect of criminal pride is the heightened sense of masculinity, desirability, and sexual prowess. Challenges to the individual's "manhood" may result in defensive actions, including violence.

Yochelson and Samenow's ideas are similar to those of Baumeister, Smart, and Boden (1996) as expressed in their theory of *threatened egotism*. Baumeister et al. assert that individuals whose high self-esteem is based on real accomplishments, such as educational achievement and legitimate success, are not likely to respond violently when their sense of self is challenged. On the other hand, individuals with high self-esteem that is not based on real accomplishments tend to react aggressively to provocation. Baumeister et al., however, posit that low self-esteem is not related to violence, while for Yochelson and Samenow, low self-esteem and criminality, including violent criminality, are closely correlated.

A great deal of research supports Baumeister's contention. It is likely that his emphasis on high unfounded egotism and violence, coupled with his rejection of the low self-esteem factor found in Yochelson and Samenow's theory, is responsible for the lack of support for the criminal personality theory. Theories vary in their degree of explanation, and Yochelson and Samenow's contribution is probably strongest in regard to treating criminal offenders. Changing criminal thinking styles, that is, the thinking distortions believed to support criminal behavior, has become a major treatment approach that holds promise for intervention aimed at altering or reducing criminal behavior.

Psychopathy

Perhaps the most significant advance in the psychological understanding of criminal behavior has emerged from the work of Robert D. Hare (1970), who devised a way of measuring and assessing the complex set of interrelated personality constructs known as *psychopathy*, having to do with affective and interpersonal traits such as egocentricity, deceit, shallow affect, manipulativeness, selfishness, and lack of empathy, guilt, or remorse. Hare conducted several studies that have helped characterize the *psychopath*—the remorseless predator who uses charm, intimidation, and, if necessary, impulsive and cold-blooded violence to attain his or her ends. These studies define the central characteristics, deficits, and behaviors of psychopathy and the relationship of psychopathy to criminal behavior.

Psychopathy can best be described and defined through Hare's measure, the Psychopathy Checklist-Revised (PCL-R) and the research that has been done using the PCL-R. The PCL-R contains 20 items that describe the psychological deficits and characteristics of the person being evaluated. Each item is rated as 0=not present, 1=possibly present, or 2=definitely present, resulting in a possible total score of 40.

"Glibness/Superficial Charm" is the description given to a smooth taker who has only a superficial knowledge of many topics, but in reality has a limited grasp of the topics. This attribute makes the psychopath quite engaging. For example, serial killer Ted Bundy had a way with words and charmed his unsuspecting victims into their demise. The next item is a "Grandiose Sense of Self Worth," the belief that one is special and superior to others. Bundy, a law student, attempted unsuccessfully to represent himself in his trial for several of the murders. His grandiosity, the belief that he had special legal knowledge and abilities in spite of his lack of experience, might have played a role in his own conviction. The third item, "Need for Stimulation/Proneness to Boredom," has to do with the individual wanting to be where the action is, and an inability to deal with routine activity.

Other items on the PCL-R deal with "Impulsivity," "Poor Behavioral Controls," "Lack of Guilt or Remorse," "Callous Lack of Empathy," and "Pathological Lying." These are all characteristics that may facilitate a criminal lifestyle. The subject is also rated on "Criminal Versatility," that is, his or her engagement in a wide variety of criminal behavior, as well as on "Shallow Affect," the inability to experience strong emotions, a concept related to poor attachment ability.

The case of a defendant who was psychologically evaluated by one of the authors, Thomas Kucharski, might be illustrative. Donald, a hitchhiker, was picked up by a driver who a short while later picked up a second hitchhiker. The driver was assaulted, tied up, and thrown in the trunk of the car. After drinking and drugging, using the driver's money, Donald pulled into a rest area, exited the car, opened the trunk, strangled the driver, and dumped the body in the woods nearby. Donald dropped off the second hitchhiker at his destination, where they both shook hands and agreed to meet in the future. To Donald's surprise, the second hitchhiker went directly to the police and later testified at Donald's trial. Donald could not believe that a "close friend" would "rat him out."

Donald exhibits several psychopathic characteristics. His shallow affect is reflected in his superficial sense of friendship. His lack of empathy is seen in the cold-blooded murder itself. Donald felt no remorse for the murder, claiming that the only reason he was in jail was because his "friend" had "ratted him out." He took no responsibility for his misdeeds, claiming that the victim had made a homosexual pass at him, thus justifying his murderous act. Donald had a long history of criminal conduct dating back to his early teens. He had been on probation many times but had violated the probation requirements, returned to the court, and was eventually reincarcerated. He was sexually promiscuous with many partners whom he exploited financially and sexually, attesting to his parasitic lifestyle. Donald was quite adept verbally and somewhat charming in his interactions with the evaluator, often complimenting him on a necktie he wore. Donald's self-report of his life history was full of contradictions, and when confronted with them, he merely stated, "OK, Doc, you don't believe me? How about this one?," instantly concocting a totally different life story.

All of these characteristics and behaviors resulted in a high PCL-R score and a classification as a psychopath. But what does the research tell us about psychopaths? In a study by Hart, Knopp, and Hare (1988), psychopaths had a 90 percent rearrest rate after release from prison, in contrast to a 30 percent rearrest rate for those without psychopathy. Compared with nonpsychopaths, psychopaths have a higher rate of rearrest for violent behavior in general as well as for rape. These results are impressive, given that a high number of crimes are committed by a relatively small number of offenders.

Box 4.5 • Diagnostic Criteria for Antisocial Personality Disorder

The Diagnostic and Statistical Manual of Mental Disorders – Fourth Edition (DSM-IV), published by the American Psychiatric Association, Washington DC, 1994, gives the following diagnostic criteria for Antisocial Personality Disorder.

A. There is a pervasive pattern of disregard for and violation of the rights of others occurring since age 18 years, as indicated by three (or more) of the following:

1. failure to conform to social norms with respect to lawful behaviors as indicated by repeatedly performing acts that are grounds for arrest

2. deceitfulness, as indicated by repeated lying, use of aliases, or conning others for personal profit or pleasure

3. impulsivity or failure to plan ahead

4. irritability and aggressiveness, as indicated by repeated physical fights or assaults

5. reckless disregard for safety of self or others

6. consistent irresponsibility, as indicated by repeated failure to sustain consistent work behavior or honor financial obligations

7. lack of remorse, as indicated by being indifferent to or rationalizing having hurt, mistreated, or stolen from another

B. The individual is at least 18 years old (under 18 see Conduct Disorder)

C. There is evidence of Conduct Disorder with onset before age 15 years.

D. The occurrence of antisocial behavior is not exclusively during the course of Schizophrenia or a Manic Episode.

Hare and his colleagues (Intrator et al., 1997) have extended this research with some interesting preliminary results that link physiological deficits to psychopathy. The future looks promising for a better understanding of the causes, prevention, and treatment of psychopathy. There is no official diagnosis of psychopathy. The closest psychiatric condition, *antisocial personality disorder* (ASPD), shares many of the characteristics of psychopathy. (For a distinction between the two disorders, see Hare [1996].) It is important to recognize that most psychopaths meet the criteria for ASPD, but most individuals with ASPD are not psychopaths.

Psychological Theories of Specific Crimes (3)

Typologies of Criminal Behavior

Before turning to criminal profiling, let us briefly consider some psychological theories that can best be described as typologies of criminal behavior. A *typology* consists of classifying offenders into categories defined by some common denominator. These typologies are central in understanding profiling, as profiling essentially involves developing classifications of different "types" of criminals. Typologies abound in the psychology of criminal conduct. Some are very general, such as those of homicide, where the perpetrator is viewed either as *instrumental* in his or her actions, killing for some financial or other gain, or as *affective*, where high emotional intensity is involved. Stalkers have been grouped by *victim type*, those who had a prior relationship with the victim versus those with no prior relationship. One useful finding from the research on this typology is that the risk of violence is much greater if there was a prior intimate relationship. Public awareness of the problem of *stalking*—a course of conduct that places a person in fear for their safety—peaked as a result of the 1989 stalking and murder of television actress Rebecca Schaeffer by an erotomanic delusional man. Cases involving celebrities, however, are perhaps less dangerous than the more common stalking of former intimates.

Other typologies of criminal behavior are quite complex. Groth (1979), for example, have focused on the personality characteristics of rapists. They created a three-group rapist typology based partly on behavior exhibited at the time of the offense and the presumed motivation of the offender. The *anger rapist* inflicts much more physical violence than is necessary to accomplish the act. Because his aim is to humiliate and degrade the victim, his motivation is seen chiefly as an expression of his anger toward women. He tends to view sex as dirty. This explains his use of rape and sex as a means of degrading the victim. His attack is quick, extremely violent, and prompted by his having been humiliated by a woman.

Groth's second type is the *power rapist,* who uses only enough violent force to accomplish the rape. He fantasizes that, because of his sexual prowess, the victim after being raped will view him positively and even be happy that the assault occurred. Rape is a means of asserting his damaged identity. Often the outcome of the rape is disappointing, not living up to his fantasized expectations. Feeling guilty, he initially senses that his need to rape is now satisfied and he will never rape again. However, he soon starts the fantasizing process and begins searching for a new victim.

Finally, Groth describes the *sadistic rapist,* whose aggression, domination, and sexuality are fused. Fitting this typology are the Hillside Stranglers—Kenneth Bianchi and Angelo Buono—who, in 1977, abducted, raped, and killed 10 women in Los Angeles. The sadistic rapist often searches or trolls for a victim, abducts and takes her to a prearranged place, tortures her, and frequently kills her. The motivation here is to gratify a sexually deviant orientation in which violence, infliction of pain, domination, and control are characteristic themes. Groth's typologies are helpful in understanding the motives of the rapist, an important factor in treatment and risk assessment.

Aside from stalkers and rapists, criminal typologies have also been formulated for domestic violence perpetrators, child molesters, and many other offenders. Understanding, describing, and predicting risk; designing treatment programs; and monitoring and supervision in the community have all profited from this descriptive approach. While typologies do not tell us what motivates the perpetrator directly, they do provide clues to the underlying psychological forces and factors that lead to criminal behavior.

Crime and Mental Illness

The stereotype of those who suffer from schizophrenia, bipolar disorder, or other severe psychiatric difficulties as violent and prone to criminal acts has long been part of the public's perception of the mentally ill. Generally, however, the research has not supported this perception. In fact, most mentally ill people are nonviolent and do not engage in criminal behavior. Recent studies, however, suggest that drug abuse in individuals with mental illness does increase the risk of violence.

Many mental health professionals have raised concerns regarding the increased incarceration of the mentally ill in jails, prisons, and juvenile detention facilities. While this increase has more to do with the lack of treatment services and changing commitment standards than it does with increased criminal conduct on the part of the mentally ill, it does point to the fact that larger numbers of ex-inmates are returning to their communities with untreated emotional or behavioral disorders.

Offender Profiling

Thus far, we have provided an overview of psychology and psychological theory as it relates to criminal behavior. We said that psychology is the scientific study of behavior, but that psychologists are also interested in underlying mental constructs such as personality, cognition, emotion, and how these manifest themselves in behavior. We discussed the various orientations of psychologists (biological, cognitive, social, clinical, and forensic) and the interests and major focus of each. The type of psychologist most involved in the criminal justice system and most interested in criminal behavior is the forensic psychologist.

One major issue of importance to forensic psychologists over the past 50 years or so has been *risk assessment*, which involves a careful examination of individuals who could cause harm to people through their crimes. The idea is to determine if enough precautions have been taken, or if more should be done, to prevent these individuals from causing harm. Risk assessment generally involves making predictions regarding the likelihood that a person will act violently in the future. Forensic psychologists must have a good understanding of general psychological theory, theories of criminal conduct, and theories of specific types of offenses as they try to predict dangerousness. They must assess the level of psychopathy, determine the magnitude of attachment and identity deficits, understand the limitations that the potentially violent person has in terms of control over their impulses, and assess particular ways the individual's cognitive processes and social influences contribute to his or her behavior.

Offender profiling can be viewed as the flip side of risk assessment. While profilers employ many of the same skills needed in risk assessment, they do not endeavor to predict the likelihood of criminal behavior. Instead, they try to determine the behavioral, cognitive, and emotional characteristics of the perpetrator of a crime that has already occurred.

At the start of each academic year we ask our students why they are studying forensic psychology, and a good number of them say they want to be profilers, and that they ultimately want to work for the Federal Bureau of Investigation or other major agencies dealing with the investigation of serious violent crimes. When we ask them what they think profiling is, and where they get their ideas about it, they inevitably point to popular movies like *The Silence of the Lambs*, *Kiss the Girls*, and *Along Came a Spider,* or TV shows like "CSI" or "Cold Case," in which a main character is either a forensic scientist or a psychological profiler investigating some complicated heinous crime. When we probe a bit further, it becomes clear that what students think about profiling is reflected in the image the popular media portrays, of an individual who, through their personal talent or skills, can "enter" the mind of the killer and understand their most internal and private fantasies, which in turn will somehow enable them to find the perpetrator based on the way they committed the crime.

This image has also been perpetuated in books written by crime investigators who recount their successes in tracking down various serial killers, books such as John E. Douglas's *Mindhunter* and Robert K. Ressler's *I Have Lived in the Monster*. In fact, when we ask the students what books they have read about profiling, these true-crime accounts are the ones they mention. These mass-market paperbacks are interesting and accessible. However, there are not many academic books that give a more objective, scientific account of what profiling is and how it is to be used.

With the increasing number of students planning to enter the fields of criminal justice and forensic psychology, with career ambitions in profiling, it is important to give a more balanced and accurate view of what the field is actually about, and where it currently stands. Indeed, one way in which we can understand offender profiling is by asking ourselves whether it is indeed the "art" we see on TV and read in true-crime books, or whether it is a "science" we can research and study in universities and a technical skill that can be learned and applied.

What is Offender Profiling?

Let's start with a case that illustrates what profiling is, its use, how it compares to other forensic science approaches, and the principal ideas behind it. In 1983, in the village of Narborough in England, a teenage girl was found raped and murdered. For three years, the police investigated the crime, but were not able to identify a suspect. Then, in 1986, another teenage girl was found raped and murdered in the same village. The police now faced an enormous amount of public, media, and political pressure to solve the crimes. The pressure was compounded by the fact that they had to determine whether they were dealing with two separate crimes, and so mount two separate investigations, or two crimes committed by a *serial killer* (typically identified as someone who kills three or more people, with a cooling-off period between killings). The latter scenario raised the chilling possibility that the offender would kill again.

Around the time of the Narborough murders, the scientific community hit upon a revolutionary identification technique with the same potential that the initial discovery of fingerprinting in criminal investigations had had in the nineteenth century. This new technique, *DNA profiling*, involved taking a sample of a person's genetic makeup from skin, blood, semen, or hair and comparing it with another DNA sample to determine if it belonged to the same person. The Narborough inquiry was one of the first in the world to use this new identification technique to successfully link two DNA samples of genetic evidence, taken from two different crime scenes, to determine conclusively that the two young women had been killed by the same person.

The reason the Narborough case is significant to our discussion of profiling has to do with the next decision made by the investigation team. Given that they had two samples of DNA, they now had to match them to the person to whom the DNA belonged. Thus, they decided to take on the painstaking task of blood-testing every male in the village, which amounted to 4,583 people. Although today this procedure would not take as long to accomplish, in the mid-1980s, blood testing was still a laborious and slow process. In addition, it was a tremendous organizational task to coordinate this effort. The result was that it took a great deal of time, resources, and manpower to test all the men in the village. Time and money are always crucial to any criminal investigation, particularly one as serious as serial murder.

Ironically, although he was eventually apprehended, the DNA investigation did not identify the murderer, Colin Pitchfork, because he asked a friend to give blood in his place. (For more information on this case, see Joseph Wambaugh's novel, *The Blooding*.) This case illustrates that DNA testing is not only time-consuming but also a controversial process, given today's climate of ethical sensitivities and the protection of privacy. Moreover, imagine the daunting task of successfully coordinating blood-testing, as they did in tiny Narborough, in a large metropolitan area such as New York City or Los Angeles. Instead of testing every citizen, it would be more useful for investigators to have a method in which the suspect pool can be narrowed to the most likely offenders during the initial stages of the investigation. This is where profiling is useful.

Offender profiling is the process of inferring the characteristics of an offender—gender, age, type of criminal record, distance of home from crime scene, social background, psychological dysfunctions—from the offender's *crime scene behavior*. Such inferences can help investigators shorten their list of suspects to the most likely culprits. This is achieved by providing those characteristics that distinguish the most likely offenders from the array of people whom the police are considering. Had the investigation team in Narborough been able to pare down their suspect pool to the most likely 50 or so men, using an offender profile, and then comparing their genetic material against the DNA samples retrieved from the crime scene as evidence, they might have solved the crime much faster.

It is important to understand that offender profiling is not intended to be used in isolation from other evidence. If we compare all of the evidence that is generally available at a crime scene (see Box 4.6), the most reliable clues come from *forensic evidence,* such as DNA, fingerprints, and fibers (from clothing, carpet, etc.).

Although forensic evidence is relatively more accurate in identifying the clues left behind, forensic evidence can effectively be removed from a crime scene or not even be left in the first place, making it difficult to link a suspect to the scene. For example, an offender can wear gloves so as not to leave fingerprints, or use a condom so as not to leave semen. One thing, however, that cannot be removed from the crime scene is the offender's

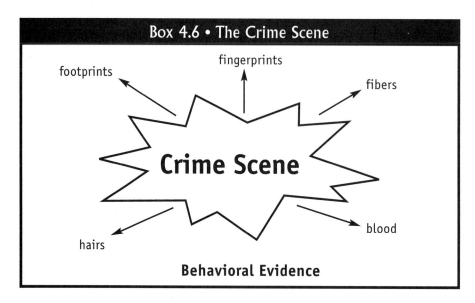

Box 4.6 • The Crime Scene

footprints

fingerprints

fibers

Crime Scene

hairs

blood

Behavioral Evidence

behavioral evidence, or those indicators from which investigators can infer the offender's *personality characteristics*. Behavioral evidence includes the type of victim targeted by the offender (in regard to gender, race, age), as well as victim grouping (such as prostitutes or children), and the behaviors the offender engaged in at the crime scene (such as the type of weapon used, evidence of a sexual assault, theft of property from the victim, method of disposing the body, etc.). Unlike forensic evidence, behavioral evidence cannot be removed and will always be present at the scene of the crime. If the chosen victim is female, she will remain female. If a knife was used to kill the victim, there will be knife wounds indicating such. If the body was removed from the original crime scene and buried in a forest, such body disposal evidence will be available. Accordingly, behavioral evidence is crucial. Indeed, how the offender deals with the forensic evidence, whether or not he or she leaves it behind, is itself a behavioral indicator pointing to the type of offender involved. The only question that remains is *how* this behavioral evidence can tell us something about the offender.

Offender Profiling as an Investigative Tool

Offender profiling is a relatively new concept in criminal justice and has only recently been regarded as an important investigative tool, particularly in cases in which the offender's identity is not immediately known, or subsequently difficult to determine. Nonetheless, the general idea of profiling has been around for a long time. The most famous historical cases of psychological profiling include that of Jack the Ripper in 1888 London, when police surgeon Thomas Bond provided detailed characteristics of the killer, who has never been identified (see Box 4.7). During World War II, British psychiatrist Walter C. Langer, on behalf of the Office of Strategic Services, produced a psychological profile of Adolph Hitler, which diagnosed Hitler's mental state and correctly predicted his response to defeat—suicide (Langer, 1972). Perhaps the most famous and successful offender profile involved the case of the "Mad Bomber" of New York City by the psychiatrist James Brussel in the 1950s. By examining his threat letters, Brussel (1969) provided detailed characteristics of the Bomber's personality, lifestyle, place of residence, and even dress sense, down to the detail of how he wore his waistcoat. When the Bomber was apprehended, the accuracy of this profile was uncanny.

Box 4.7 • Profiling Jack the Ripper

Excerpts from letter dated November 10, 1888 from Dr. Thomas Bond to Sir Robert Anderson, head of the Criminal Investigation Department, in reference to the murders attributed to Jack the Ripper.

1. All five murders were no doubt committed by the same hand. . . .

2. All the circumstances surrounding the murders lead me to form the opinion that the women must have been lying down when murdered and in every case the throat was first cut. . . .

3. In all the cases there appears to be no evidence of struggling and the attacks were probably so sudden and made in such a position that the women could neither resist nor cry out. . . .

4. In the first four cases the murderer must have attacked from the right side of the victim. . . .

5. The mutilations in each case . . . were all of the same character and showed clearly that in all the murders the object was mutilation. . . .

6. In each case the mutilation was inflicted by a person who had no scientific nor anatomical knowledge. . . .

7. The instrument must have been a very strong knife at least six inches long, very sharp, pointed at the top and about an inch in width. . . .

8. The murderer must have been a man of physical strength and of great coolness and daring. There is no evidence that he had an accomplice. He must in my opinion be a man subject to periodical attacks of Homicidal and erotic mania. The character of the mutilations indicate that the man may be in a condition sexually, that may be called Satyriasis. . . . The murderer in external appearance is quite likely to be a quiet inoffensive looking man probably middle-aged and neatly and respectably dressed. I think he must be in the habit of wearing a cloak or overcoat or he could hardly have escaped notice in the streets if the blood on his hands or clothes were visible.

9. Assuming the murderer to be such a person as I have just described, he would be solitary and eccentric in his habits, also he is most likely to be a man without regular occupation, but with some small income or pension. He is possibly living among respectable persons who have some knowledge of his character and habits and who may have grounds for suspicion that he isn't quite right in his mind at times. . . .

Donald Rumbelow, *Jack the Ripper: The Complete Casebook* (1988), pp. 139-141.

All of these profiles, however, were based on the profiler's individual sensibilities, thus contributing to the notion that profiling is an art for which only some people have a talent. Through their extensive experience with criminals, these profilers were able to draw certain conclusions about the offenders by examining their actions during their crimes. Many criminal profilers since Bond, Langer, and Brussel have also relied on their personal experiences to determine the possible characteristics of an offender. Indeed, the Federal Bureau of Investigation, which is credited with inventing modern profiling as an applied investigative tool (e.g., Ressler, Burgess, and Douglas, 1988), uses this same basis of professional field experience. Since the 1970s, the FBI has operationalized the process and trained its agents in the methods of profiling by condensing many years of criminal investigation experience into a short course designed for future agents and profilers.

With the increased attempts to bring profiling into court as evidence, the method has come under close scrutiny by law enforcement officials and scholars, and there have been more demands for demonstrating its *validity* (how well it does at what it claims to do, that is, identify the most likely offender responsible for the crime) and *reliability* (how well it works from case to case). Indeed, since the 1990s, a number of scholars began to question the inference process used in offender profiling because it was generally not supported by the rigorousness of empirical scientific study.

In the first study done on the validity of profiling, Pinizzotto and Finkel (1990) concluded that much of the psychological profiling used in criminal investigations, though based on years of investigative experience, had been more a matter of guesswork and the use of anecdotal information that is vulnerable to errors and misinterpretation. When we look at the psychological literature on how people make decisions, we find that people, including professional investigators, are apt to believe they are unbiased in the way they analyze evidence regardless of how subjectively they perceive the world. When people are faced with a complicated judgement or decision, they tend to rely on general "rules of thumb," based on their experiences in similar situations, which can oversimplify a complicated situation and lead to the wrong answers.

The recognition of inherent perceptual bias, combined with a lack of empirical support between subjective profiles and case evidence, have been the main causes for questioning the accuracy of profiling as an applied psychological tool in police investigations. For example, Alison, Smith, and Morgan (2003) examined the validity and reliability of 21 investigative profiles, which sought to construct identifiable characteristics of suspects based on behavioral indices at the crime scene. Of nearly 4,000 claims made in the 21 profiles, as much as 80 percent of the information provided was not supported by the evidence. There was also a great lack of substantiation to the claims made, such as, "It is 80 percent likely that the offender is between 25 and 30 years old." In short, it did not appear that the offender profiles were very useful.

Most recently, research has been conducted to establish a scientific basis for profiling by thoroughly analyzing criminal behavior and the people responsible for engaging in such activities. More specifically, studies have endeavored to distinguish between different *types of criminals* and the way they commit their crimes. This is done in order to more accurately relate crime scene activity to offender characteristics, thus depicting the type of person responsible for a particular set of behaviors at a crime scene.

Offender Profiling and Psychological Theory

As previously indicated, the absence of conclusive, empirical studies of offender profiling has led to a lack of validity and reliability of current investigative profiling methods. One concern about inferring behavioral profiles is whether the process of classifying offenders' criminal actions is clear and consistent enough for accurate application in police investigations. Indeed, determining what evidence *can* be used from the crime scene and exactly *how* it links to the offender's personality characteristics are important steps to establish. In addition, the disregard of principles derived from psychological theories of criminal behavior has, to date, also contributed to profiling's lack of refinement.

Social learning theory, as already mentioned, posits that an individual's experiences are determined by his or her social environment. Indeed, its main advocate, B.F. Skinner (1965), contended that all our behaviors and attitudes are acquired through learning from the world around us. Understanding the influence of social environment is important to profiling because it sharpens our understanding of how the offender interacts with the victim at the crime scene, and whether these interactions fit a pattern of how the offender has related to people in the past. For example, assuming that aggression is best understood as a behavioral reaction to a social situation rather than as a biological trait, the next step is to determine how and why individuals learn these aggressive behaviors.

Psychologist Hans Toch (1969) maintains that for some people, violent behaviors are rooted in well-learned, systematic strategies of violence that have proven to be effective in dealing with interpersonal conflict. Indeed, Toch postulates that the life histories of violent persons reveal surprising consistency in their approaches to interpersonal relationships. In all likelihood, these individuals learned in childhood that violence is an effective way of dealing with conflict; they see violence as a means to obtain rewards and avoid costs. Toch further posits that when such individuals experience humiliation or threats to their reputations and social status, they are incited to violence. A blow to the self-esteem of a person who has few coping mechanisms (such as verbal skills) for resolving disputes and conflicts, may precipitate violence. This is particularly true if the individual's subcultural values (i.e., the values of the group or community of which he or she is a member) include settling disputes through physical aggression.

Huesmann and Eron (1989) claim that the manner in which an offender demonstrates aggression, as well as the intensity of that aggression, can be attributed to social learning. They hypothesize that social behavior is largely controlled by responses learned early in life. Learned responses for social behavior in general, and for aggressive behavior in particular, are largely controlled by *cognitive scripts*, which are like "behavioral instruction booklets" on how to act in certain situations. Cognitive scripts are stored in a person's memory and used as guides for behavior and social problem-solving, suggesting how one should respond to events, and what the likely outcomes of these responses are. They are formed during childhood and persist throughout life. From this perspective, a habitually aggressive child is one who regularly mentally retrieves violent cognitive scripts and externally displays belligerent behavior. This regular retrieval results in the accumulation of numerous aggressive scripts stored in memory, making them readily available for use as particular situations arise. Additionally, continuously drawing on these scripts makes them easier to retrieve when faced with a problematic situation. If aggression has been the repeated response to interpersonal conflict, for example, when this type of situation occurs again in the future, aggression will likely be employed. In other words, people under high states of emotional arousal, during a time when their capacity for calm and logical thought is diminished, will automatically resort to strongly established habits to guide their behavior.

Not only does aggression as a characteristic way of solving problems emerge early in life, it is also likely that each individual develops a particular type of aggressiveness that remains fairly consistent across social situations and throughout the life course. In a study spanning 22 years, Huesmann et al. (1984) collected data on the behavior of more than 600 subjects, their parents, and their children. They found that subjects who were the more aggressive eight-year-olds at the beginning of the study were also the more aggressive 30-year-olds at the end of the study. They further found that early aggressiveness was predictive of later serious antisocial behavior, including criminality, spouse abuse, self-reported physical aggression, and traffic violations.

The importance of this work is clear: If we can understand the link between an offender's early life experiences and the actions during the commission of a crime, we can better determine the offender's psychological characteristics and behavioral patterns in general. As previously indicated, behavioral profiling tries to empirically link offenders' criminal actions at the crime scene with other aspects of their lives, including the details of their home life (e.g., do they live alone? are they married?); their social patterns (e.g., do they own a car? do they travel far to commit their crimes?); their lifestyle (e.g., are they loners? in what contexts do they interact with others? do they engage in violent sports?); how they relate to other people (e.g., do they become aggressive and out of control? get into bar fights? abuse their partners?); and any other activities that might aid police investigating a crime, especially the persistence, severity, range, and specialization of previous crimes committed by suspects. In this way, a connection can be established between crime scene behaviors and the general behaviors in the offender's life, a link that can aid police in narrowing suspects or identifying geographical areas for their investigation.

However, just understanding the range of activities that offenders may engage in outside of their criminal activities is not enough. Although we learn more about offenders as a *group* (that is, the general demographics of offenders), the most important goal of behavioral profiling is to devise a method for determining what in psychology we call *individual differentiation,* or comparing individuals in terms of conceptual categories. In behavioral profiling, that means differentiating among behavioral styles at the crime scene, and then matching these crime-scene styles to various offender lifestyle and criminal background patterns. The idea behind this is that offenders engage in a number of different ways of acting at the crime scene. We call these *behavioral subtypes*. These behavioral subtypes generally include subgroups of behaviors with the same underlying psychological theme or meaning to the offender, such as controlling the victim (e.g., gagging and binding) or trying to establish a pseudo-relationship with the victim (e.g., kissing or complimenting the victim). The case study in Box 4.9 illustrates how psychologists might differentiate behavioral subtypes based on evidence of certain behaviors in homicide cases. These different types of behavior at the crime scene can then be associated with information about criminal backgrounds and home lives, so that an offender who engages in Subtype A behaviors at the crime scene will have Subtype A lifestyle characteristics and Subtype A criminal histories. The same goes for Subtype B offenders, Subtype C offenders, and so on.

Let's take serial crime as an example of how using the underlying psychological theme of behavior can aid profiling. In order to profile a series of crimes and connect them to one offender, we need to demonstrate that offenders act in a similar way across their succession of crimes. Imagine a situation in which 10 rapes have been committed, and have been linked to one offender because in each case the offender gagged his victim. What would happen if another rape victim, instead of being gagged, was bound? If we focus on the behavior itself (gagging), this latter victim would not be connected to the series. However, if we recognize the underlying *psychological meaning* behind gagging and binding, we adopt a different perspective. Let's say that for the offender the most important thing is to accomplish the rape with the least possible resistance from the victim. To do this he needs to totally control the victim. If early on in his crime spree the serial rapist encountered a victim who screamed, he would need to gag her. As we discussed earlier, the offender has now learned a useful strategy that he will employ in future rapes. Imagine, though, that the last victim does not scream; instead, she tries to run away. There is no need to gag her, but because the offender still needs to control her, he adapts his behavior to the

controlling type vs. pseudo-intimate type

particular situation, and binds her. While the physical behavior is different, the psychological meaning behind the behavior remains the same—control. Put another way, we may say that the offender possesses a variety of offending behaviors with the same function, but which are used in a different context. As such, relying on psychological themes allows for establishing context-victim connections that are typically ignored in offender-focused approaches to analyzing behavior.

In the first study attempting to identify different behavioral styles of offenders in cases of sexual assault, Canter and Heritage (1990) suggested that the controlling rapist was one such type. They also suggested that another type of rapist had no interest in controlling the victim but instead wanted to establish a "pseudo-intimate" connection with her by encouraging a forced intimacy. This type of rapist engaged in behaviors such as kissing and complimenting the victim, behaviors that are psychologically similar but nonetheless different than the behavioral pattern (gagging and binding) of a controlling rapist.

By determining the different types of crime scene behavior, we can look for differences between how offenders employ them. Then we can establish different *crime scene types*, and ultimately link them to specific offender characteristics associated with each type (see Box 4.8).

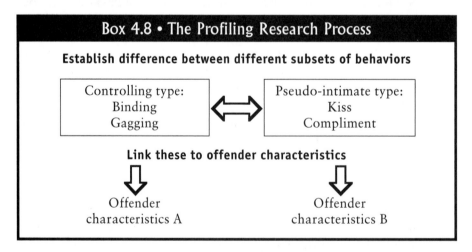

Box 4.8 • The Profiling Research Process

Establish difference between different subsets of behaviors

| Controlling type: Binding Gagging | ⟷ | Pseudo-intimate type: Kiss Compliment |

Link these to offender characteristics

⬇   ⬇

Offender   Offender
characteristics A   characteristics B

A more systematic approach to analyzing criminal behavior than has previously existed will allow a more coherent and reliable use of underlying psychological patterns for profiling purposes. As Box 4.8 shows, the key is to *differentiate* (indicated by the horizontal arrows) between different ways of behaving at a crime scene, and to *relate* (indicated by the vertical arrows) these different behavioral types to offender characteristics.

Most of the early research on profiling was based on interviewing famous criminals. There are, however, several problems with this strategy (see Salfati and Canter, 1999), the most notable being that unstructured interviews with incarcerated offenders have very low levels of reliability and validity. Offenders who agree to be interviewed may have a different type of personality compared to those who do not. In addition, offenders may not always tell the truth, or may not disclose the whole story. In addition, unless interviewers ask exactly the same questions in the same way in every interview, they may not collect the same type of information from each respondent. All of these issues of research methodology need to be seriously considered because they may elicit biased responses. The key issue here is that the information we collect tells us something about individuals, but *how* we collect it influences this information directly. Consequently, how we approach data collection will determine how we conceptualize an offender's behavior at the crime scene.

Today, psychological researchers using an empirical approach to profiling are less likely to rely on interviewing during the *initial* stages of research, although it may be used later to add depth of understanding. Instead researchers should focus on the offender's behaviors as described in the crime files. Obviously, using crime files is also problematic, given that they are not intended for psychological research but to develop a legal case for prosecuting a suspect. Thus, the information contained in the files may not be helpful in understanding who the offender is or how he or she acts at the crime scene.

During the initial stage of any research, using an objective measure, such as behavior, provides a more valid basis upon which to make assertions. The offender's *internal motivations* or mental reasonings, which are often the focus of interviews, although interesting and useful in psychological treatment, are less reliable in understanding the differences between types of offenses in terms of how the offender *acted* at the crime scene. What is needed is the physical measure of internal motivations. If we can ascertain how certain motivations are physically exhibited at crime scenes, we will be able to much more accurately account for why the offender committed the crime.

In the case of homicides in which the identity of the offender is not immediately known, there is little information directly available to investigators other than what is present at the crime scene and associated aspects of the crime, such as the details of the victim (age, gender, occupation, etc.) and the time and location of the crime. In such cases it is necessary that the profiler start with information concerning the offender's behavior. The next step is to identify the behavioral type (e.g., "pseudo-intimate rapist"), based on the examination of the offender's actions at the crime scene. These actions are then related to the offender's age, gender, previous criminal history, and the distance they live from the crime scene. The case study in Box 4.9 illustrates how psychological theory can be used in investigating and profiling criminal behavior.

Box 4.9 • Case Study: An Empirical Study of Profiling Homicide

Salfati and Canter (1999), in an attempt to relate offender profiling to current methodological and theoretical issues, conducted a pioneering study specifically focusing on cases in which the police did not know the offenders' identities early on in the investigation. The aim was to determine the different "types" of homicide crime scenes and relate these different types to the offender's psychological characteristics, and by so doing, provide a solid scientific classification for the purposes of offender profiling.

They examined police reports of 82 single-offender/single-victim, solved homicide cases from the 1980s to the early 1990s and identified three distinct types of homicide crime scenes, all of which reflected a link to the psychological theories that distinguish between different types of aggression, in terms of the meaning and functional use the aggressive behavior has for the offender.

Type 1: The Violent Type

A young woman was found brutally murdered in her living room. The victim had sustained numerous stab wounds and had bruises on her forearms and head. Her jaw had been fractured in two places. It also appeared that some of her wounds had been inflicted after her death. The tip of a knife blade was found lodged in one of her vertebrae.

This type of homicide, also known as expressive-impulsive, exhibits a collection of frenzied and impulsive behaviors, including the offender inflicting multiple wounds on the victim's body in a variety of ways (e.g., using different types weapons or wounding in different ways—stabbing, hitting, kicking, etc.). Many of the victims in these cases had sustained injuries to the face, an action that is assumed in most of the psychological literature to signify the offender was striking at the identity of the person. In many cases, the offender used a weapon available at the crime scene, further supporting the element of impulsiveness that is inherent in these types of homicides. (However, in other cases, the offender brings a weapon to the scene, suggesting that the offender has come prepared for a violent confrontation.) Here, the woman is the victim of an emotionally charged attack, as evidenced by the number and type of wounds inflicted on her.

Offenders associated with these types of homicides often have a past of impulsive and violent offences, which shows that they have previously dealt with other people in a violent way, and, as such, may illustrate how they approach conflict with other people in general.

Type 2: The Vulnerable Victim Type

An 86-year-old woman, found in her living room, had been sexually assaulted with a wooden stake, which was left at the crime scene. Her head and face were covered with a brown nylon bed cover, which, together with an electric cord, was tied around her neck. The house had been ransacked and the key to the backdoor taken. Seven hundred and fifty dollars in cash had also been taken, as well as a handbag containing an additional $15, personal papers, and the victim's bank and pension books.

Many of the offenders who commit Type 2 homicides, also known as instrumental-opportunistic crimes, target vulnerable victims of opportunity, such as women and senior citizens, who are often alone at home at the

Box 4.9, *continued*

time of the crime. Injuries are inflicted manually, emphasizing that a weapon is not needed to incapacitate the victim. However, in many of these cases, the manual attack is ferocious, involving kicking and punching the victim to death. Victims are frequently strangled.

In many of these cases, the offender steals valuables from the victim's person or house, and sometimes sexually assaults the victim, almost as if they were "stealing" sex. In the offender's mind, the victim is no more than an object, to be used for the offender's own purposes, over and beyond the murder itself.

In some Type 2 homicides, the victim's face is covered after the crime, either by a piece of clothing, a pillow, or other object, suggesting that the offender may have feelings of shame, most probably in relation to either the violence or the sex. This suggests that these offenders may be uncomfortable with this element of the crime, possibly because it is not something they have done before. These offenders, who may have criminal histories of robbery and burglary (which again relates to the idea of forcibly taking from people what they want), may in this instance have gone too far in the "taking," and having completed their crimes, may be shocked and uncomfortable with their own actions.

This case illustrates a typical instrumental crime scene. These types of offenders frequently exhibit a similar psychological theme in their previous thefts and burglaries. The best way of understanding this type of offender is as someone accustomed to breaking into people's homes and stealing from them. Many of these offenders are relatively young (17-21 years), are generally acquainted with their victims, and have identified them as vulnerable and easy targets.

Type 3: The Forensically Aware and Experienced Type

The body of 29-year-old male was found dumped near a river bank. He was lying face down, and was naked. His throat had been cut, and a serious attempt had been made at severing his arms and legs.

Behaviors of the third type, also known as instrumental-cognitive crimes, have a highly cognitive emphasis to them. Most commonly in homicide, we see Type I crime scenes in which the offender has lost control and acted impulsively, without thinking. In Type 3 cases, however, the offender remains calm during and after the crime, and engages in behaviors that suggest a great deal of advance planning, such as removing forensic evidence from the crime scene, transporting the body away from the original crime scene, and disposing of the body by hiding or burying it. These activities suggest that offenders are actively distancing themselves from the victim and the crime, and by so doing, distancing themselves as the suspect. Many of these offenders are aware of forensic evidence (e.g., the weapon, blood, semen, etc.), which they make sure not to leave behind.

This case gives an extreme example of this type of crime, an example in which the offender has engaged in activities over and beyond the norm of just hiding the body. In this case, the offender has gone as far as trying to cut the body of the victim into several pieces for easy disposal, but failed.

The offenders associated with Type 3 homicides, which have a cognitive focus, choose aggression and violence as a lifestyle. Some of these offenders are also likely to have committed prior violent offenses.

Results from recent empirical studies on the behavior and psychological characteristics of killers, such as the study summarized above, have established a classification system of homicide crime scenes and its related offenders, one that goes beyond the personal and anecdotal experience of any one profiler. This demonstrates that by using our understanding of human behavior, derived from general psychology, for differentiating criminal behavior in a way that is relevant to police investigations, it is possible to establish the foundations for a repeatable scientific approach. By so doing, we can begin to demystify the previously obscured process of psychological profiling and establish what can be expected from profiling and what needs to be done in order to make it a more valid and reliable investigative tool.

Summary

Psychology, as we have described, is a complex discipline, which encompasses a wide spectrum of theoretical approaches. In this chapter, we have by no means been exhaustive in our overview of the discipline, but instead have attempted to give a summary of some of the main psychological theories as they relate to criminal behavior. In order to situate the work of a forensic psychologist, we provided some general background on the discipline of psychology. We highlighted the notion that psychology is the scientific study of behavior, but that psychologists are also interested in understanding underlying mental constructs—such as personality, cognition, emotion—and how these are manifested in behavior. We discussed the various orientations of psychologists (biological, cognitive, social, clinical, and forensic) and the interests and major focus of each. We then closely considered the forensic psychologist, the type of psychologist most involved in the criminal justice system and most interested in criminal behavior.

Because the subject matter of forensic psychology itself is nearly as wide as that of the general discipline of psychology, we narrowed our focus on one of the newest and most controversial areas of forensic psychology: offender profiling. This investigative technique is one that many students find interesting, but at the same time it is also the technique that is most erroneously depicted in the media—and, as such, it is the investigative technique about which the least is known.

Although new and controversial, offender profiling highlights many of the key issues—theoretical, methodological, and applied—that are common to many areas of psychology. Specifically, profiling was used as an example of how we may want to utilize psychological theory in explaining how an individual grows up to be violent, ultimately expressing their aggression in different ways, against different people, in different situations. The key concern of the general discipline of psychology is the classification of individuals in terms of their similarities and their differences, that is, which criminal behaviors are found among all offenders, and what personality character-istics differentiate the offenders. Finally, we looked at the main factors involved in how we think about and interpret behavior, how these influence our ideas about criminal behavior, and ultimately how they may affect our use of psychology in understanding crime.

Suggested Further Reading

Ainsworth, P. (2001). *Offender Profiling and Crime Analysis.* Devon, UK: Willan.

Bartol, C.R., and A.M. Bartol (2005). *Criminal Behavior: A Psychosocial Approach.* Upper Saddle River, NJ: Pearson.

Blackburn, R. (1993). *The Psychology of Criminal Conduct: Theory, Research and Practice.* Chichester, UK: John Wiley.

Canter, D. (2000). *Criminal Shadows, Inner Narratives of Evil.* Irving, TX: Authorlink Press.

Gottfredson, M., and T. Hirschi (1990). *A General Theory of Crime.* Stanford, CA: Stanford University Press.

References

Ainsworth, P. (2001). *Offender Profiling and Crime Analysis.* Devon, UK: Willan.

Alison, L., M. Smith, and K. Morgan (2003). "Interpreting the Accuracy of Offender Profiles." *Psychology, Crime and Law,* 9(2):185-195.

Bandura, A. (1973). *Aggression: A Social Learning Analysis.* Englewood Cliffs, NJ: Prentice Hall.

Baumeister, R.F., L. Smart, and J.M. Boden (1996). "Relation of Threatened Egotism to Violence and Aggression: the Dark Side of Self Esteem." *Psychological Review,* 103(1):103-33.

Bowby, J. (1944). "Forty-Four Juvenile Thieves." *International Journal of Psychoanalysis,* 25:1-57.

Brussel, J.A. (1969). *Casebook of a Crime Psychiatrist.* London: New English Library.

Canter, D. (1995). "Psychology of Offender Profiling." In R. Bull and D. Carson (eds.), *Handbook of Psychology in Legal Contexts,* pp. 335-343. Chichester, UK: John Wiley.

Canter, D. (1994). *Criminal Shadows.* London: Harper Collins.

Canter, D., and R. Heritage (1990). "A Multivariate Model of Sexual Offence Behavior: Developments in 'Offender Profiling.'" *Journal of Forensic Psychiatry,* I(2):185-212.

Cleckley, H. (1976). *The Mask of Sanity,* 5th ed. St. Louis: Mosby.

Copson, G. (1995). "Coals to Newcastle? Part 1: A Study of Offender Profiling." *Police Research Group Special Interests Series: Paper No. 7.* London: Home Office Police Department.

Douglas, J.E., and M. Olshaker (1996). *Mindhunter: Inside the FBI's Elite Serial Crime Unit.* New York: Pocket Books.

Eysenck, H.J. (1977). *Crime and Personality*, 2nd ed. London: Routledge & Kegan Paul.

Freud, S. (1916). "Criminals From a Sense of Guilt." *The Standard Edition of the Complete Psychological Works of Sigmund Freud.* Vol. 14, pp. 332-33. London: Hogarth Press.

Groth, A.N., with H.J. Birnbaum (1979). *Men Who Rape: The Psychology of the Offender.* New York: Plenum.

Hare, R.D. (1996). "Psychopathy and Antisocial Personality Disorder: A Case of Diagnostic Confusion." *Psychiatric Times,* 13(2):39-40.

Hare, R.D. (1970). *Psychopathy: Theory and Research.* New York: John Wiley.

Hart, S., P. Knopp, and R.D. Hare (1988). "Performance of Criminal Psychopaths Following Conditional Release from Prison." *Journal of Consulting and Clinical Psychology,* 56:227-232.

Hirschi, T., and M. Gottfredson (1988). "Towards a General Theory of Crime." In W. Buikhuisen & S. A. Mednick (eds.), *Explaining Criminal Behaviour*, pp. 8-26. Leiden, Netherlands: Brill Academic.

Huesmann, L.R., and L.D. Eron (1989). "Individual Differences and the Trait of Aggression." *European Journal of Personality*, 3:95-106.

Huesmann, L.R., L.D. Eron, M.M. Lefkowitz, and L.O. Walder (1984). "The Stability of Aggression Over Time and Generations." *Developmental Psychology,* 20:1120-1134.

Intrator, J., R.D. Hare, P. Stritzke, and K. Brichtswein (1997). "A Brain Imaging Study of Semantic and Affective Processing in Psychopaths." *Biological Psychiatry,* 42:96-103.

Knight, R.A., and R.A. Prenky (1987). "The Developmental Antecedents and Adult Adaptations of Rapist Subtypes." *Criminal Justice and Behavior,* 14:403-426.

Langer, W. (1972). *The Mind of Adolph Hitler.* New York: Basic Books

Pinizzotto, A.J., and N.J. Finkel (1990). "Criminal Personality Profiling—An Outcome and Process Study." *Law and Human Behavior*, 14(3):215-232.

Redl, F., and H. Toch (1979). "The Psychoanalytic Perspective." In H. Toch (ed.), *Psychology of Crime and Criminal Justice*, pp. 183-187. Prospect Heights, IL: Waveland.

Ressler, R.K., and T. Shachtman (1998). *I Have Lived in the Monster: Inside the Minds of the World's Most Notorious Serial Killers.* New York: St. Martin's.

Ressler, R.K., A.W. Burgess, and J.E. Douglas (1988) *Sexual Homicide.* Lexington, MA: Lexington Books.

Rumbelow, D. (1988). *Jack the Ripper: The Complete Casebook*. Chicago: Contemporary Books.

Salfati, C.G., and D.V. Canter (1999). "Differentiating Stranger Murders: Profiling Offender Characteristics From Behavioural Styles." *Behavioural Sciences and the Law.* 17:391-406.

Skinner, B.F. (1965). *Science and Human Behavior.* New York: The Free Press.

Toch, H. (1969). *Violent Men: An Inquiry into the Psychology of Violence.* Chicago: Aldine.

Wambaugh. J. (1989) *The Blooding.* New York: Bantam.

Wolfgang, M.E. (1958). *Patterns in Criminal Homicide.* Philadelphia: University of Pennsylvania.

Yochelson, S., and S.E. Samenow (1976).*The Criminal Personality.* Northvale, NJ: Jason Aronson.

Commentary

Lode Walgrave

At the beginning of their chapter, Salfati and Kucharski point out that a layperson would find it difficult to define psychology. Likewise, even many professional criminologists would have problems defining their science. Compared to psychologists, who are nearly unanimous in describing their discipline as "the scientific study of human behavior," criminologists find that there is ambiguity in articulating the scope of their field. "Criminology," some would say in a halfhearted attempt at describing the discipline, "is what criminologists do." But this begs the question, "Who are the criminologists?" The response: "Those whom one can meet at professional conferences in criminology." This inside joke illustrates the embarrassing situation in which criminologists endeavor to describe the kind of scientific enterprise commonly called "criminology."

Since its early beginnings 100 years ago, criminology was clearly understood as "the scientific study of crime and the criminal." But particularly during the 1960s and 1970s, criminology shifted its focus toward critical and radical initiatives in the discipline that were chiefly concerned with the workings of the criminal justice system, not criminal behavior. It is now generally acknowledged that the discipline's shift away from the criminal went too far. The discipline today encompasses the dual subjects of crime and the criminal, its primary concerns, along with the study of political beliefs and practical operations involved in the state's control of crime and criminals. Due to their study of politics, laws, and societal influences on crime, criminologists are well aware that crime itself is not a neutral concept, but one loaded with political meaning. From this standpoint, the purely psychological approach to understanding crime, which does not take political context into account, has limitations for criminologists.

Psychologists generally approach the study of crime with three assumptions in mind:

1. "Crime" is a concept that defines a particular aspect of human nature. It is a category of behavior that is fundamentally distinct from noncriminal behavior.

2. The person who commits crime is deviant. The problem of criminal behavior lies with the person who commits it.

3. Deviance can be best understood in psychological—individualistic—terms. It is the person and his particular behavior that should be the focus of investigation and scholarly exploration.

Given these three assumptions, psychologists believe that certain individual psychological characteristics are related to certain types of crimes. At first sight, this conceptual relationship, or convergence, seems obvious. After all, it is individuals who forcefully impose their behavior on others, for example by stealing or committing an act of violence. Even if an individual's criminal behavior is provoked by his or her social environment or peers, that behavior is also the result of his or her (wrong-minded) decisions and psychological processes. Consequently, the operative question is: Why do some people who experience such crime-producing social processes decide to break the law while others do not? For example, not all socially disadvantaged adolescents engage in street violence. Why is it that some do and others do not?

Salfati and Kucharski provide an excellent survey of the various theoretical approaches in psychology that may be employed in answering such questions. Moreover, they give a most interesting account of offender profiling, which is fast becoming one of the most intriguing and useful applications of psychological analysis. Most criminologists, however, take a more complex approach. They see crime as a *social* phenomenon. Social processes and social structures are responsible, at least in part, for both *defining* certain behaviors as criminal, as well as for *causing* criminal behavior. A purely psychological, or individualistic, approach does not account for these larger social influences. In the next sections, I will briefly explain why this is the case. I do so in order to clarify the difference between a strictly psychological approach to understanding crime, and a more comprehensive criminological perspective.

Crime is a Relative Concept

Although psychologists associate crime with psychological categories such as mental disorders, crime does not necessarily stem from the pathological nature of certain individuals. It is a truism that what is defined as criminal conduct—such as abortion, drug use, homosexuality, traffic violations, and tax fraud—depends on the particular point in history and on the particular society or culture being considered. What is regarded as criminal behavior has changed throughout history. Further, different cultures prohibit different behaviors to different degrees. For example, Amsterdam, the capital of the Netherlands, permits the sale of recreational drugs that are prohibited in the United States, while the island nation of Singapore imposes the death penalty on drug dealers. Economic interests, cultural and religious values, and political power fundamentally influence which actions are criminalized and the degree of punishment associated with them.

All this notwithstanding, there *are* some behaviors that are prohibited by criminal law in *every* culture. One might argue the need for two categories of law: a "hard core" criminal law to protect property and ensure personal safety, and another type of criminal law to govern social life. The first category would disallow acts that are inherently wrong, such as murder or theft (the so-called *mala in se* offenses), while the second category of criminal law would consider certain behaviors as wrong only because they are forbidden by the legislature (the so-called *mala prohibita* offenses). Psychology, following this argument, would have relevant application only to those individuals who commit *mala in se* crimes. However, the distinction between the two types of crimes is not always so clear. Both tax fraud and armed robbery are ways of taking away property that belongs to another. Not only assault and battery, but also the conscious polluting of the environment, threaten the physical well-being of others. The definition of who is a criminal is not based on absolute "natural" laws, a notion well illustrated by the fact that one-time "terrorists," such as former President of Ireland, Eamon de Valera, and former Prime Minister of Israel, Menachem Begin, ended their careers as respected politicians (because they won their "terrorist wars").

It also is the case that psychological characteristics do not inevitably coincide with criminal categories. Offenders are psychologically very different from each other. Committing tax fraud versus committing a ruthless murder, for example, involve different psychological factors, based on motivation, skills, emotions, relationship to the victim, and moral convictions. What is more, the psychology of people who engage in tax fraud is probably more comparable to the legitimate behavior of corporate executives involved in manipulative business practices.

Mental Illness is Not Associated with Criminal Behavior

Criminal behavior alone is not a sufficient reason to suspect a person of being psychologically deviant. Originally, in the nineteenth century, criminology assumed that all offenders had some form of psychological or biological dysfunction. Particularly in Europe, the discipline of criminology began as a specialized clinical science with the objective of investigating the psychiatric and psychopathologic origins of criminal conduct. Much has changed since then. Now, the link between criminality and psychological pathology is far from evident, due in part to sociology's contribution to criminology and the criticism of psychologically based treatment models during the 1960s and 1970s. In the film, *The Godfather,* for example, the mafia boss, Don Vito Corleone (portrayed by Marlon Brando) is not depicted as a crazed criminal, but as a loving husband, a caring father to his children, and a loyal friend. Moreover, research on youth crime has convincingly demonstrated that offense behavior is age-linked to adolescence. Statistically and social-psychologically, youth offending is not pathological, but, rather, "normal." The main distinction in youth crime exists between normal age-linked delinquency and more frequent, serious, and persistent forms of adolescent criminal behavior (Rutter, Giller, and Hagell, 1998).

There are numerous studies indicating the individual psychological, neurological, and family differences between individuals who exhibit such patterns of persistent, serious offending, which tends to begin early in life, and adolescents who are not known as such offenders. There is also ample sociological research available to explain why juveniles from certain demographic groups, such as young black men, risk more than others and risk arrest by committing criminal acts (Rutter, Giller, and Hagell, 1998). It is difficult, then, to isolate psychological characteristics from their social backgrounds. While psychological characteristics alone sometimes contribute to criminal behavior, it is more likely the case that they mediate between social relationships and conditions and the actual behavior. Sociological criminologists would say that most of the patterned youth offending is committed by normal persons living in "pathological"—that is, anomic, disorganized, disadvantaged—social environments.

Psychological Patterns Exist in Persistent, Serious Offenders

Psychological peculiarities do exist in some offenders. How do we explain them? Given the psychological profile of persistent offenders, genetic and neuropsychological factors should not be overlooked. On the basis of their biological and psychological condition, some children may be at a higher risk of becoming hyperactive, impulsive, or less intelligent, but the process toward criminality is far from direct. It involves complex interpersonal experiences in the family, school, neighborhood, and other social environments. "There is not a gene for crime . . . genetic influences operate through effects on vulnerability to environmental adversities and stressors, and some through their role with respect to behaviors concerned with the shaping and selecting of environments" (Rutter, Giller, and Hagell, 1998:165-66). The same biological and psychological traits may lead to totally different and socially prized characteristics in sports, business, politics, or the military.

The family is frequently regarded as the most influential social environment in the emergence of crime. The presence of an authoritarian type of socialization or a chaotic and/or lax parental discipline toward children appears to explain much of an offender's potential delinquency. However, most of these environmental factors are not just a matter of unique family features, they are frequently the result of social and economical stressors that may have burdened the family over repeated generations. Or they may be the result of traumatic life events such as death of a parent, unemployment, or divorce.

Basically, individual characteristics are not just individual. They emerge during social interactions and other experiences, which are themselves influenced by social institutions such as the family, school, and work. The relatively stable way in which the individual experiences the "here and now," and copes with it, is a product of his or her personality, which has been formed through past social interactions, life opportunities, and cultural experiences. These are partly determined by the social environment in which he or she has been living. Accordingly, individual characteristics are always related to interpersonal relations and social environments.

Failure to acknowledge this greatly restricts our analysis of social reality and our efforts at understanding crime. It brings us to a kind of sophism, illustrated in Wilson and Herrnstein's influential volume, *Crime and Human Nature* (1985). The authors compare their approach to the scientific study of animal behavior and consider the relationship among four levels of analysis: the developmental, the situational, the adaptive, and the biological. Wilson and Herrnstein thus analyze criminal behavior strictly from a "biologic adaptive" perspective. They consider society as if it were, like nature, an unproblematic, unchangeable given. They therefore "problematize" only the individual offender, and disregard those broader social factors—social structures, social processes, and social environments—that may explain part of the criminogenic process.

Psychology Can Improve Knowledge about Decisionmaking

I am not arguing that the discipline of criminology should reject individual psychology. Psychology, as the scientific study of human behavior, remains an important discipline, even if it frequently focuses on the behavior of individuals and offers only a partial understanding of crime. In criminology, psychology is needed to understand the fact that individuals do—more or less frequently, and more or less consciously—decide to commit crime and risk being labeled as criminals and punished in society.

Psychological traits, such as impulsivity or low self-control, may be easier to measure than group or societal factors such as social interactions and culture. Individual behavior can more easily be observed than large-scale social structures such as bureaucracies. Because of this consideration, some psychologists regard the individualistic approach as being more scientific, and disregard all sociological factors from their theoretical and research work. By doing so, they reverse the scientific process. Instead of employing the research methods most appropriate for providing answers to the most important topics on crime, some limit themselves to those research topics that can be measured by a small number of methods. Such a reversal is not only unscientific; it is also counterproductive because it engenders the popular notion that crime is a result of the pathological condition of individuals. Those social factors that determine why certain behaviors are defined as criminal are not even considered.

Inversely, purely sociological approaches also have their shortcomings. They fail to account for differences between individuals who live in the same social environment or who are members of the same population group. Not all socially disadvantaged juveniles commit crime, but social exclusion increases the risk for engagement in persistent youth crime. How that risk actually leads to serious levels of criminality depends on how the unfavorable social environment is experienced and manifested, and that may be peculiar to the individual.

There is much interdisciplinary work that seeks to understand crime by taking into account the individual dimension. One example is the rational choice perspective, to which cognitive psychological processes are crucial. Another is the life-course paradigm, in which experiential psychology seems to play an important role. Yet another is reintegrative shaming theory, which considers moral emotions as essential to human development and social relations. These theories place psychological factors and processes within a comprehensive framework of psychological and societal factors.

Psychology Can Enhance our Understanding of the Criminal Justice System

To be sure, the discipline of psychology has much to contribute to criminology. Many sociologists who consider themselves criminologists often fail to understand the essential contributions that psychology has made in explaining human (criminal) behavior. Accordingly, many of their theories in criminology are not sufficiently detailed and thus limit our understanding of individual responses to crime as well as an understanding of the treatment or reintegration of offenders. Psychology's contribution to criminology goes far beyond the study of criminals. Now that criminology has broadened its disciplinary scope to consider society's reaction to the criminal as well as critically analyzing law and punishment, the field of psychological research in criminology has also expanded considerably.

Consider that social psychological factors are an essential component in the public's attitudes about crime and punishment. Consider also that research on deterrence reveals great differences in the way people are restrained from committing crime by the threat of punishment. There is no doubt that effective deterrence strategies are based on an understanding of psychological factors and processes. Similarly, understanding people's fear of crime is also enhanced by psychology. In certain individuals, fear of crime appears to be part of a more general feeling of vulnerability, which itself is more a matter of mental perception than of the actual statistical risk of being victimized by crime.

The criminal justice system is rife with other issues of special interest to psychology, such as studying the reliability of witness testimony in court; the consequences of long-term incarceration; the effects of prison life on the intellectual, emotional, and social functioning of inmates; and the possible (mis)uses of authority by police officers, judges, or corrections officers.

Recent developments in the area of restorative justice, to be discussed in Chapter Seven, have brought to light many new topics that await psychological research. Such topics include the sentiments and thoughts underlying victims' and offenders' willingness to meet each other; the complex and intense emotions—anger, resentment, shame—that are invariably present during victim-offender mediation, conferencing, or circles; and the psychological meaning of what is "just" and how injustice is repaired. Many other examples of psychology's contribution to understanding crime could be mentioned, but the aforementioned suffice to illustrate the discipline's potential.

Contemporary criminology has stripped the concept of crime of its simplistic meaning. Given that crime is not seen as intrinsically "bad" or "sick" behavior, but as a matter of social definition, it is difficult to apply psychological concepts without reservation. This shift in the conceptualization of crime undermines many of the traditional psychological explanations of criminality. All this notwithstanding, the extension of criminology has now opened promising avenues for psychological work on the new, emerging topics of interest to criminology.

Endnotes

1. Individual responsibility is not always clearly the case, as in, for example, corporate crime, in which CEOs are often not held criminally responsible.

2. As argued by, for example, Wilson and Herrnstein (1985).

References

Rutter, M, H. Giller, and A. Hagell (1998). *Antisocial Behavior by Young People*. Cambridge, UK: Cambridge University Press.

Wilson, J.Q., and R. Herrnstein (1985). *Crime and Human Nature*. New York: Simon and Schuster.

Chapter Five

Biological Perspectives on Crime

Lee Ellis

[handwritten: behavior is regulated by the brain ⇒ biological factors.]

Biology is the study of all forms of life. Because behavior is regulated by the brain, one can reasonably assume that human behavior—including that defined as *criminal*—is influenced by biological factors. In fact, human behavior itself can be thought of as a biological phenomenon because no behavior would be possible without a functioning brain. Typically, however, biologists leave the study of most forms of human behavior up to social scientists.

The biggest question addressed by biologists is how life came to be. This is a controversial issue mainly because the answer provided by the so-called *fossil record* is that life evolved over billions of years from very humble microbial origins, a view that conflicts with biblical teachings. *Evolution* refers to the many changes in the forms of life revealed by fossils embedded in successive layers of rock and sediment. For example, the fossil record indicates that for more than 100 million years dinosaurs dominated the planet, during which time there were virtually no mammals as we know them today. Following a large meteor collision about 65 million years ago, the dinosaurs became extinct, and soon thereafter a primitive rodent-like insectivore, which eked out a modest nocturnal living near the end of the dinosaur era, began to proliferate into numerous species of mammals. As more and more fossils have been discovered, and as advances have been made in genetics, scientists have slowly pieced together the puzzles of how the millions of species that exist today are related to one another and to even more millions of species that lived eons ago.

[handwritten: Evolution ↓ Changes in the forms of life to adapt]

What does evolution have to do with criminology? This chapter will argue that evolution—along with other biological forces—is in fact central to understanding crime. The perspective from which this proposal is made departs from mainstream sociology. One reason for my unusual perspective as a sociologist and criminologist is that I received quite a bit of academic training in biology and continued to read much of its rich literature. Throughout my career, I have been primarily interested in human social behavior and social institutions, with a special focus on criminal behavior and the workings of the criminal justice system. However, I have always been open to the view that human behavior, even that which is learned, is highly influenced by biology.

This perspective has been referred to by various names such as *sociobiology, biosociology, evolutionary psychology,* and even *neuropsychology*. Each of these disciplines has slightly different emphases, but they all share the belief that human behavior can only be well understood when biology is part of the picture. Because this chapter focuses on criminal behavior, its perspective can be most closely linked to what is known as *biosocial criminology*. This term is now widely applied to the view that biological and social learning factors *interact* to give each human being a unique probability of engaging in criminal behavior.

Box 5.1 • On Genes

Genes are rarely about inevitability, especially when it comes to humans, the brain, or behavior. They're about vulnerability, propensities, tendencies.

Matt Ridley *The Origins of Virtue: Human Instincts and the Evolution of Cooperation* (1998), p. 293.

A Short History of Biosocial Criminology

The first person to make an academic case for biological influences on criminality was an Italian military physician by the name of Cesare Lombroso. Writing in the mid-1800s, his most famous assertion was that persistent criminals were *atavistic,* meaning throwbacks to a more primitive stage in human evolution. Since then, Lombroso's proposal has been frequently ridiculed. Even those of us who work from a biosocial perspective have now largely set aside his theory because considerably more sophisticated arguments about how evolutionary forces could be influencing criminal behavior are now available, a few of which will be presented in this chapter.

Today, the opinions of criminologists about the relevance of biology to the study of crime can be placed into three categories:

1. Biology is of overwhelming importance.
2. Biology and the social environment are both important.
3. Only the social environmental is important.

According to a recent survey (Ellis and Walsh, 1999), few if any crimi- nologists subscribe to the first idea. Regarding the other two categories, 85 percent contend that people's varying tendencies to commit crime are almost entirely the result of social circumstances; they are the sociological (or environmental) criminologists. I am among the 15 percent who believe that both biological and social factors interact to affect criminal behavior; we are the biosocial criminologists.

Methods Used by Biosocial Criminologists

Most of the research methods employed by biosocial criminologists are the same as those used by criminologists in general. We rely heavily on ques- tionnaires and on statistical information maintained by the criminal justice system. What distinguishes us most is that we try to keep abreast of what is happening in various fields of biology and psychology that affect human behavior, especially when it is of a criminal nature, and incorporate that information for understanding crime.

. One of the main reasons biosocial criminology is still relatively unpop- ular is the fact that most criminologists have little or no training in biology. Without such training, they are unlikely to be aware of the tremendous advances that have been made in understanding how the brain responds not only to sociocultural experiences, but to a whole host of biological factors, many of which could affect people's tendencies to engage in crime. Read- ers of this chapter who become convinced of the wisdom of the biosocial perspective should take at least a few basic courses in biology before delv- ing very deeply into criminology.

To provide a foundation for readers with limited training in biology, I will begin to make the case for biology's relevance to the field of criminology by describing a memorable childhood experience that impressed me regarding the power of biology in relationship to behavior. Later in the chap- ter, I will present a relatively new biosocial theory of criminal behavior that I have formulated based on my work as well as the efforts of other social and biological scientists. The chapter closes with a discussion of several bio- logical variables that studies suggest are associated with criminal behavior.

Life on the Farm

While growing up on a Kansas farm, I noticed that male and female farm animals behaved differently. Of course, this is true of humans, but I was impressed by sex differences in animals as well. Among cattle, for example, bulls (males) were more likely than cows (females) to pick fights with one another (and even with humans). About the only time I ever saw cows being aggressive was when they were protecting their calves, which bulls never did. I wondered why bulls were so frequently chasing one another, snorting, scratching their hooves in the dirt, and butting heads. Of course, when boys wrestle and scuffle more than most girls do, people (including social scientists) often attribute the difference to socialization, but this would have been a farfetched explanation for sex differences in aggression among farm animals.

Years later, from some of the courses I took in college, along with a lot of reading I did on my own, I learned about a hormone that males have more of than females. This powerful biochemical, called *testosterone*, dramatically alters genital development in mammals. Testosterone also increases the development of muscle tissue, especially following the onset of puberty. Another bodily organ that is influenced by testosterone is the brain. The full extent of these neurological changes is still being identified, but there appears to be no major part of the brain that is unaffected, and several of the alterations involve areas associated with aggression and violence (Hines, 2004; Niehoff, 1999).

I witnessed firsthand evidence of testosterone's influence on aggression when I watched my father—usually with the help of his brother or a farmhand—round up yearling calves each spring. Besides vaccinating them for various diseases, Dad would corral more than 90 percent of the young bulls into a rusty old stanchion and castrate each one of them using a pocketknife. This painful procedure removed the primary organ (the testes) that produces testosterone. Within a year, the effects of castration were obvious: Not only were the few "intact" males more muscular than castrated males (steers), but only the "intact" males spent time snorting and engaging in ritualistic combat.

By the time I studied criminology in college, I recall learning something that is just as true today as it was in the 1960s: Men engage in more crime than women do, especially violent crime. I took my first criminology course during the mid-1960s, when the women's liberation movement was just beginning to attract national attention, and I remember my instructor predicting that as women became more liberated, their involvement in crime would eventually come to resemble that of men. Has it? Nearly half a century later, criminologists have yet to find a society in which women's involvement in violent crime comes close to that of men's (Ellis and Walsh, 2000:102-107). Furthermore, in countries where the greatest progress has been made toward gender equality in the home, workplace, and society in general (mainly Western Europe, Australia/New Zealand, and North America), the wide gap between men and women in the commission of violent offenses still persists (Ellis and Walsh, 2000:388-391; Steffensmeier and Streifel, 1991).

As I became increasingly intrigued by the well-documented sex differences in criminal behavior, a simple idea came to me. Perhaps the same hormone that causes male farm animals to be so aggressive has similar effects in humans. If so, criminologists ought to learn about testosterone and how it affects the human brain and, consequently, human behavior. This conclusion is one that I still share with students who wish to study crime from a biosocial perspective.

Box 5.2 • The Blank Slate

Aggressive parents often have aggressive children, but people who conclude that aggression is learned from parents in a 'cycle of violence' never consider the possibility that violent tendencies could be inherited as well as learned.

Steven Pinker, *The Blank Slate: The Modern Denial of Human Nature* (2002), p. 310.

It is not possible in the space of this chapter to provide a detailed discussion of the numerous threads of evidence about the effects that testosterone (and various related hormones) has on the brain, and how several of these effects appear to impact criminal behavior. However, I can provide a sense of how much has been learned along these lines by presenting a biosocial theory of criminal behavior that I have formulated during 30-plus years of working in the area.

The Evolutionary Neuroandrogenic Theory

The biosocial explanation of criminal behavior that I have come to embrace is called the *evolutionary neuroandrogenic (ENA) theory*. It is so named because major elements of the theory have to do with evolution, the brain, and male sex hormones. (The term *androgens* refers to several hormones that are more prevalent in males than in females, of which testosterone is the most important.) Despite its biological emphasis, ENA theory specifies several ways in which biological variables interact with social and learning variables to affect criminal behavior.

The theory's central tenet is that testosterone and other androgens have evolved the ability to affect the brain in ways that increase a general type of behavior called *competitive/victimizing tendencies*. To be more specific, ENA theory consists of two central propositions. The first one focuses on evolution, and the second involves the influence of sex hormones on the brain.

The idea of evolution remains controversial largely for religious reasons. Among biologists, however, there is no doubt that the dazzling array of life forms we see today can all trace their origins to single-celled organisms via millions of extinct creatures whose remains are strewn throughout the fossil record. In other words, life began with relatively simple forms and gradually expanded into today's species, including humans. Theoretically, life will continue to slowly evolve as current species adapt to ever-changing environmental conditions.

In their attempts to explain the fossil record, scientists have devised a variety of theories. So far, the theory that has stood up best to the evidence both from the fossil record and from contemporary knowledge of genetics is one proposed by Charles Darwin a century and a half ago (before the concept of genetics had even been invented). The crux of Darwin's theory is that new species evolve from earlier species by slowly changing their physical forms over hundreds, if not thousands, of generations in response to continually changing environmental conditions. In other words, as environments change over time, existing species must either devise new adaptations to those changes or they will eventually become extinct.

Darwin theorized that most of the time when living things reproduce, they "breed true," meaning that offspring resemble their parents. If this were *always* the case, the species would have no opportunities to evolve. But mutations—odd traits such as extra-long fur for warmth or extra-sensitive ears for hearing over longer distances—occasionally present themselves. Geneticists have discovered that mutations are caused by tiny random "errors" in the DNA molecules, and that it is these molecules that make evolution possible.

For a species that is well adapted, nearly all mutations will detract from survival, and so any individual with a mutation will be at a survival disadvantage. However, to the extent that the environment is changing, some mutations will actually promote survival, allowing individuals carrying these mutations to thrive and to have more offspring than those lacking the mutations. As mutations accumulate, members of a species will eventually exhibit such a large number of physical changes that they will look distinctly different from their forebears hundreds of generations earlier. At this point, a new species is said to have evolved.

The central concept in Darwin's theory is that of *natural selection*. This term refers to any environmental pressure on members of an existing species that forces them to either adapt to a changing environment or become extinct. Darwin argued that natural selection (the biological version of "shape up or ship out") is what drives evolution. This, of course, runs contrary to the view that a supernatural or divine force is responsible for the emergence and disappearance of species.

Of what relevance are evolution and natural selection to the study of criminal behavior? The answer is contained in the first proposition of ENA theory.

The Evolutionary Proposition

According to ENA theory, competitive/victimizing behavior has been naturally selected among humans primarily in the case of males rather than females. As part of the evidence for this assumption, an interesting sex difference in mating preferences has now been well documented: Unlike men, when most women choose mates, they give serious consideration to the prospective mate's "ability to make a living" (i.e., to procure resources). So many studies have found this "female bias" toward mates who are able resource provisioners that it is now considered a cultural universal (e.g., Buss et al., 1990; Davis, 1990; Kemper and Bologh, 1980).

ENA theory assumes that a female preference for men who are capable of resource procurement occurs primarily through an evolutionary process of natural selection, not through cultural training (although socialization may augment the evolutionary process). Being more specific, over countless generations, women who have chosen mates who are stable providers of resources (such as food and shelter) have produced more children than females who have used other criteria for choosing mates (Ellis, 2001). A similar sort of "biased" mating preference has been found in nearly all other mammals, because females generally mate more with dominant rather than subordinate males (Ellis, 1995a). Because dominance must be won, this female bias has had the effect of selecting for genes that facilitate competitive/victimizing tendencies among males.

The main types of crimes that ENA theory is intended to explain are those causing harm to others, either by physically injuring them (such as assault and murder) or by depriving them of their property (such as theft and fraud). To distinguish these injurious and property-depriving offenses from crimes that do neither, so-called victimless crimes, the term *victimful crimes* will be used.

Victimful criminality can be thought of as a type of competitive/victimizing tendency. This is illustrated in Box 5.3. The "victimizing" end of the continuum consists of acts that intentionally and directly injure others (such as murder and assault) or take their property (such as robbery and fraud). In all societies with written laws, these harmful acts are criminalized (Ellis and Walsh, 2000:8). At the "competitive" end of the competitive/victimizing continuum are acts that usually involve making per-item or per-service profits from commercial ventures (such as selling products and services for more than they cost to produce or provide).[1] Most of these commercial forms of the behavior have potential victimizing elements, especially when the accumulated profits are large, as, for example, through price gouging, or when they cause harm, such as when defective products are produced and sold.

Any theory that rests on a Darwinian foundation (as this one does) must assume that genes contribute to variations in the traits being investigated. Accordingly, ENA theory stipulates that males have a greater *genetic* propensity toward competitive/victimizing behavior than do females. If so, where would these male-only genes be located? Humans have 46 chromosomes, all but one of which males and females share. The exception is the Y-chromosome. With a few technical qualifications that are beyond the limits of this chapter, individuals who have it are male; those who do not are female.

Box 5.3 • A Continuum of Competitive/Victimizing Behavior			
Type of Behavior	very crude-----------------------------intermediate ----------------------------very sophisticated		
Degree of Criminalization	highly certain----------------------------intermediate ----------------------------highly limited		
Examples	Violent and property offenses ("street crimes")	Embezzlement, fraud ("white collar crimes")	Deceptive business practices, price gouging	General profit-making

Consequently, ENA theory necessitates that genes located on the Y-chromosome contribute to criminal behavior. Without this assumption, the theory is unable to account for the universally higher male involvement in victimful criminality. The question of how genes on the Y-chromosome (or elsewhere) actually exercise such behavioral influences is addressed by the theory's second proposition.

The Neuroandrogenic Proposition

ENA theory stipulates that five different aspects of brain functioning are responsible for competitive/victimizing behavior. Three aspects promote the behavior, while the remaining two help to direct the behavior away from victimful offending toward more socially acceptable (commercial) forms.

Genes responsible for the production of high (male-typical) levels of testosterone are located on the Y-chromosome (Maxson, 1992; Van Oort-merssen, Benus, and Sluyter, 1992). Early in fetal development, these genes promote the formation of testes from what otherwise would become ovaries. Once the male testes have formed, testosterone production begins to surpass the minute amounts produced by females. As shown in Box 5.4, androgen production is especially high prior to birth and following puberty.

Experiments with laboratory animals such as rats and monkeys have shown that testosterone has powerful effects on how the brain functions, particularly before birth and after puberty. The most permanent and irreversible effects occur shortly before birth or within a few months afterward (Compaan et al., 1993). In humans, most of the perinatal phase roughly spans the third through the seventh months of pregnancy (Ellis and Ames, 1987; Macke et al., 1993:845). Basically, when testosterone levels are high (typical of males), the brain is masculinized; when testosterone is low (typical of females), the brain remains in its default feminine mode (Burr, 1993:51). Although the most dramatic differences in testosterone level are between males and females, considerable variations within each sex have also been documented.

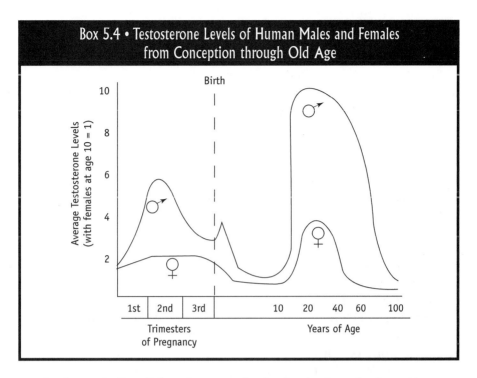

Box 5.4 • Testosterone Levels of Human Males and Females from Conception through Old Age

As shown in Box 5.4, puberty marks the beginning of a dramatic surge in male testosterone production. When high postpubertal levels of testosterone are combined with high perinatal levels, many changes ensue. Muscles strengthen, a growth spurt begins, the vocal cords enlarge, and the brain begins to function in ways that promote sexual interest.

In addition to promoting a strong interest in sexual activity, the brain of males must ensure that behavior generally attractive to females is exhibited. ENA theory asserts that it is for this reason that competitive/victimizing behavior roughly accompanies the onset of puberty, and that its crudest expressions are in the form of assaulting and stealing from others. I will now specify the types of effects that testosterone has on the brain that seem to incline males toward competitive/victimizing behavior in general, and toward victimful criminality specifically.

Promoting Competitive/Victimizing Behavior

While much remains to be learned about brain functioning and competitive/victimizing behavior, enough is now known to offer some specific theoretical proposals. In particular, three interrelated aspects of brain functioning appear to promote competitive/victimizing behavior, and all three are enhanced by exposing the brain to male-typical levels of testosterone.

First, exposing the brain to male-typical levels of testosterone causes a general subduing of the brain's responsiveness to incoming stimuli, a phenomenon called *suboptimal arousal* (Ellis, 1995b). A suboptimally aroused brain inclines individuals to prefer above-average levels of sensory stimulation, such as noises, colors, and sensations. Among the behavioral patterns that result from a suboptimally aroused brain are childhood hyperactivity, conduct disorders, and difficulty in sustaining one's focus of attention. Numerous studies have found that these sorts of traits are more characteristic of males than of females even before the onset of puberty (Lavigne et al., 1996; Luk et al., 1991; Maughan and Rutter, 1998; Moffitt, Caspi, and Silva, 2001; Stallard, 1993).

Second, exposing the brain to testosterone appears to make males more volatile with respect to "negative emotions," such as anger and rage. The most affected area appears to be the *limbic system*, a primitive region of the mammalian brain that wields great influence on emotions. When the limbic system is exposed to high levels of testosterone (and some of its metabolites), any number of environmental stressors can trigger strong emotional outbursts in the form of what psychologists call *episodic dyscontrol* (Creaby et al., 1993; Kandel and Freed, 1989:406). When episodic dyscontrol occurs, an individual temporarily loses voluntary control over his or her actions, and often carries out a series of near-automated actions of rage. The crimes that may result from episodic dyscontrol by susceptible individuals range from assaults to arson and vandalism.

Third, testosterone appears to promote competitive/victimizing behavior by shifting some of the functioning of the outer portion of the brain, called the *neocortex*, away from the left hemisphere toward the right hemisphere (Reite et al., 1993; Shucard, Shucard, and Cummings, 1981:93). As a result of this rightward shift, individuals rely less on language-based reasoning (which occurs predominantly in the left hemisphere), and emphasize spatial, temporal, and mathematical thinking instead (Ellis, 2003a). Among the evidence that brain exposure to testosterone causes this shift is the finding that males surpass females in being able to "mentally rotate" three-dimensional objects (Galea and Kimura, 1993; Silverman et al., 2000), make sense of complex algebraic formulas (Benbow and Stanley, 1983; Koivula, Hassmén, and Hunt, 2001), as well as perform other nonlanguage cognitive tasks (Alexander, Packard, and Peterson, 2002; Hamilton 1995). On the other hand, because rules of conduct, including laws, are inherently language-based, persons whose brains have been exposed to high levels of testosterone will take longer to conform to linguistic rules, making criminal violations more common.

From a Darwinian perspective, the above three androgen-enhanced brain functioning patterns are hypothesized to have evolved to a greater extent in males than in females because they have collectively contributed to competitive/victimizing behaviors. Additionally, it is important to bear in mind that engaging in crude forms of competitive/victimizing behavior, such as assault, make the offender vulnerable to retaliation efforts by victims and their relatives. Thus, in the interest of their own well-being, it behooves males who are prone to competitive/victimizing behaviors to develop the more sophisticated forms of such behavior. How adolescent males tend to move from the crude to the sophisticated forms of competitive/victimizing behavior will now be addressed.

HOW to make them control this behavior

Diverting Males Away from a Life of Crime

The final two neurological factors envisioned by ENA theory help to direct competitive/victimizing behavior away from their crude (criminal) expressions toward more socially acceptable and financially rewarding expressions (such as engaging in competitive business practices). The first factor involves learning ability, and the second involves foresight and planning ability. Theoretically, the more rapidly males learn and the more foresight and planning they engage in, the faster they will shift away from crude expressions of competitive/victimizing behaviors toward the more sophisticated expressions.

While the concept of learning ability is complex and impossible to define precisely, especially in neurological terms, it is most often measured in terms of standardized tests of intelligence. ENA theory therefore asserts that high scores on these tests will be associated with rapid transitioning from crude to sophisticated forms of competitive/victimizing behaviors. Consistent with this prediction are studies showing that persistent offenders score lower on intelligence tests than do persons who are relatively law abiding (Ellis and Walsh, 2003).

Regarding foresight and planning ability, the brain's prefrontal regions closely monitor the limbic region, where most emotions reside (Davidson, Cave, and Sellner, 2000:592; Strayhorn, 2002:11). When emotional impulses are sent to the frontal lobes, they respond, although always within the context of past experiences (Tomarken and Keener, 1998:401). For the brain to weave past experiences with strategies for reaching future goals, the frontal lobes perform what is known as *executive functioning* (Barkley, Godzinsky, and Du Paul, 1992; Passler, Isaac, and Hynd, 1985). *executive functioning*

Executive functioning can be thought of as the brain's master control center. To illustrate, several nonfrontal parts of the brain coordinate physical movement such as walking, swimming, riding a bike, or driving a car. However, decisions about *where* one should move, and for what *purpose*, are primarily made by the frontal lobes.

Reasoning about moral/legal issues appears to be heavily dependent upon executive functioning because such reasoning often requires accurately anticipating the long-term consequences of one's actions (Anderson, Holmes, and Ostresh, 1999). The brain's ability to perform executive functioning can be disturbed by prenatal complications and by various types of physical and chemical trauma throughout life (Barkley, 1990; Mann, 1995:1922).

According to ENA theory, executive functioning often plays a key role in criminal behavior as well as in *psychopathy,* a mental condition closely linked to persistent criminality, which was discussed in Chapter Four. Among the main traits associated with psychopathy are the lack of a conscience along with a chronic tendency to be deceitful, manipulative, arrogant, and socially irresponsible (Kiehl et al., 2001). Despite difficulties measuring deficits in executive functioning, these deficits have been found to be unusually common among criminals and psychopaths (Miller et al., 1997; Morgan and Lilienfeld, 2000; Raine, 1993).

To summarize, in ENA theory three aspects of brain functioning—suboptimal arousal, limbic seizuring, and a rightward shift in neocortical functioning—promote competitive/ victimizing behaviors. With minimal learning, such behavior is often expressed in criminal forms. Theoretically, males are more prone toward competitive/victimizing behavior because their brains are exposed to higher levels of testosterone than female brains, and all three of these brain functions are promoted by testosterone exposure. Furthermore, according to ENA theory, two additional brain functioning patterns help to refine competitive/victimizing behavior into less overtly victimizing expressions. One pattern promotes high intelligence, while the other promotes efficient executive functioning, each of which helps direct competitive/victimizing behavior away from crime and toward commercial activities. Commercial forms of competitive/victimizing behaviors are tolerated, and even encouraged. Even commercial forms that involve considerable deception—"ruthless capitalism," if you will—is considered acceptable in many societies.

ENA theory is summarized in a flow chart shown in Box 5.5. Beginning at the far left, genes and prenatal factors are shown influencing two sets of neurological factors. If a particular influence is positive, the arrow points upward; if the influence is negative, the arrow points downward.

The three neurological factors that promote victimful criminality—suboptimal arousal, limbic system seizuring, and a rightward shift in neocortical functioning—appear in the upper left portion of Box 5.5. Presented in the lower left portion of the chart are the two factors that shift such behavior away from its crudest, most criminal forms—learning ability and executive control. Theoretically, not only do these two sets of neurological factors affect victimful criminality, they also impact a variety of other behavior patterns, including recreational drug use, sensation seeking, Attention Deficit Hyperactivity Disorder (ADHD) symptoms, school performance, and even the stability of one's work history.

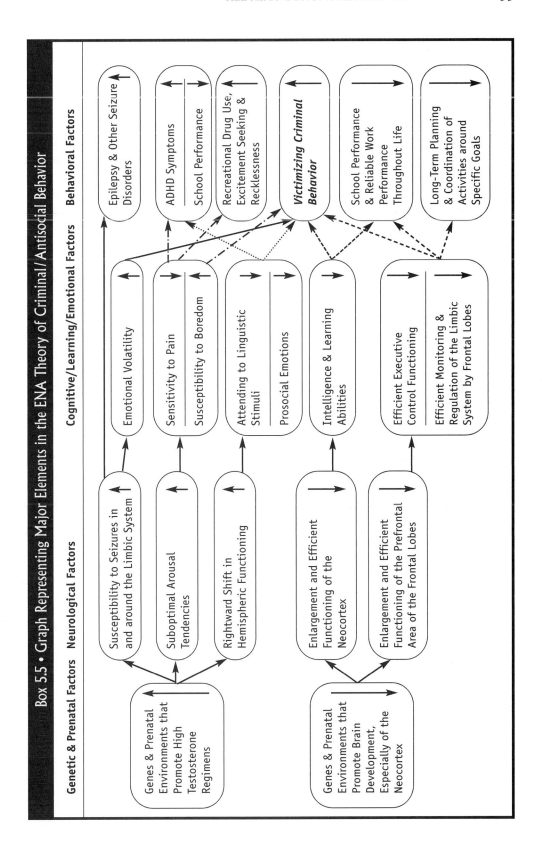

Box 5.5 • Graph Representing Major Elements in the ENA Theory of Criminal/Antisocial Behavior

Correlates of Criminal Behavior

Correlates of criminal behavior are variables that have been repeatedly investigated and found to exhibit consistent (or at least fairly consistent) relationships with offending. Age and sex are two well-documented correlates of crime. Twelve biological correlates of criminal behavior are examined here: (1) testosterone, (2) mesomorphy, (3) maternal smoking during pregnancy, (4) hypoglycemia, (5) epilepsy, (6) heart rate, (7) skin conductivity, (8) cortisol, (9) serotonin, (10) monoamine oxidase, (11) slow brainwave patterns, and (12) P300 amplitude. As these correlates are reviewed, keep in mind that a scientific theory of criminal behavior should be able to explain why these and other documented correlates of crime exist.

Testosterone

As previously noted, testosterone is central to ENA theory, especially regarding the well-documented sex differences in offending probabilities. Comparing males to females, the theory leads one to expect that criminality will be more prevalent among males, because their testosterone levels are much higher than females, especially beyond puberty. However, given the fact that testosterone alters brain functioning not only following the onset of puberty, but also even before birth, and does so in interaction with other hormones, the relationship between testosterone and offending probabilities is not likely to be simple. Virtually all of the research on this relationship has relied on measuring testosterone levels in the blood or saliva, both of which are imperfect indicators of brain levels of testosterone. Nevertheless, most of the studies of blood and saliva testosterone and persistent offending among males have found modest positive correlations (e.g., Banks and Dabbs, 1996; Dabbs, Jurkovic, and Frady, 1991; Mazur, 1995; Virkkunen et al., 1994). Modest links have also been found between saliva levels of testosterone and male involvement in domestic violence (Soler, Vinayak, and Quadagno, 2000:735), "acting out" and conduct disorders among children (Maras et al., 2003), and even aggressive play among boys in primary school (Sanchez-Martin et al., 2000).

Mesomorphy

An unusually muscular body build, called *mesomorphy,* has been investigated by numerous studies in relationship to crime and delinquency. All of these studies have concluded that mesomorphic persons are more likely to be offenders than their less muscular counterparts (Blackson and Tarter,

1994; Hartl, Monnelli, and Eldeken, 1982). ENA theory predicts such a finding given that testosterone not only affects the brain, but also increases muscle mass, especially in the shoulders and arms (Bhasin et al., 1996).

Maternal Smoking during Pregnancy

Since the early 1990s, six studies have investigated links between smoking during pregnancy and subsequent offending by the mother's offspring. Four of these studies indicate that women who smoke run an elevated risk of having children who are unusually delinquent as adolescents (Bagley 1992; Rantakallio et al., 1992) or criminal as adults (Brennan, Grekin, and Mednick, 1999; Rasanes et al., 1999). The other two studies provide qualified support for the same conclusion (Gibson, Piquero, and Tibbetts, 2000; Gibson and Tibbetts, 1998).

ENA theory can account for these findings in three ways. First, fetal exposure to carbon monoxide and other neurotoxins found in cigarette smoke may disrupt brain development in ways that adversely affect either intelligence or executive functioning.

Second, some of the genes contributing to nicotine addiction also appear to increase the risk of offending. Relevant to this point is evidence that nicotine affects the reticular formation, an area of the brain mentioned earlier regarding arousal control (Polich and Kok, 1995:126; Pritchard, 1991:1191). If genes affecting the regulation of arousal cause individuals to be more prone to nicotine addiction, one would expect inherited tendencies both for cigarette smoking and criminal involvement.

Third, research with rats indicates that maternal exposure to nicotine during pregnancy increases fetal testosterone production, especially for female fetuses (Smith et al., 2003). This, in turn, may cause a greater overall masculinization of the fetus' developing brain than what normally occurs (Kandel and Udry, 1999).

Hypoglycemia

The main fuel for the brain is a type of natural sugar known as *glucose*. Its production is regulated by the pancreas in response to chemical messages from the brain's hypothalamus via the blood system. When glucose levels become "too high" or "too low," the hypothalamus signals the pancreas to alter glucose production, which it does by regulating insulin output. In most people, this feedback regulatory process maintains a stable level of glucose in the brain.

For a variety of reasons, some people have difficulty stabilizing their production of glucose, and therefore suffer from what is termed *hypoglycemia* (Bonnet and Pfeiffer, 1978:197; Chollar, 1988:33). Dramatic fluctuations in brain glucose can cause temporary disturbances in thoughts and moods, with the most common symptoms being confusion, difficulty concentrating, and irritability (Adlersberg and Dolger, 1939:1805; Virkkunen, 1988:153).

Four studies have found unusually high rates of violent crimes among hypoglycemics (Groesbeck, D'Asaro, and Nigro, 1975; Virkkunen, 1986; Virkkunen and Huttunen, 1982; Yaruara-Tobias and Neziroglu, 1975). Two additional studies have found hypoglycemia to be significantly more prevalent among persons diagnosed with antisocial personality disorder than those without such a diagnosis (Virkkunen, 1982, 1983). Basically, while hypoglycemia is rare even among criminals, its prevalence still appears to be several times greater among violence-prone offenders than among the general population.

ENA theory accounts for this relationship by pointing to the need for stable and efficient functioning of the brain. In particular, erratic fluctuations in glucose levels in the frontal lobes or in the limbic system, particularly during times of stress, could result in violent behavioral responses.

Epilepsy

Epilepsy is a neurological disease typified by "electrical storms" in the brain called seizures. People vary in their genetic susceptibilities to these seizures, but factors such as brain injuries, viral infections, birth trauma, and exposure to a variety of chemicals can trigger seizures as well.

The main behavioral symptoms of epilepsy are known as convulsions or "fits," although not all epileptics exhibit these symptoms. A mild epileptic seizure may manifest itself as little more than a momentary pause in one's ongoing activities accompanied by a glazed stare. Even though such mild seizures have few noticeable effects on physical movement, they may profoundly affect emotions if their epicenter happens to be in or around the limbic system.

Epilepsy appears to affect about one in every 150 to 200 persons (Rose, Smith, and Sato, 1987:330), but its rates among incarcerated offenders is at least three times as high (Ellis, 1987:504). Adults convicted of violent offenses are especially likely to have been diagnosed with epilepsy (Mendez, Doss, and Taylor, 1993; Mungas, 1983; Okasha, Sadek, Moneom, 1975).

ENA theory explains the relationship between epilepsy and criminal behavior by noting that very basic and primitive emotional responses such as rage and jealousy can emanate from the limbic region. And behavioral manifestations of limbic seizures can include spontaneous acts of violence. Theoretically, research will show that exposing the brain to testosterone increases the probability of most types of brain seizures.

Resting Heart and Pulse Rates

Elevations in heart and pulse rates can be caused by emotional stress. Relative to persons in general, the resting heart and pulse rates of delinquents (Raine and Venables, 1984; Wadsworth, 1976) and adult offenders (Farrington, 1997:94; Mezzacappa et al., 1997:463; Raine et al., 1995) have been found to be low, suggesting that their feelings of stress are somewhat below normal. One study found that the heart and pulse rates of children under standard testing conditions predicted their probability of offending in adolescence (Raine et al., 1995). In addition, the heart and pulse rates of delinquents and criminals seem to rise more slowly in response to mild physical exertion or emotional stress than is true for people generally (Raine et al., 1995; Raine, Venables, and Williams, 1990a, 1990b).

If one assumes that low heart and pulse rates under standard testing conditions are physiological indicators of suboptimal arousal, ENA theory explains why these physiological measures would be associated with offending.

Skin Conductivity (Galvanic Skin Response)

One physical symptom of nervousness is the degree to which people sweat. An instrument known as the *galvanic skin response* (GSR) sensor or meter assesses the degree of sweating in the palms. The device contains two electrodes that must be connected in order to conduct a current of electricity that is too small to be felt. By placing fingers on the two electrodes, a subject's hand completes the electric circuit. Because salt water in sweat is an excellent electrical conductor, the more one sweats, the stronger the electrical current becomes. Temperature obviously affects how much people sweat, but once temperature is controlled, the main determinant of GSR fluctuations is stress. Several studies have found that persons convicted of crime exhibit lower skin conductivity under standardized testing conditions than do people in general (Buikhuisen, Eurelings-Bontekoe, and Host, 1989; Raine, Venables, and Williams, 1996). This suggests that they remain unusually "cool" emotionally when confronted with stressful experiences.

As with heart and pulse rates, ENA theory accounts for offenders' comparatively low nervousness with the premise that offenders tend to be suboptimally aroused. Future studies are needed to determine if testosterone contributes to lower GSR readings as well as to lower heart and pulse rates, as the theory hypothesizes.

Cortisol

Cortisol is generally considered a stress hormone. Several studies have found low levels of cortisol associated with involvement in crime (Bergman and Brismar, 1994; King et al., 1990; Lindman, Aromaki, and Eriksson, 1997; Virkkunen, 1985). This evidence is consistent with ENA theory to the extent that low cortisol levels diminish an individual's feelings of tension and threat in the face of punishment risks. In other words, low cortisol levels may be another indication of suboptimal arousal.

Serotonin

Serotonin is an important neurotransmitter, which means that it plays an essential role in transferring messages from one nerve cell to another. Without these transfers, animals would be incapable of coordinating movement, experiencing feelings, or generating thoughts. The main types of feelings associated with serotonin are those of contentment and calm. When serotonin activity is low in the brain, feelings of irritability and "edginess" are common (Kalus, Asnis, and Van Praag, 1989; Plaznik, Kostowski, and Archer, 1989). Many studies have found abnormally low levels of serotonin activity in the brains of violent offenders (Blumensohn et al., 1995; Matykiewicz et al., 1997; Pliszka et al., 1988; Virkkunen et al., 1996). Impulsive violent offenses appear to be especially common among persons with low serotonin brain activity (Coccaro et al., 1997; Dolan et al., 2002; O'Keane et al., 1992; Virkkunen and Linnoila, 1993).

ENA theory explains the association between low serotonin and violent criminal behavior by noting that in a normal brain, active serotonin pathways run between the prefrontal (planning) areas and the limbic (emotion-control) centers of the brain (Davidson, Purtnam, and Larson, 2000:592; Strayhorn, 2002:11). Persons diagnosed with antisocial personality disorder have limbic systems that are relatively nonresponsive to stimuli of an emotional nature, such as a crying child, and are below normal in the transmission of emotional impulses from the limbic system to prefrontal areas of the brain (Kiehl et al., 2001). Poor communications between the planning and emotion-control centers of the brain—which serotonin helps to foster—may underlie the relationship between low serotonin levels and criminality.

Monoamine Oxidase

Within the brain, an enzyme known as *monoamine oxidase* (MAO) helps to break down and clear away neurotransmitter molecules (including serotonin) that linger in the synaptic gap connecting nerve cells (Westlund et al., 1985). Without this "cleansing function," signals being sent from one nerve cell to another appear to get garbled. Unfortunately, the sampling source used in most MAO research is from the blood rather than from the brain, and findings do not all agree regarding how well blood levels and brain levels of MAO correlate. One study found them to correlate highly (Bench et al., 1991), while an earlier study found virtually no correlation (Young et al., 1986).

Studies indicate that individuals with low MAO activity in the blood tend to have higher rates of criminal behavior (Alm et al., 1996a, 1996b; af Klinteberg, 1996) as well as antisocial personality disorder (Samochowiec et al., 1999; von Knorring, Oreland, and von Knorring, 1987). In addition, low MAO activity has been found to be statistically associated with traits frequently linked to criminality, especially alcoholism (Devor et al., 1993; Faraj et al., 1994; Rommelspacher et al., 1994; von Knorring and Oreland, 1996) and drug abuse (Gade et al., 1996; Norman et al., 1982).

To account for why criminal behavior would be correlated with low MAO activity, ENA theory focuses on the fact that MAO activity is distinctly lower among males than females, especially after the onset of puberty (Ellis, 1991). In functional terms, low MAO activity may contribute to suboptimal arousal.

Brain Waves and P300 Amplitude

Brain waves are low-voltage electrical impulses that can be measured using electrodes placed on the scalp. While these waves are quite varied, they have been classified into bands that range from being exceedingly rapid and regular (alpha brain waves) to relatively slow and irregular (delta brain waves). Five studies have indicated that offenders exhibit greater proportions of slower brain waves than do persons in general (Low and Dawson, 1961; Okasha, Sadek, and Moneom, 1975:39; Mednick et al., 1981; Petersen et al., 1982; Verdeaux and Verdeaux, 1955), with one failure to replicate (Raine et al., 1995).

In recent years, the measurement of brain waves has been refined by computerized averaging of numerous electrical responses to dozens of identical stimuli (like a flash of light) presented at irregular intervals in a laboratory environment. These averaged responses yield a distinctive brain wave "signature" for each subject. One of the most unique patterns in these brain-wave signatures involves a dip that occurs in the electrical voltage approximately one-third of a second following the test stimuli; this dip is called the *P300 amplitude* (Kalat, 1992:91). The P300 dip is thought to reflect brain activity having to do with attention and memory (Polich, 1998).

Research linking the P300 amplitude with criminal behavior has thus far been equivocal (Branchey, Buydens-Branchey, and Lieber, 1988). However, several studies have found an unusually subdued P300 response signature (termed a *decrement*) in individuals diagnosed with antisocial and conduct disorders (Bauer, 1997; Costa, Savage, and Valenzuela, 2000; Raine and Venables, 1988; Raine et al., 1990). A decrement in the P300 amplitude of alcoholics and their close genetic family members (Hesselbrock et al., 2001) has also been found. This is noteworthy given the well-established relationship between alcoholism and criminality (Andreasson, Allebeck, and Brandt, 1993; Greenfield and Weisner, 1995; Modestin, Berger, and Ammann, 1996).

To explain these brain-wave patterns, the suboptimal arousal component of ENA theory can again be invoked. In particular, both a slower-than-average brain-wave pattern and a decrement in P300 amplitude in neurological responses to stimuli could be interpreted as suboptimal arousal.

Box 5.6 • Case Study: Dunedin Longitudinal Study

An unusually ambitious research project, called the Dunedin Multidisciplinary Health and Development Study, followed 1,000 males and females from age three to 21 in Dunedin, a city of 120,000 on New Zealand's South Island, for the purpose of studying sex differences in antisocial behavior. The 1,000 young people represented a complete *cohort*, or age-based population, of children born in that region between April 1972 and March 1973. Perinatal information about any difficulties during pregnancy was obtained from parents as the children were born; the children were subsequently tracked as research subjects beginning at age three. Every year, near their birthday, each child was interviewed to learn about such life experiences as dental and medical visits, asthma and allergies, injuries, relationships, job experiences, and delinquency. To maintain reliability, interviewers were blind to information measuring other indicators. In addition to the interview data, a variety of other material was obtained from sources including direct observers hired by the project, parents, teachers, peers, police, courts, and diagnostic interviews. Unlike other *longitudinal* cohort studies, which examined the age effect on crime by assessing research subjects at regular intervals over time, this study was designed to measure the effects of both age *and* sex, and it used a multidisciplinary perspective that incorporated biological, psychological, and sociological variables.

After analyzing the extensive database, the researchers drew two major conclusions about antisocial behavior, which included "fighting" as well as more serious violent offenses (simple and aggravated assault, rape, armed robbery, and gang fighting). Subjects were rated on antisocial behavior by means of behavioral checklists completed by parents, teachers, subjects, and others who knew the youths well. When it came to ordinary adolescent antisocial behavior, that is, delinquency that the adolescent eventually grew out of, the explanations for males as well as females tended to be similarly related to the adolescents' social context—generally, their peer group, as well as the effects of drugs and alcohol. However, when the researchers analyzed the causal factors related to those subjects who displayed a *persistent* pattern of antisocial behavior that continued into adulthood, they

---

Box 5.6, *continued*

found a marked gender difference both in frequency of the risk factors that best explained the behavior as well as in the behavior itself. While the sex-ratio for the ordinary "adolescence-limited" delinquency was only 1.5 males per female, the researchers found a sex-ratio of 10 males per female for the persistent antisocial offenders. Subjects exhibiting this persistent pattern exhibited four main risk factors that were associated with long-term antisocial behavior: neurocognitive deficits, undercontrolled temperament, a personality trait called weak constraint, and hyperactivity. The researchers found that compared to females, males, in general, experienced greater vulnerability to the very risk factors that proved to be the best predictors of antisocial behavior. The authors of the study recommend that further research include, in addition to the four primary risk factors, molecular genetic data to measure neural development in infancy and childhood.

Moffit, T.A., A. Caspi, M. Rutter, and P.A. Silva (2001). *Sex Differences in Antisocial Behaviour; Conduct Disorder, Delinquency, and Violence in the Dunedin Longitudinal Study.* Cambridge, UK: Cambridge University Press.

Conclusions and Discussion

This chapter reflects an out-of-the-mainstream approach to understanding crime in the sense that it asserts that the causes of criminal behavior are not limited to the social environment. The biosocial perspective assumes that biological factors also need to be incorporated into any comprehensive theory of criminality.

The particular biosocial theory advocated here is primarily intended to explain violent and property offenses, the main so-called victimful offenses. Driving the theory is evidence that throughout the world most serious crimes are committed by males in their teens and twenties. Two overarching premises are central to the theory.

First, it assumes that a broad spectrum of behavior called *competitive/victimizing behavior* has evolved to facilitate reproduction. Theoretically, this behavior is more prevalent in males because females have evolved tendencies to prefer to mate with males who are competent at resource provisioning. Among young males, most of the expressions of competitive/victimizing behavior are crude in the sense that they directly victimize others, and, as a consequence, they are socially condemned and criminalized. Within a few years after reaching puberty, most males learn how to exhibit competitive/victimizing behavior in more socially acceptable forms. Those who fail to do so become persistent criminals.

Second, the theory explains how male brains have evolved greater tendencies toward competitive/victimizing behavior than is true for female brains. The theory asserts that genes on the Y-chromosome play a crucial role.

In part, these genes cause the testes to develop during the first five months of gestation. Once formed, the testes produce testosterone and other androgens that help to masculinize the brain in at least three ways relevant to criminality. Specifically, exposing the brain to testosterone (or its metabolites) causes *suboptimal arousal*, *seizuring proneness*, and *a rightward shift in neocortical functioning*. All three of these neurological conditions are hypothesized to increase the probability of competitive/victimizing behavior, especially in its crudest forms. Two remaining neurological factors—*learning ability* and *executive functioning*—help to shift competitive/victimizing behavior away from its crudest (criminal) expressions toward sophisticated (commercial) expressions. When learning ability is high and/or executive functioning is efficient, individuals will transition quickly from crude to sophisticated forms of competitive/victimizing behavior.

In support of the theory, 12 biological correlates of criminal behavior were briefly reviewed: testosterone, mesomorphy, maternal smoking during pregnancy, hypoglycemia, epilepsy, heart rate, skin conductivity, cortisol, serotonin, monoamine oxidase, and two types of brain-wave patterns. The nature of their relationships to criminal behavior can be fairly well explained within the framework of ENA theory.

Overall, ENA theory is an expression of the biosocial approach to criminology. Advocates of this approach maintain that biological factors interact with social environmental factors to give each individual a unique probability of learning criminal behavior (Ellis and Walsh, 1997; Lykken, 1995; Mealey, 1995; Raine, 1993; Rowe, 2002; Walsh, 2002; Walsh and Ellis, 2003). Future advances in biosocial criminology will depend on how well today's criminology students are able to combine some basic "biological literacy" with conventional training in the social and behavioral sciences (Ellis, 2003b).

End Note

1. Profit-making is not a necessary aspect of competitive/victimizing activity. Individuals take advantage of others in noncommercial settings as well, such as academic institutions, to increase their status or position.

Suggested Further Reading

Ellis, L., and Hoffman, H. (eds.) (1990). *Crime in Biological, Social, and Moral Contexts*. New York: Praeger.

Lykken, D.T. (1995). *The Antisocial Personalities*. Hillsdale, NJ: Lawrence Erlbaum.

Raine, A., P.A. Brennan, D.P. Farrington, and S.A. Mednick (eds.) (1997). *Biosocial Bases of Violence*. New York: Plenum.

Raine, A. (1993). *The Psychopathology of Crime: Criminal Behavior as a Clinical Disorder*. San Diego, CA: Academic Press.

Walsh, A. (2002). *Biosocial Criminology: Introduction and Integration*. Cincinnati: Anderson.

Walsh, A., and L. Ellis (Eds.) (2003). *Biosocial Criminology: Challenging Environmentalism's Supremacy*. New York: Nova.

References

Adlersberg, J., and J. Dolger (1939). "Medico-Legal Problems of Hypoglycemic Reactions in Diabetics." *Annals of Internal Medicine*, 12:1804-1807.

af Klinteberg, B. (1996). "Biology, Norms, and Personality: A Developmental Perspective." *Neuropsychobiology*, 34:146-454.

Alm, P. O., B. af Klinteberg, L. Humble, J. Leppert, S. Sorensen, L.H. Thorell, and L. Lidberg (1996a). "Criminality and Psychopathy as Related to Thyroid Activity in Former Juvenile Delinquents." *Acta Psychiatrica Scandinavica*, 94:112-117.

Alm, P. O., B. af Klinteberg, K. Humble, J. Leppert, S. Sorensen, L.H. Thorell, L. Lidberg, and L. Oreland (1996b). "Psychopathy, Platelet MAO Activity and Criminality Among Former Juvenile Delinquents." *Acta Psychiatrica Scandinavica*, 94:105-111.

Alexander, G. M., M.G. Packard, and B.S. Peterson (2002). "Sex and Spatial Position Effects on Object Location Memory Following Intentional Learning of Object Identities." *Neuropsychologia*, 40:1516-1522.

Anderson, B. J., M.D. Holmes, and E. Ostresh (1999). "Male and Female Delinquents' Attachments and Effects of Attachments on Severity of Self-reported Delinquency." *Criminal Justice and Behavior*, 26:435-452.

Andreasson, S., P. Allebeck, and L. Brandt (1993). "Predictors of Alcoholism in Young Swedish Men." *American Journal of Public Health*, 83:845-850.

Bagley, C. (1992). "Maternal Smoking and Deviant Behavior in 16 Year Olds: A Personality Hypothesis." *Personality and Individual Differences*, 13:377-378.

Banks, T., and J. Dabbs, Jr. (1996). "Salivary Testosterone and Cortisol in a Delinquent and Violent Urban Subculture." *Journal of Social Psychology*, 136:49-56.

Barkley, R.A. (1990). *Attention Deficit Hyperactivity Disorder: A Handbook for Diagnosis and Treatment*. New York: Guilford Press.

Barkley, R.A., G. Godzinsky, and G. Du Paul (1992). "Frontal Lobe Functions in Attention Deficit Disorder with and without Hyperactivity: A Review and Research Report." *Journal of Abnormal Child Psychology*, 20:163-188.

Bauer, L.O. (1997). "Frontal P300 Decrements, Childhood Conduct Disorder, Family History, and the Prediction of Relapse among Abstinent Cocaine Abusers." *Drug and Alcohol Dependence*, 44:1-10.

Benbow, C.P., and J.C. Stanley (1983). "Sex Differences in Mathematical Reasoning Ability: More Facts." *Science*, 222:1029-1031.

Bench, C. J., G.W. Price, A.A. Lammertsmaa, J.C. Cremer, S.K. Luthra, D. Turton, R.J. Dolan, R. Kettler, J. Dingemanse, M. Da Prada, K. Biziere, G.R. McClelland, V.L. Jamieson, N.D. Wood, and R.S.J. Frackowiak (1991). "Measurement of Human Cerebral Monoamine Oxidase Type B (MAO-B) Activity with Positron Emission Tomography (PET): A Dose Ranging Study with the Reversible Inhibitor Ro 19-6327." *European Journal of Clinical Pharmacology*, 40:169-173.

Bergman, B., and B. Brismar (1994). "Hormone Levels and Personality Traits in Abusive and Suicidal Male Alcoholics." *Alcoholism: Clinical and Experimental Research*, 18:311-316.

Bhasin, S., T.W. Storer, N. Berman, C. Callegari, B. Clevenger, J. Phillips, T. Bunnell, R. Tricker, A. Shirazi, and R. Casaburi (1996). "The Effects of Supraphysiologic Doses of Testosterone on Muscle Size and Strength in Normal Men." *New England Journal of Medicine*, 335:1-7.

Blackson, T.C., and R.E. Tarter (1994). "Individual, Family, and Peer Affiliation Factors Predisposing to Early-age Onset of Alcohol and Drug Use." *Alcoholism: Clinical and Experimental Research*, 18:813-821.

Blumensohn, R., G. Ratzoni, A. Weizman, M. Israeli, N. Greuner, A. Apter, S. Tyano, and A. Biegon (1995). "Reduction in Serotonin 5HT Receptor Binding on Platelets of Delinquent Adolescents." *Psychopharmacology*, 118:354-356.

Bonnet, P.L., and C.C. Pfeiffer (1978). "Biochemical Diagnosis for Delinquent Behavior." In L.J. Hippchen (ed.), *Ecologic-Biochemical Approaches to Treatment of Delinquents and Criminals*, pp. 183-205. New York: van Nostrand Reinhold.

Branchey, M. H., L. Buydens-Branchey, and C.S. Lieber (1988). "P3 Alcoholics with Disordered Regulation of Aggression." *Psychiatry Research*, 25:49-58.

Brennan, P.A., E.R. Grekin, and S.A. Mednick (1999). "Maternal Smoking During Pregnancy and Adult Male Criminal Outcomes." *Archives of General Psychiatry*, 56:215-224.

Buikhuisen, W., E.H.M. Eurelings-Bontekoe, and K.B. Host (1989). "Crime and Recovery Time: Mednick Revisited." *International Journal of Law and Psychiatry*, 12:29-40.

Burr, C. (1993). "Homosexuality and Biology." *The Atlantic Monthly*, 271(March):47-65.

Buss, D.M., M. Abbott, A. Angleitner, A. Biaggio, A. Blanco-Villasenor, M. Bruchon Schweitzer (& 45 additional authors) (1990). "International Preferences in Selecting Mates: A Study of 37 Cultures." *Journal of Cross-Cultural Psychology*, 21:5-47.

Carrasco, J. L., J. Saiz-Ruiz, E. Hollander, J. Cesar, and J.J.J. Lopez- Ibor (1994). "Low Platelet Monoamine Oxidase Activity in Pathological Gambling." *Acta Psychiatrica Scandinavica*, 90:427-431.

Chollar, S. (1988). "Food for Thought." *Psychology Today*, 22(April):30-34.

Coccaro, E. F., R.J. Kavoussi, T.B. Cooper, T.B., and R.L. Hauger (1997). "Central Serotonin Activity and Aggression: Inverse Relationship with Prolactin Response to d-fenfluramine, but not CSF 5-HIAA Concentration in Human Subjects." *American Journal of Psychiatry*, 154:1430-1435.

Compaan, J.C., G. van Wattum, A.J.H. de Ruiter, G.A. van Oortmerssen, J.M. Koolhaas, and B. Bohus (1993). "Genetic Differences in Female House Mice in Aggressive Response to Sex Steroid Hormone Treatment." *Physiology and Behavior*, 54:899-902.

Costa, E.T., D.D. Savage, and C.F. Valenzuela (2000). "A Review of the Effects of Prenatal or Early Postnatal Ethanol Exposure on Brain Ligand-gated Ion Channels." *Alcoholism: Clinical and Experimental Research*, 24(5):706-715.

Creaby, M., M. Warner, N. Jamil, and S. Jawad (1993). "Ictal Aggression in Severely Mentally Handicapped People." *Irish Journal of Psychological Medicine,* 10:12-15.

Dabbs, J.M., Jr. (1990). "Salivary Testosterone Measurements: Reliability Across Hours, Days, and Weeks." *Physiology and Behavior,* 48:83-86.

Dabbs, J.M., G.J. Jurkovic, and R.L. Frady (1991). "Salivary Testosterone and Cortisol Among Late Adolescent Male Offenders." *Journal of Abnormal Child Psychology,* 19:469-478.

Davidson, H., K.R. Cave, and D. Sellner (2000). "Differences in Visual Attention and Task Interference Between Males and Females Reflect Differences in Brain Laterality." *Neuropsycholgia,* 38:508-519.

Davidson, R J., K.M. Purtnam, and C.L. Larson (2000). "Dysfunction in the Neural Circuitry of Emotion Regulation: A Possible Prelude to Violence." *Science,* 289:591-594.

Davis, S. (1990). "Men as Success Objects and Women as Sex Objects: A Study of Personal Advertisements." *Sex Roles,* 23:43-50.

Devor, E.J., C.R. Cloninger, P.L. Hoffman, and B. Tabakoff (1993). "Association of Monoamine Oxidase (MAO) Activity with Alcoholism and Alcoholic Subtypes." *American Journal of Human Genetics,* 48:209-213.

Dolan, M., W.J.F. Deakin, N. Roberts, and I. Anderson (2002). "Serotonergic and Cognitive Impairment in Impulsive Aggressive Personality Disordered Offenders: Are There Implications for Treatment?" *Psychological Medicine,* 32:105-117.

Ellis, L. (2003a). "Biosocial Theorizing and Criminal Justice Policy." In S. Peterson and A. Somit (eds.), *Human Nature and Public Policy: An Evolutionary Approach.* New York: Palgrave.

Ellis, L. (2003b). "So You Want to be a Biosocial Criminologist? Advice From the Underground." In A. Walsh and L. Ellis (eds.), *Biosocial Criminology: Challenging Environmentalism's Supremacy.* New York: Nova.

Ellis, L. (2001). "The Biosocial Female Choice Theory of Social Stratification." *Social Biology,* 48:297-319.

Ellis, L. (1995a). "Dominance and Reproductive Success among Nonhuman Animals: A Cross-Species Comparison." *Ethology and Sociobiology,* 16:257-333.

Ellis, L. (1995b). Arousal Theory and the Religiosity-Criminality Relationship." In L. Siegel and P. Cordella (eds.), *Contemporary Criminological Theory.* Boston: Northeastern University Press.

Ellis, L. (1991). "Monoamine Oxidase and Criminality: Identifying an Apparent Biological Marker for Antisocial Behavior." *Journal of Research on Crime and Delinquency,* 28:227-251.

Ellis, L. (1987). "Neurohormonal Bases of Varying Tendencies to Learn Delinquent and Criminal Behavior." In E. K. Morris and C. J. Braukmann (eds.), *Behavioral Approaches to Crime and Delinquency,* pp. 499-518. New York: Plenum.

Ellis, L., and M.A. Ames (1987). "Neurohormonal Functioning and Sexual Orientation: A Theory of Homosexuality-Heterosexuality." *Psychological Bulletin,* 101:233-258.

Ellis, L., and A. Walsh (2003). "Crime, Delinquency, and Intelligence: A Review of the Worldwide Evidence." In H. Nyborg (ed.), *The Scientific Study of General Intelligence: Tribute to Arthur R. Jensen.* New York: Elsevier.

Ellis, L., and A. Walsh (2000). *Criminology: A Global Perspective.* Boston: Allyn & Bacon.

Ellis, L., and A. Walsh (1999). "Criminologists' Opinions about Causes and Theories of Crime and Delinquency." *The Criminologist,* 24:3-6.

Ellis, L., and A. Walsh (1997). "Gene-Based Evolutionary Theories in Criminology." *Criminology,* 35:229-276.

Faraj, B.A., D.C. Davis, V.M. Camp, A.J. Mooney, III, T. Holloway, and G. Barika (1994). "Platelet Monoamine Oxidase Activity in Alcoholics, Alcoholic with Drug Dependence, and Cocaine Addicts." *Alcoholism: Clinical and Experimental Research,* 18:1114-1120.

Farrington, D. P. (1997). "The Relationship between Low Resting Heart Rate and Violence." In A. Raine, P.A. Brennan, D.P. Farrington, and S.A. Mednick (eds.), *Biosocial Bases of Violence,* pp. 89-105. New York: Plenum.

Fergusson, D., J. Horwood, and M. Lynskey (1993). "Maternal Smoking Before and After Pregnancy: Effects on Behavioral Outcomes in Middle Childhood." *Pediatrics,* 92:815-822.

Fuster, J. M. (1995). "Memory and Planning: Two Temporal Perspectives of Frontal Lobe Function." In H.H. Jasper, S. Riggio, and P.S. Goldman-Rakic (eds.), *Epilepsy and the Functional Anatomy of the Frontal Lobe,* pp. 9-18. New York: Raven.

Gade, R., D. Muhleman, J. MacMurray, and D. Comings (1996). "Monoamine Oxidase Gene Variants in Tourette Syndrome and Drug Abuse." *Psychiatric Genetics,* 6:168.

Galea, L.A., and D. Kimura (1993). "Sex Differences in Route Learning." *Personality and Individual Differences,* 14:53-65.

Gibson, C.L., A.R. Piquero, and S.G. Tibbetts (2000). "Assessing the Relationship between Maternal Cigarette Smoking during Pregnancy and Age at First Police Contact." *Justice Quarterly,* 17:519-542.

Gibson, C. L., and S.G. Tibbetts (1998). "Interaction between Maternal Cigarette Smoking and Apgar Scores in Predicting Offending Behavior." *Psychological Reports,* 83:579-586.

Greenfield, T.K., and C. Weisner (1995). "Drinking Problems and Self-Reported Criminal Behavior, Arrests and Convictions: 1990 U.S. Alcohol and 1989 County Surveys." *Addiction,* 90:361-373.

Groesbeck, C., B. D'Asaro, and C. Nigro (1975). "Polyamine Levels in Jail Inmates." *Orthomolecular Psychiatry,* 4:149-152.

Hamilton, C.J. (1995). Beyond Sex Differences in Visuo-Spatial Processing: The Impact of Gender Trait Possession." *British Journal of Psychology,* 86:1-20.

Hartl, E.M., E.T. Monnelli, and R.D. Eldeken (1982). *Physique and Delinquent Behavior.* New York: Academic Press.

Hesselbrock, V., H. Begleiter, B. Porjesz, S. O'Connor, and L. Bauer (2001). "P300 Event-Related Potential Amplitude as an Endophenotype of Alcoholism: Evidence from the Collaborative Study on the Genetics of Alcoholism." *Journal of Biomedical Science,* 8:77-82.

Hines, M. (2004). *Brain Gender.* New York: Oxford University Press.

Joubert, Y., C. Tobin, and C. Lebart (1994). "Testosterone-Induced Masculinization of the Rat Levator Ani Muscle During Puberty." *Developmental Biology,* 162:104-110.

Kalat, J.W. (1992). *Biological Psychology.* Belmont, CA: Wadsworth.

Kalus, O., G.M. Asnis, and H.M. Van Praag (1989). "The Role of Serotonin in Depression." *Psychiatric Annals,* 19:348-353.

Kandel, E., and D. Freed (1989). "Frontal-Lobe Dysfunction and Antisocial Behavior: A Review." *Journal of Clinical Psychology,* 45:404-413.

Kandel, D.B., and J.R. Udry (1999). "Prenatal Effects of Maternal Smoking on Daughters' Smoking: Nicotine or Testosterone Exposure?" *American Journal of Public Health,* 89:1377-1383.

Kemper, T.D. (1990). *Social Structure and Testosterone: Essays on the Socio-Bio-Social Chain.* New Brunswick, NJ: Rutgers University Press.

Kemper, T.D., and R.W. Bologh (1980). "The Ideal Love Object: Structural and Family Sources." *Journal of Youth and Adolescence,* 9:33-48.

Kiehl, K.A., A.M. Smith, R.D. Hare, A. Mendrek, B.B. Forster, J. Brink, J., and P.F. Liddle (2001). "Limbic Abnormalities in Affective Processing by Criminal Psychopaths as Revealed by Functional Magnetic Resonance Imaging." *Biological Psychiatry,* 50:677-684.

King, R.J., J. Jones, J.W. Scheuer, D. Curtis, and V.P. Zarcone (1990). "Plasma Cortisol Correlates of Impulsivity and Substance Abuse." *Personality and Individual Differences,* 11:287-291.

Koivula, N., P. Hassmén, and D.P. Hunt (2001). "Performance on the Swedish Scholastic Aptitude Test: Effects of Self-Assessment and Gender." *Sex Roles,* 44:629-645.

Lavigne, J.V., R.D. Gibbons, K.K. Christoffel, R. Arend, D. Rosenbaum, H. Binns, N. Dawson, H. Sobel, and C. Isaacs (1996). "Prevalence Rates and Correlates of Psychiatric Disorders Among Preschool Children." *Journal of the American Academy for Child and Adolescent Psychiatry,* 35:204-214.

Lindman, R.E., A.S. Aromaki, and C.J.P. Eriksson (1997). "Sober-State Cortisol as a Predictor of Drunken Violence." *Alcohol and Alcoholism,* 32:621-626.

Low, N., and S. Dawson (1961). "Electroencephalographic Findings in Juvenile Delinquency." *Pediatrics,* 28:452-457.

Luk, S., P.W. Leung, J. Bacon-Shone, S. Chung, P.W. Lee, R. Ng, F. Lieh-Mak, L. Ko, V.C.N. Wong, and C.Y. Yeung (1991). "Behaviour Disorder in Pre-School Children in Hong Kong." *British Journal of Psychiatry,* 158:213-221.

Lykken, D.T. (1995). *The Antisocial Personalities.* Hillsdale, NJ: Lawrence Erlbaum.

Macke, J.P., N. Hu, S. Hu, M. Bailey, V.L. King, T. Brown, D. Hamer, and J. Nathans (1993). "Sequence Variation in the Androgen Receptor Gene is Not a Common Determinant of Male Sexual Orientation. *American Journal of Human Genetics,* 53:844-852.

Mann, J.J. (1995). "Violence and Aggression." In Bloom and Kupfer (eds.), *Psychopharmacology,* pp. 1919-1928. New York: Raven Press.

Maras, A., M. Laucht, D. Gerdes, C. Wilhelm, S. Lewicka, D. Haack, L. Malisova, and M.H. Schmidt (2003). "Association of Testosterone and Dihydrotestosterone with Externalizing Behavior in Adolescent Boys and Girls." *Psychoneuroendocrinology,* 28:932-940.

Matykiewicz, L., L. La Grange, P. Vance, M. Wang, and E. Reyes (1997). "Adjudicated Adolescent Males: Measures of Urinary 5-Hydroxyindoleacetic Acid and Reactive Hypoglycemia." *Personality and Individual Differences,* 22:327-332.

Maughan, B., and M. Rutter (1998). "Continuities and Discontinuities in Antisocial Behavior from Childhood to Adult Life." In T.H. Ollendick and R.J. Prinz (eds.), *Advances in Clinical Child Psychology, Volume 20*, pp. 1-47. New York: Plenum Press.

Maxson, S.C. (1992). "Potential Genetic Models of Aggression and Violence in Males." In P. Driscoll (ed.), *Genetically Defined Animal Models of Neurobehavioral Dysfunctions*, pp. 174-188. Basel, Switzerland: Birkhauser.

Mazur, A. (1995). "Biosocial Models of Deviant Behavior Among Male Army Veterans. *Biological Psychology,* 41:271-293.

Mealey, L. (1995). "The Sociobiology of Sociopathy: An Integrated Evolutionary Model. *Behavioral and Brain Sciences,* 18:523-599.

Mednick, S.A., J. Volavka, W.F. Gabrielli, Jr., and T.M. Itil (1981). "EEG as a Predictor of Antisocial Behavior." *Criminology,* 19:219-229.

Mendez, M.F., R.C. Doss, and J. Taylor (1993). "Interictal Violence in Epilepsy: Relationship to Behavior and Seizure Variables." *Journal of Nervous and Mental Disease,* 181:566-569.

Mezzacappa, E., R.E. Tremblay, D. Kindlon, J.P. Saul, L. Arseneault, J. Seguin, R.O. Pihl, and F. Earls (1997). "Anxiety, Antisocial Behavior, and Heart Rate Regulation in Adolescent Males." *Journal of Psychiatry,* 38:457-469.

Miller, B.L., A. Darby, D.F. Benson, J.L. Cummings, and M.H. Miller (1997). "Aggressive, Socially Disruptive and Antisocial Behaviour Associated with Fronto-Temporal Dementia." *British Journal of Psychiatry,* 170:150-155.

Modestin, J., A. Berger, and R. Ammann (1996). "Mental Disorder and Criminality: Male Alcoholism." *Journal of Nervous and Mental Disease,* 184, 393-402.

Moffitt, T.E., A.M.R. Caspi, and P.A. Silva (2001). *Sex Differences in Antisocial Behavior: Conduct Disorder, Delinquency, and Violence in the Dunedin Longitudinal Study*: Cambridge, UK: Cambridge University Press.

Morgan, A.P., and S.O. Lilienfeld (2000). "A Meta-Analytic Review of the Relation between Antisocial Behavior and Neuropsychological Measures of Executive Function." *Clinical Psychology Review,* 20:113-156.

Mungas, D. (1983). "An Empirical Analysis of Specific Syndromes of Violent Behavior." *The Journal of Nervous and Mental Disease,* 171:354-361.

Nee, L.E., E.D. Caine, and R.J. Polinsky (1980). "Gilles de la Tourette's Syndrome: Clinical and Family Study of 50 Cases." *Annals of Neurology,* 7:41.

Niehoff, D. (1999). *The Biology of Aggression.* New York: Simon and Schuster.

Norman, T.T., M.A. Chamberlain, M.A. French, and G.F. Burrows (1982). "Platelet Monoamine Oxidase Activity and Cigarette Smoking." *Journal of Affective Disorders,* 4:73-77.

Okasha, A., A. Sadek, and S.A. Moneom (1975). "Psychosocial and Electroencephalographic Studies of Egyptian Murderers." *British Journal of Psychiatry,* 126:34-40.

O'Keane, V., E. Maloney, H. O'Neill, A. O'Connor, C. Smith, and T.G. Dinan (1992). "Blunted Prolactin Response to D-Fenfluramine in Sociopathy: Evidence for Subsensitivity of Central Serotonergic Function." *British Journal of Psychiatry,* 160:643-646.

Orlebeke, J.F., D.L. Knol, and F.C. Verhulst (1997). "Increase in Child Behavior Problems Resulting from Maternal Smoking During Pregnancy." *Archives of Environmental Health,* 52:317-321.

Passler, M.A., W. Isaac, and G.W. Hynd (1985). "Neuropsychological Development of Behavior Attributed to Frontal Lobe Functioning in Children." *Developmental Neuropsychology,* 1:349-370.

Pauls, D L., D.J. Cohen, R. Heimbuch, J. Detlor, and K.K. Kidd (1981). "Familial Pattern and Transmission of Gilles de la Tourette Syndrome and Multiple Tics." *Archives of General Psychiatry,* 38:1091.

Petersen, K.G.I., M. Matousek, S.A. Mednick, J. Volovka, and V. Pollock (1982). "EEG Antecedents of Thievery." *Acta Psychiatrica Scandinavica,* 65:331-338.

Pinker, S. (2002). *The Blank Slate: The Modern Denial of Human Nature.* New York: Viking.

Plaznik, A., W. Kostowski, and T. Archer (1989). "Serotonin and Depression: Old Problems and New Data." *Progress in Neuro-Psychopharmacology and Biochemical Psychiatry,* 13:623-633.

Pliszka, S.R., G.A. Rogeness, P. Renner, J. Sherman, and T. Broussard (1988). "Plasma Neurochemistry in Juvenile Offenders." *Journal of the American Academy of Child and Adolescent Psychiatry,* 27:588-594.

Polich, J. (1998). "P300 Clinical Utility and Control of Variability." *Journal of Clinical Neurophysiology,* 15:14-33.

Polich, J. and A. Kok (1995). "Cognitive and Biological Determinants of P300: An Integrative Review." *Biological Psychology,* 41:103-146.

Pritchard, W.S. (1991). "The Link between Smoking and Pregnancy: A Serotonergic Hypothesis. *Personality and Individual Differences,* 12:1187-1204.

Raine, A. (1993). *The Psychopathology of Crime: Criminal Behavior as a Clinical Disorder.* San Diego, CA: Academic Press.

Raine, A., D. Phil, P.H. Venables, and M. Williams (1995). "High Autonomic Arousal and Electrodermal Orienting at Age 15 Years as Protective Factors Against Crime Development at Age 29 Years." *American Journal of Psychiatry,* 152:1595-1600.

Raine, A., M. O'Brien, N. Smiley, A.S. Scerbo, and C.J. Chan (1990). "Reduced Lateralization in Verbal Dichotic Listening in Adolescent Psychopaths." *Journal of Abnormal Psychology,* 99:272-277.

Raine, A., and P.H. Venables (1988). "Enhanced P3 Evoked Potentials and Longer P3 Recovery Times in Psychopaths." *Psychophysiology,* 25:30-38.

Raine, A., and P.H. Venables (1984). "Tonic Heart Rate Level, Social Class, and Antisocial Behavior." *Biological Psychology,* 18:123-132.

Raine, A., P.H. Venables, and M. Williams (1996). "Better Autonomic Conditioning and Faster Electrodermal Half-Recovery Time at Age 15 Years as Possible Protective Factors Against Crime at Age 29 Years." *Developmental Psychology,* 32:624-630.

Raine, A., P.H. Venables, and M. Williams (1990a). "Autonomic Orienting Responses in 15-year-old Male Subjects and Criminal Behavior at Age 24." *American Journal of Psychiatry,* 147:933-937.

Raine, A., P.H. Venables, and M. Williams (1990b). "Relationships between Central and Autonomic Measures of Arousal at Age 15 Years and Criminality at Age 25 Years." *Archives of General Psychiatry,* 47:1003-1007.

Rantakallio, P., E. Laara, M. Isohanni, and I. Moilanen (1992). "Maternal Smoking During Pregnancy and Delinquency of the Offspring: An Association without Causation? *International Journal of Epidemiology*, 21:1106-1113.

Rasanes, P., H. Hakko, M. Isohanni, S. Hodgins, M.-R. Jarvelin, and J. Tiihonen (1999). "Maternal Smoking during Pregnancy and Risk of Criminal Behavior among Adult Male Offspring in the Northern Finland 1966 Birth Cohort." *American Journal of Psychiatry,* 156:857-862.

Reite, M., C.M. Cullum, J. Stocker, P. Teale, and E. Kozora (1993). "Neuropsychological Test Performance and MEG-Based Brain Lateralization: Sex Differences." *Brain Research Bulletin,* 32:325-328.

Ridley, M. (1998). *The Origins of Virtue: Human Instincts and the Evolution of Cooperation.* New York: Penguin Books.

Rommelspacher, H., T. May, P. Dufeu, and L.G. Schmidt (1994). "Longitudinal Observations of Monoamine Oxidase B in Alcoholics: Differentiation of Marker Characteristics." *Alcoholism: Clinical and Experimental Research,* 18:1322-1329.

Rose, D.F., P.D. Smith, and S. Sato (1987). "Magnetoencephalography and Epilepsy Research. *Science,* 238:329-335.

Rowe, D.C. (2002). *Biology and Crime.* Los Angeles: Roxbury.

Samochowiec, J., K.P. Lesch, M. Rottman, M. Smolka, Y.V. Syagailo, O. Okladnova, H. Rommelspacher, G. Winterer, L.G., Schmidt, and T. and Sander (1999). "Association of a Regulatory Polymorphism in the Promoter Region of the Monoamine Oxidase: A Gene with Antisocial Alcoholism." *Psychiatric Research,* 86:67-72.

Sanchez-Martin, J.R., E. Fano, L. Ahedo, J. Cardas, P.F. Brain, and A. Azpiroz (2000). "Relating Testosterone Levels and Free Play Social Behavior in Male and Female Preschool Children." *Psychoneuroendocrinology,* 25:773-783.

Shucard, J.L., D.W. Shucard, and K.R. Cummings (1981). "Auditory Evoked Potentials and Sex-Related Differences in Brain Development." *Brain and Language,* 13:91-102.

Silverman, I., J. Choi, A. Mackewn, M. Fisher, J. Moro, and E. Olshansky (2000). "Evolved Mechanisms Underlying Wayfinding: Further Studies on the Hunter-Gatherer Theory of Spatial Sex Differences." *Evolution and Human Behavior,* 21:201-213.

Smith, L.M., C.C. Cloak, R.E. Poland, J. Torday, and M.G. Ross (2003). "Prenatal Nicotine Increases Testosterone Levels in the Fetus and Female Offspring." *Nicotine and Tobacco Research,* 5:369-374.

Soler, H., P. Vinayak, and D. Quadagno (2000). "Biosocial Aspects of Domestic Violence." *Psychoneuroendocrinology,* 25:721-739.

Stallard, P. (1993). "The Behaviour of 3-year-old Children: Prevalence and Parental Perception of Problem Behaviour: A Research Note." *Journal of Child Psychology and Psychiatry and Allied Disciplines,* 34:413-421.

Steffensmeier, D., and C. Streifel (1991). "Age, Gender, and Crime Across Three Historical Periods: 1935, 1960, and 1985." *Social Forces,* 69:869-894.

Strayhorn, J.M. (2002). "Self-Control: Theory and Research." *Journal of the American Academy of Child and Adolescent Psychiatry,* 41:7-16.

Thornton, J., and R.W. Goy (1986). "Female-Typical Sexual Behavior of Rhesus and Defeminization by Androgens Given Prenatally." *Hormones and Behavior,* 20:129-147.

Tomarken, A.J., and A.D. Keener (1998). "Frontal Brain Asymmetry and Depression: A Self-Regulatory Perspective." *Cognition and Emotion,* 12:387-420.

Van Oortmerssen, G.A., R.F. Benus, and F. Sluyter (1992). "Studies on Wild House Mice IV: On the Heredity of Testosterone and Readiness to Attack." *Aggressive Behavior,* 18:143-148.

Verdeaux, G., and J. Verdeaux (1955). "Etude Electro-Encephalographic d'un Groupe Important de Delinquants Primaires ou Recidvistes au Cours de Leur Detention." *Annales Medico-Psychologiques,* 113:643-658.

Virkkunen, M., R. Rawlings, R. Tokola, R.E. Poland, A. Guidotti, D. Nemoff, D.G. Bisette, K. Kalogeras, S.L. Karonen, and M. Linnoila (1994). "CSF Biochemistries, Glucose Metabolism, and Diurnal Activity Rhythms in Alcoholic, Violent Offenders, Fire Setters, and Healthy Volunteers." *Archives of General Psychiatry,* 51:20-27.

Virkkunen, M. (1988). "Cerebrospinal Fluid: Monoamine Metabolites among Habitually Violent and Impulsive Offenders." In T.E. Moffitt and S.A. Mednick (eds.), *Biological Contributions to Crime Causation,* pp. 147-157. Boston: Martinus Nijhoff.

Virkkunen, M. (1986). "Reactive Hypoglycemic Tendency among Habitually Violent Offenders." *Nutrition Reviews,* 44 (Supplement):94-103.

Virkkunen, M. (1985). "Urinary Free Cortisol Excretion in Habitually Violent Offenders." *Acta Psychiatrica Scandinavica,* 72:40-44.

Virkkunen, M. (1983). "Insulin Secretion During the Glucose Tolerance Test in Antisocial Personality." *British Journal of Psychiatry,* 142:598-604.

Virkkunen, M. (1982). "Reactive Hypoglycemic Tendency among Habitually Violent Offender: A Further Study by Means of the Glucose Tolerance Test." *Neuropsychobiology,* 5:35-40.

Virkkunen, M., M. Eggert, R. Rawlings and M. Linnoila (1996). "A Perspective Follow-up Study of Alcoholic Violent Offenders and Fire Starters." *Archives of General Psychiatry,* 53:523-529.

Virkkunen, M., and M.O. Huttunen (1982). "Evidence for Abnormal Glucose Tolerance Test among Violent Offenders." *Neuropsychobiology,* 8:30-34.

Virkkunen, M., and M. Linnoila (1993). "Brain Serotonin, Type II Alcoholism, and Impulsive Violence." *Journal of Studies on Alcohol,* 11(Supplement):163-169.

von Knorring, L., and L. Oreland (1996). "Platelet MAO Activity in Type 1/Type 2 Alcoholics." *Alcoholism: Clinical and Experimental Research,* 20 (Supplement):224A-230A.

von Knorring, L., L. Oreland, and A.L. von Knorring (1987). "Personality Traits and Platelet MAO Activity in Alcohol and Drug Abusing Teenage Boys." *Acta Psychiatrica Scandinavica,* 75:307-314.

Wadsworth, M.E.J. (1976). "Delinquency, Pulse Rate and Early Emotional Deprivation." *British Journal of Criminology,* 16:245-256.

Wakschlag, L.S., B.B. Lahey, R. Loeber, S.M. Green, R.A. Gordon, and B.L. Leventhal (1997). "Maternal Smoking During Pregnancy and the Risk of Conduct Disorder in Boys." *Archives of General Psychiatry,* 54:670-676.

Walsh, A. (2002). *Biosocial Criminology: Introduction and Integration.* Cincinnati: Anderson.

Walsh, A., and L. Ellis (eds.) (2003). *Biosocial Criminology: Challenging Environmentalism's Supremacy.* New York: Nova.

Westlund, K.N., R.M. Denney, L.M. Kochersperger, R.M. Rose, and C.W. Abell (1985). "District Monoamine Oxidase A and B Populations in Primate Brain." *Science,* 230:181-183.

Yaruara-Tobias, J.A. and F.A. Neziroglu (1975). "Violent Behavior, Brain Dysrythmia, and Glucose Dysfunction. A New Syndrome." *Journal of Orthomolecular Psychiatry,* 4:182-188.

Young, W.F., E.R.J. Laws, F.W. Sharbrough, and R.M. Weinshilboum (1986). "Human Monoamine Oxidase: Lack of Brain and Platelet Correlation." *Archives of General Psychiatry,* 43:604-609.

Commentary

Deborah W. Denno

One of many curiosities about the academic discipline of criminology is the negligible role it assigns to biology. As Ellis rightly contends, criminal behavior results from both biological *and* social factors. Yet, most criminologists still believe that only the social environment is an important predictor of crime. This circumstance raises a key question: Who took the biology out of crime?

In this commentary I want to briefly hone a few additional points on the intersection of biology and crime, while relying on select reviews of biosocial research (e.g., by Tehrani and Mednick, 2002). In my attempt to answer the question—Who took the biology out of crime?—I will focus on some examples of criminological research that analyze biosocial interactions with crime. Because of the close tie between biological and social factors and the frequent muddling of the terms "biological" and "genetic," my discussion begins by defining these concepts.

Definitions and Dilemmas

In general, *social variables*, such as socioeconomic status, consist of environmental influences on a person's behavior (Tehrani and Mednick, 2002). *Biological variables*, on the other hand, constitute "physiological, biochemical, neurological, and genetic" effects on a person's behavior (Tehrani and Mednick, 2002:292). Genetic factors are a subset of biological variables, distinguishable because they are inherited; in contrast, social factors are not inherited (Tehrani and Mednick, 2002). All of these factors—social, biological, and genetic—are related in interesting ways. For example, Ellis emphasizes that being male is a genetic factor that strongly predicts crime. Yet many men never commit a crime, particularly a violent crime. Likewise, other biological factors and a wide range of social factors mediate the relationship between sex and criminal behavior, so much so that social factors greatly dominate our ability to determine who among a small group of people will engage in criminality.

175

As Ellis notes, early biological theories of crime, such as those put forth by Cesare Lombroso, were later justifiably ridiculed for both their concepts and methods. Not only theory but biological evidence was viewed with skepticism due to a number of moral and ethical dilemmas, which included the following: (1) biology's link to the abhorrent experimental abuses inflicted by the Nazis on prisoners during the Holocaust; (2) the belief that if nature were found to be more significant than nurture there would be little basis for society's vision of free will; (3) fears that indications of "biological inferiority" would stigmatize certain groups—concerns tragically fueled by the preventive detention of individuals in the criminal justice system, or past efforts to screen for "biologically different" children; (4) the potential deflection of societal responsibility for the social factors that cause crime (e.g., poverty, racism, limited opportunities) if the criminal justice system focused primarily or exclusively on biological factors; and (5) suggestions that juries may be more readily swayed in court by biological evidence because it seems to be more objective and precise than social evidence (Denno, 1996; Dreyfuss and Nelkin, 1992; Robinson, 2004).

These issues remain unresolved. As such, I do not want to promote naive and dangerous policies of crime control, but rather to point out the power of biology to shed light on social influences on criminal behavior in ways that would probably not be detected otherwise. Indeed, during the past two decades criminological research has increasingly incorporated both biological and social factors as vehicles for understanding crime. When criminological studies employ a wide range of both kinds of variables, they show that biology continually accentuates the significance of social factors on behavior (Denno, 1990; Tehrani and Mednick, 2002). As Ellis suggests, criminologists can learn from biology; but I emphasize that biologists can also learn from sociology and criminology, disciplines that have been sorely neglected in the medical, psychological, and neurological sciences.

A Biosocial Link: Lead Poisoning and Crime

A particularly apt example of the value of multidisciplinary research is found in studies of lead poisoning's effect on children's behavior. Recent statistics show that more than 10 percent of all children in the United States are severely impacted by toxic levels of lead. While lead poisoning is considered one of the most destructive conditions among young children, it is also highly preventable (Denno, 1993, 1999; Needleman et al., 1996, 2002).

Children acquire lead poisoning in insidious ways—primarily in homes where they eat lead-based paint chips. Other lead sources include drinking water, soil, food, gasoline, and industrial waste. Studies indicate that both high and low lead levels adversely affect children's physiological development, resulting in problems ranging from reading and learning disabilities to dropping out of school and delayed nervous system functioning. The behavioral manifestations of lead-poisoned children have been thoroughly documented. These include hyperactivity, hypoactivity, impulsivity, disorganization, restlessness, and atypical social and aggressive behavior. Criminological research has consistently demonstrated that these kinds of physiological and behavioral variables are associated with crime. Therefore, it is not surprising that a growing body of research shows lead poisoning to be a strong predictor of crime among males, even controlling for other influential biological and social variables (Denno, 1990, 1993, 1999; Needleman et al., 1996, 2002).

The first major statistical finding of a relationship between lead poisoning and crime was documented by the Biosocial Study,[1] one of this country's largest longitudinal studies of biological and sociological predictors of crime. The Biosocial Study was unique because it analyzed more than 3,000 variables in a group of nearly 1,000 male and female subjects during the first 22 years of their lives—beginning when the subjects' mothers were admitted to the same Philadelphia hospital to give birth. Biological data included early central nervous system development, neurological status, attention deficit disorder, hyperactivity, and general physical health. Social data included parents' occupation, education, employment history, marital stability, welfare status, and number of people supported in the household (Denno, 1990, 1993).

The Biosocial Study's results confirmed past criminological studies showing an association between academic ability and behavior in predicting crime. However, a number of never-examined factors, such as lead poisoning, were also analyzed. The results were striking: lead poisoning among males was the most significant predictor of school disciplinary problems. Lead was among the top five predictors of officially recorded juvenile delinquency and adult criminality (Denno, 1990, 1993, 1999). Subsequent research has confirmed similar results with lead poisoning. For example, two prospective studies of young males have demonstrated significant associations among bone lead levels, aggression, and juvenile delinquency, while also accounting for social variables (Needleman et al., 1996, 2002).

The tie between lead poisoning and crime exemplifies the interrelationship between biological and social factors. Research suggests that lead can produce neurochemical changes in the brain that can affect inhibitory processes that encourage impulsive behavior. Likewise, impulsivity and related factors (such as aggression, hyperactivity, and academic difficulty) tend to be highly significant predictors of delinquency and crime. Other kinds of social factors also encourage the connection between lead and crime, including diet, alcohol or other drug use, and family stressors, such as a large family size or a single-parent household (Denno, 1990, 1993, 1999; Needleman et al., 1996, 2002).

It is significant that many repercussions of children's exposure to lead toxins may not initially appear to have been caused by social factors, because they are manifested biologically over time. In other words, social factors affect the body physiologically. By examining biological and social factors in tandem, however, it can be seen more easily that social factors are the true culprits in these disorders, a finding that may not have been realized by simply looking at both types of factors in isolation.

Other Biosocial Interactions with Crime

Interactions between biological and social factors that lead to crime account for many associations that may appear, on the surface, to be purely biological. For example, Ellis states that maternal smoking during pregnancy is a correlate of criminal behavior, and refers to six studies as evidence. Yet none of these studies sufficiently accounts for the intervening influence of social factors on the supposed direct link between maternal smoking and crime. In the Biosocial Study, for example, maternal smoking during pregnancy was related to criminality when social factors were not controlled. Indeed, numerous biological variables showed strong and interesting connections to crime when they were examined either in isolation or with a limited number of other variables. These associations disappeared, however, when key social factors—such as socioeconomic status—were introduced as controls. This result illustrates that even within a relatively socioeconomically homogenous group of individuals (such as the Biosocial Study's subjects), social factors are critical and should not be ignored. If researchers choose to exclude a range of social factors, they may get results that are intriguing (for example, indications that maternal smoking predicts crime) but highly misleading. Such results also risk diverting resources away from the more significant—social—sources of criminality, such as low socioeconomic status.

Modern studies of adopted twins separated at birth from their biological parents provide another pointed example of the interaction between biological and social influences. Researchers regard traits that the adoptees share with their biological parents as evidence of the impact of genetic factors, while characteristics the adoptees share with their adopted parents are evidence of the effect of social factors.

Some of the adoption research suggests a genetic component to criminal behavior. For example, there seems to be a significant concordance between the criminality of adopted sons and that of their biological parents (Tehrani and Mednick, 2002). This research is relatively sophisticated, extensive, and international (conducted in the United States, Sweden, and Denmark). That said, the studies also demonstrate the significance of the interaction between genetic and social factors. Of course, there is no "crime gene," but rather the potential inheritance of proclivities that enhance the likelihood that an individual may engage in crime. A person's sex is a good example of this proclivity. Although being male is a substantially stronger predictor of criminality than being female, positive social factors, such as upper socioeconomic status, greatly reduce the likelihood that an individual of either sex will engage in crime (Denno, 1990). Likewise, individuals with a genetic predisposition to alcoholism and mental illness appear more likely to commit crime, although social stressors, such as negative family influences, can substantially enhance these proclivities in the same way that social buffers, such as advanced income and education, can decrease them (Tehrani and Mednick, 2002). In all of these associations, social variables affect the outcome.

Other kinds of research further demonstrate the nuances of biosocial interrelationships. According to some clinical studies, for example, children and adults exposed to early life stress show neurobiological changes, which could in turn increase the risk of psychopathy (Heim and Nemeroff, 2001). Such physiological impairment seems to be particularly egregious in cases of child abuse (Glaser, 2000). Intervention efforts to prevent the harmful effects of this stress on the central nervous system could successfully block the chain of causation leading to crime. These findings are important because they demonstrate how social factors affect biological conditions (Robinson, 2004), a reverse pattern from that which many criminologists typically presume, if they consider biological factors at all.

This discussion of the interaction of biosocial factors and crime returns us to the initial question: Who took the biology out of crime? The answer appears to be: Both biologists and criminologists. Each group has neglected the insights of the other, perhaps because both believe outside fields of study have nothing to contribute. With time, disciplines considered to be "outside" may be welcomed. A multidisciplinary approach can bring benefits still waiting to be realized.

ACKNOWLEDGMENT: I am most grateful to Marianna Politzer for her editorial assistance with this commentary.

End Note

1. The 987 subjects who were the focus of the Biosocial Study were born at Pennsylvania Hospital, in Philadelphia, between 1959 and 1962. The subjects and their families were originally part of the Collaborative Perinatal Project, a nationwide study of biological and environmental influences on pregnancy and infant and childhood mortality as well as physical, neurological, and psychological development in children. Nearly 60,000 pregnant women participated in the study between 1959 and 1966 in 15 different medical centers. Examination of the study children from the time of their birth through age seven continued until 1974. In 1978, the Sellin Center for Studies in Criminology and Criminal Law at the University of Pennsylvania was awarded a grant by the National Institute of Justice to examine those Perinatal Project children who were born in Philadelphia. As part of the grant, public school and police record data were collected on a total sample of about 10,000 youths. Thereafter, detailed data were organized and analyzed on a subsample consisting of the 987 youths who constituted the subjects for this study (Denno, 1990).

References

Denno, D.W. (1999). "Health and Medical Factors: Lead." In R. Gottesman and R. Maxwell Brown (eds.), *Violence in America: An Encyclopedia*, pp. 106-108. New York: Charles Scribner's Sons.

Denno, D.W. (1996). "Legal Implications of Genetics and Crime Research." In G. Bock and J. Goode (eds.) *Genetics of Criminal and Antisocial Behaviour*, pp. 248-264. New York: John Wiley & Sons (Ciba Foundation Symposium 194).

Denno, D.W. (1993). "Considering Lead Poisoning as a Criminal Defense." *Fordham Urban Law Journal,* 20:377-400.

Denno, D.W. (1990). *Biology and Violence: From Birth to Adulthood.* New York: Cambridge University Press.

Dreyfuss, R.C., and D. Nelkin (1992). "The Jurisprudence of Genetics." *Vanderbilt Law Review,* 45:313-348.

Glaser, D. (2000). "Child Abuse and Neglect and the Brain — A Review." *Journal of Child Psychology and Psychiatry,* 41(1):97-116.

Heim, C., and C.B. Nemeroff (2001). "The Role of Childhood Trauma in the Neurobiology of Mood and Anxiety Disorders: Preclinical and Clinical Studies." *Biological Psychiatry,* 49:1023-1039.

Needleman, H.L., J.A. Riess, M.J. Tobin, G.E. Biesecker, and J.B. Greenhouse (1996). "Bone Lead Levels and Delinquent Behavior." *Journal of the American Medical Association,* 275 (5):363-369.

Needleman, H.L., C. McFarland, R.B. Ness, S.E. Fienberg, and M.J. Tobin (2002). "Bone Lead Levels in Adjudicated Delinquents." *Neurotoxicology and Teratology,* 24 (6):711-717.

Robinson, G.E. (2004). "Beyond Nature and Nurture." *Science,* 304:397-399.

Tehrani, J.A., and S.A. Mednick (2002). "Crime Causation: Biological Theories." In J. Dressler, T.J. Bernard, D.W. Denno, R.S. Frase, J. Hagan, D.M. Kahan, and C.S. Streiker (eds), *Encyclopedia of Crime and Justice*, pp. 292-302. New York: Macmillan Reference.

Chapter Six

Philosophy and Crime

Stephen Mathis

The oldest of all academic disciplines, philosophy covers a wide range of subjects, from the moral character of the individual lawbreaker to justifying how far the law should reach into our lives. In contemporary times, we find that philosophy contributes to our understanding of crime in many ways, but that philosophers are drawn to different aspects of the subject than criminologists. While criminologists seek to understand the "criminal justice system"—how it "works," how *well* it functions—philosophers develop *justifications* that demonstrate why laws and punishments should exist. Criminologists may find it interesting to track a particular type of offender through the system, say all assault and battery cases, noting trends in arrest, conviction, disposition, and so on, while philosophers will instead break down the definition of "assault and battery," trying to identify the full range of activities that the definition covers (from a drunken argument to a domestic dispute to a schoolyard fight) so that they can then ask why the law seeks to control such human behavior. For instance, a man insults another man by making a remark about his girlfriend. The insulted man responds by sucker-punching the first man in the nose. Satisfied, he walks away—only to learn later that he has been charged with assault and battery. Why is assault and battery a crime? Why do certain acts fit the definition while others do not? How much punishment should one receive for assault and battery? Philosophers believe that such questions are crucial because they get at the proper balance between the government and the individual. Because the government must infringe on the liberties of individuals to control their behavior, philosophers insist on justification.

Some areas of philosophy (in particular *ethics,* or the study of morality) focus on why it's wrong to do bad things to other people, whether against the law or not. Such approaches explain, in an abstract sense, how particular activities are wrong (certain behaviors may infringe on people's rights, decrease the overall happiness of society, violate an implied social contract between people, or have other negative implications). Philosophical approaches tend to offer no real concrete responses to wrong behavior, other than simply identifying it as wrong or *immoral*. But when it comes to *crime*, or behavior that violates the law of the land, philosophers want to be able to show not only why criminal acts are wrong, but also why and how governments should deal with people who engage in those activities. So while some people believe, for example, that lying is always wrong, philosophers of crime will note that in most cases, lying poses no real threat to the state or the well-being of its citizens (even if it is wrong to lie), and laws against most kinds of lying would be too costly to enforce, especially when balanced against the benefit of such enforcement. In fact, where would the "liar's police" even begin? [1]

The range of behaviors that are against the law does not overlap perfectly with "immorality," but philosophers still argue that for an "act" to become a "crime," they must show some justification for it being against the law. Not all crimes are easily justified—consider drug abuse, prostitution, blackmail, gambling, hate speech, suicide, pornography, ticket scalping, insider trading, and gun control. Even crimes that seem straightforward, such as assault, can get very complicated very quickly. A good example of this is the notion of *responsibility*. In the criminal law it is not enough to say that a given action violates the law. The state has immense power over the liberty and life of the defendant, and before it can punish the accused individual, it must demonstrate that he or she is responsible for that action. If the accused assailant were sleepwalking or having an epileptic seizure when she struck her roommate in the head, for example, then even though it was her arm that smashed up against the victim's skull, she did not knowingly perform any actions that caused the harm. Although the victim was struck by another individual, the sleepwalker would not be held responsible for the crime of assault and battery, and it would be wrong to punish her for that action. Within the legal category of responsibility, philosophers also scrutinize other concepts such as intention, negligence, foresight, recklessness, ignorance, and duress, which are needed to provide coherent, principled ways of dealing with offenders. One of the most concrete examples in this area is the 1962 Model Penal Code, drawn up by U.S. philosophers and legal scholars, which made principled recommendations for sentencing convicted offenders that many states have since adopted into their own criminal codes.

Beyond questioning legal definitions of crimes and trying to justify criminalizing particular actions, philosophers examine how governments deal with and respond to crimes, particularly in the area of punishment. The rule of law, as opposed to governance by the will of particular individuals or groups, is fundamental to constitutional political systems such as in the United States. A society fails to be ruled by law in either of two situations, each of which is devastating to a free society: First, when violations of the law go unpunished, and second, when governmental power is exercised either oppressively or arbitrarily. When philosophers seek to justify punishment in the United States, *political questions* about the government's aims and individuals' rights to act without government interference are considered alongside questions about the unwanted actions themselves.

Whereas criminologists tend to take the legal system for granted, philosophers do not assume that any aspect *must* be the way it is. In fact, philosophers do not assume that governments should be the only ones punishing offenders, although they eventually reach that conclusion. One argument for governments' exclusive authority to punish criminals is based on *fairness:* If individual citizens were allowed to respond to criminals however they chose, then the "punishments" would vary widely (and arbitrarily) from case to case. Just consider how some families of murder victims would push for the death penalty, while others would try to forgive the murderer. A related argument against allowing victims to exact their own revenge is based on the notion of *desert*, or the idea that people should get what is due them. Are victims of crime the best judge of deserved punishment? Or do victims tend to lean toward excessive punishment, making them biased judges of what criminals deserve?

Another argument against civilians taking punishment into their own hands considers the high priority that most of us place on *individual liberty*. If the government were not responsible for the determination of guilt or innocence, there would likely be more innocent individuals punished for crimes that they did not commit. "Better that ten guilty persons go free than that one innocent person be convicted" is a key underpinning of the rule of law, which features uniform application and enforcement of laws, standards of evidence, and procedures for determining guilt or innocence. If there were no rule or sovereignty of law, even innocent individuals, going about their daily business, would have a hard time avoiding misguided punishment by irate vigilante groups.

While most people would agree with the argument that governments, not individuals, should punish criminals, there is no widespread agreement on exactly what constraints should be placed on governments. While few people would dispute the idea that more serious crimes should receive more serious punishments, there is no consensus on what the most serious punishment should be. Should we execute criminals who have committed the most heinous crimes or sentence them to life in prison? Another potential constraint is the insistence that laws demonstrate consistency. For example, should the courts be allowed to punish possession of crack cocaine 100 times more severely than possession of powder cocaine (which it does)? Should prosecutors file murder charges on people who directly cause another's death, but not on those who fail to give assistance or call for help (which they do not)? Does it make sense to punish individuals for attempted crimes, or for unintentionally causing harm to another (which happens at times)?

Political issues involving the government's use of power are always pitted against moral issues, such as the *harm* caused by certain behaviors, according to philosopher Leo Katz (1996). The major questions posed by philosophers fall into three categories: (1) justifying punishment, (2) issues in the "General Part" of the criminal law, and (3) issues in the "Specific Part" of the criminal law. Philosophers often talk about the moral justification for punishing those who violate the law, but the imposition of punishment is tempered by limits that we set on the government. Similarly, philosophers must balance moral, social, and political considerations when they examine the concepts of the "General Part" of criminal law (such as "intent," "attempt," "act," and "duress") that play key roles in most crimes. Finally, in the "Specific Part" of the criminal law, philosophers use moral, political, and legal arguments to justify or question laws against specific crimes such as blackmail.

In these three categories of topics, we find methods, types of inquiry, and assumptions that are characteristic of philosophy as a discipline. Before addressing these three categories, however, more needs to be said about philosophical methods and about the relationship between law and morality generally.

Philosophical Methods

The discipline of philosophy falls under the category of the "humanities," which can be distinguished from social science fields such as criminology, sociology, or economics. While criminologists and other social scientists use "research methods" that guide how they conduct observational studies or collect survey data, for example, philosophers use *forms of argument* or *types of reasoning* to examine their subject matter.

Perhaps the most important emphasis of philosophy is its focus on how things *should or should not be,* instead of how they are in fact. Focusing on judgments about how things should be (also known as "evaluative" judgments) influences how philosophers of crime go about their work and influences the assumptions they make. Most philosophers of crime (and more generally, most philosophers of *law*) assume that at least some criminals act out of *free will,* meaning that crime is a choice. A social scientist, by contrast, might find it worthwhile to study whether the claim about criminals' free will is in fact true.

Philosophers also assume that the punishments convicted criminals receive—especially imprisonment and execution—are generally bad things to do to people and require some justification in order for a state to be able to impose them. By "bad things," I mean things that most people would prefer to avoid, all other things being equal. Consider what people go through to avoid punishment, and how those who evade capture and punishment are viewed as "lucky." Viewing punishment as a bad thing is what philosophers call a *pre-theoretical starting point*. It is a *pre*-theoretical point, rather than a given, because many philosophical theories end up concluding that punishing criminals is a *good* thing—once properly justified by a theory and arguments (some of which we will discuss later in the chapter). But it is the theory that eventually leads to this view. You can't *begin* with the position that punishment is a good thing, because that is what you are trying to argue. Plus, in the absence of some argument, it is hard to assume that punishments are good things. So philosophers go with the commonsense front-end assumption and take it as a given that punishments are nasty enough things to do to people that societies must have some justification for using them on people. By contrast, a social scientist might do extensive research (and in fact, some social scientists have) on whether criminals actually perceive or experience certain punishments negatively.

Philosophers also question whether it should be the government's or someone else's responsibility to control crime, while social scientists may take it for granted that the government has that responsibility and will instead question whether the state controls crime *effectively* using one means or another. Philosophers use hypotheticals: *If* a given approach to punishment (like using prison to deter drunk driving) is effective in practice as a deterrent, it would be justifiable in theory. Philosophers are less interested in the mechanics of determining whether the prison sentences actually deter would-be drunk drivers (it would take a social scientist collecting the data on the success of that approach to arrive at a practical answer to the question) than in *justify*ing the claim that a given approach to punishment *would be* better or worse, more defensible or less, while putting aside the question of effectiveness. All of these examples underscore the key feature of philosophy's approach to crime—an *evaluative* approach, or one concerned with judging how we *should* deal with crime, not a description of the criminal justice system as it is. All of philosophy's unique contributions to the study of crime stem from this aspect of the discipline.

In examining how governments should deal with crime, philosophers make use of several key types of reasoning. For philosophers of crime, the most important type is probably *analogical reasoning*. Analogical reasoning begins with the idea of treating like cases alike, and then looks for relevant similarities and dissimilarities between cases. Philosophers of crime hope to find an analogy between the case in question and a case that has already been decided, without any lingering controversy, so that they can use the decided case as a guide for the case in question. Philosophers of crime might use this type of reasoning to justify stiffer penalties for some crimes, to argue that certain circumstances reduce the criminal's responsibility and, by extension, the appropriate punishment, and to explain why the law should distinguish unintentional actions from those done knowingly, recklessly, or negligently.

Consider cases of killing in self-defense versus premeditated murder. If like cases should be treated alike and if one wants to treat cases of self-defense differently from cases of cold-blooded murder, then one has to pick out the relevant differences between killing someone in cold blood and killing someone in self-defense. Why are those differences important to the law, and why should they dictate different treatment? Philosophers provide an answer: When one kills another person in cold blood, the killer has a very different state of mind compared to someone killing another in self-defense. The person killing in self-defense must be in imminent danger and has no real *choice* in the matter. Either he must kill his attacker or he must allow himself to be killed—but the second alternative is not a reasonable option. Some people may think it a *good* thing to defend oneself against criminal violence, perhaps to send a message to other would-be attackers. For these reasons, killing in self-defense is considered to be a *justified* killing of another person. In contrast, a cold-blooded murderer chooses to perform a wrongful action, despite all kinds of alternatives available to him or her, including the choice of simply leaving the would-be victim alone. But what is the state of mind of a battered woman who kills her abuser when she is not in imminent danger? Is the "battered women's syndrome," a psychological condition caused by repeated cycles of abuse, a relevant factor to consider when evaluating state of mind and deserved punishment?

Box 6.1 • Governor Grants Clemency in Case of Battered Women's Syndrome

For the second time in New York State's history, a woman convicted of killing a man she said had terrorized and battered her was granted clemency. In his announcement, Governor George E. Pataki noted that a Queens jury had rejected Linda White's battered-woman defense at her trial in 1990. "However," he said, "the extraordinary powers of clemency allow me to exercise compassion and recognize not only that domestic violence was a factor in this case, but that Linda White has demonstrated a true commitment to rebuilding her life through her exemplary prison record."

W. Glaberson (2002). "Pataki Grants Clemency to Four in Prison." *The New York Times*, (December 25):B.1.

In addition to analogical reasoning, another form of argument for philosophers of crime is the *reductio ad absurdum* (from the Latin, meaning "reducing to absurdity"). Generally, in a *reductio* argument, a philosopher will try to show how a given argument or position leads to absurd or indefensible conclusions. Philosophers contend that an argument that leads to absurd conclusions must itself be absurd. Philosophers of crime might use this form of argument to expose the flaws of some legal or moral principle. Consider the following possible legal principle: "In order to commit a crime, one must act intentionally." If this principle were true, then no reckless or negligent action, or unintentional act that results in harm, could be a crime. This seems like an absurd conclusion because many uncontroversial laws, for example drunk driving and reckless endangerment laws, criminalize reckless and negligent actions. Having reached an absurd conclusion, philosophers would argue that the proposed legal principle must be flawed. Philosophers sometimes refer to this form of argumentation as *providing counterexamples* (which counter or prove false the principle or general claim in question). To go back to the example of intentionality, the act of killing someone while driving drunk, resulting in a charge of manslaughter, would be a counterexample to the claim that one must act intentionally to commit a crime.

Other types of reasoning are used by philosophers of crime, but analogical reasoning and providing counterexamples are the predominant ways such cases are analyzed. These two types of reasoning represent the primary "methodologies" philosophers of crime employ, usually within the framework of how we *should* deal with crime. The sections that follow discuss more examples and applications of these two main types of reasoning. The next section examines an important issue in the philosophical study of crime—distinguishing the legal from the moral.

Distinguishing the Legal from the Moral

One of the fundamental issues in the philosophical study of crime is distinguishing acts that are "illegal" from those that are "immoral." Various groups, subcultures, and individuals living in a diverse society might have different ideas about morality, yet they are all bound by one set of formal laws. Democratic nations like the United States place great value on tolerance and seek to maximize moral and religious boundaries by ensuring that laws do not unnecessarily restrict group or individual values. Philosophers today devote a great deal of time and energy to distinguishing between morality and the law, despite the fact that (or perhaps because) many of them disagree about where the exact boundary between the two *should* be. Identifying the lines between morality and law reveals some of the government's political interest in defining certain acts as "criminal."

A Little History

Philosophers have not always tried to separate the legal from the moral. In ancient Greece, Socrates, Plato, and Aristotle all suggested that moral principles should govern all aspects of life, especially public ones like the law. Ancient philosophers believed that the law and morality were almost completely overlapping. They saw the law as a product of moral values or the exercise of certain moral rules. Plato believed that law shared the same goals as morality: In his work *The Republic*, he claimed that the morally ideal state would have no need for laws because to a society of morally upright citizens, laws would be an annoyance and something of an insult.[3] For Aristotle, the political and the moral were the same thing: To be moral was to be part of the right kind of state and to participate in its political associations, and states should take responsibility for the moral education of their citizens. Identifying the legal with the moral remained the dominant philosophical approach for quite some time. Later, in the thirteenth century, St. Thomas Aquinas re-articulated these arguments. Aquinas judged the appropriateness of the legal systems of his day according to their ability to achieve moral justice. He suggested that the best legal systems would use *natural law*, which he believed was based on humans' rational understanding of human nature, as a response to misbehavior. Even though today's philosophers no longer view morality and the law as overlapping so completely, the ancient Greek identification of the law with morality continues to have its advocates, mostly in the form of *natural law theory*, based largely on Aquinas's work.

It was not until the Scientific Revolution was well underway that philosophers began to describe significant differences between morality and the law. In the seventeenth century, English philosopher Thomas Hobbes argued that society's legal system was needed to protect individuals and their property from others in society because people act out of self-interest. In this way, Hobbes was one of the first to suggest that the law and morality have different founding principles, and he opened the door to possibilities other than complete overlap of the legal with the moral.

Many philosophers responded to and refined Hobbes's ideas. John Austin, an English jurist in the early nineteenth century, proposed a perspective known as *legal positivism*, meaning that philosophers should study only existing law, or law "simply and strictly so called," rather than evaluate alternatives to the law. *Positive law* for Austin was simply what those in power said it was or what they wrote into statutes, and one could figure out how a given statute would apply to a given situation by looking at exactly what the commands of the political leaders were and by reasoning from there. Austin, and many positivists who followed him, found that there was a great deal of clarity and understanding to be gained from focusing on the law as it *is* (commands from above, backed by the threat of punishment) and not on the law as it *should* be.

Toward the end of the nineteenth century, American jurist Oliver Wendell Holmes Jr. offered a similar view, later called *legal realism*. Holmes argued that because the law similarly affects moral and immoral individuals alike, by giving them reason to avoid punishment, the law must be different from morality (because many immoral people are law-abiding at least some of the time). For Holmes, the most important consideration was the ability to predict whether or not the law would eventually punish a given individual for a given act—in other words, the reach of the law. The morality of the act itself was irrelevant from Holmes's point of view. Unlike Austin, Holmes did not look closely at the letter of the law (or at the explicit commands of political leaders) for insight into difficult cases, because he cynically believed that judges could always adjust their reasoning to justify whatever decisions they preferred. Despite their differences, the views of Austin and Holmes mark significant shifts away from the views that came before them because they both sought to separate the law from morality.

Despite the fact that they broke new ground by distinguishing the law from morality, the views of Austin and Holmes were deeply flawed. Austin's view of law as commands from above was not well-suited to civil law, while Holmes's model did not acknowledge that there may be logic or merit to judges' legal reasoning. In the mid- to late-twentieth century, several philosophers offered reformulations of the views of Holmes and Austin that are still very influential today, especially H.L.A. Hart's refining of legal positivism into a sophisticated and powerful theory. Hart's view was so influential that it single-handedly popularized philosophy of law to the point that it became established as a separate subdiscipline within philosophy.

Hart replaced Austin's command model of law with a procedural model that defined laws as special *rules* that had come from the "right" place (e.g., from political leaders or the legislature), that had been created in the "right" way (e.g., passed by a majority of representatives), and that were legitimate for their adherence to procedure rather than their relationship to morality. Nevertheless, some of Hart's basic requirements (e.g., laws had to be public and announced in advance of being applied) provided the legal system with the means to consider moral issues.

Nearly as important as Hart's refining of legal positivism was the subsequent natural law–based approach of Ronald Dworkin. Focusing more on judicial decisionmaking than Hart, Dworkin suggested that laws do not operate as mechanistically as rules do, especially when judges have to interpret them and apply them in new and different situations. Drawing on his observations of lawyers and judges, Dworkin argued that in hard cases the key issues are often resolved by analyzing competing *principles*, many of which are moral in nature such as principles of liberty or justice, rather than using rigid rules to decide the case. For Dworkin, these principles, in conjunction with the letter and history of the law, lead to specific legal *rights* for individuals. Dworkin believed in the importance of determining exactly how principles and rights work within the legal system. He argued that judges should interpret the law in a principled way so as to improve the system as a whole, not just arrive at a particular case's outcome. The result is that for Dworkin, legal decisions not only drew on moral principles, but also had moral consequences.

This very brief historical overview of the relationship between law and morality is admittedly incomplete and inconclusive, but it should give some hint of how philosophy's approach has developed and where the current thinking is on the subject. It should also make clear that even among the most influential thinkers in the field, there is disagreement about exactly how much of a role morality does and should play in the law. Finally, it's important to note that the contributions of the philosophers mentioned above cover more than just crime. The topic of the relationship between the law and morality is too broad for a more careful treatment than I can offer here. For that reason, I will leave the larger topic aside and move now to examine morality from the perspective of contemporary philosophers of crime.

Criminal vs. Merely Immoral Behavior

The primary way that contemporary philosophers concerned with issues of crime distinguish the legal from the moral is by differentiating between criminal behavior and merely immoral behavior. There are many reasons that philosophers distinguish between criminal and merely immoral behavior, and several of them may seem rather obvious. To begin with, states punish their citizens for crimes, but not usually for merely immoral behavior such as lying. If you consider why there are punishments and statutes for crimes like robbery and not for mere immorality like adultery, it is easy to find social and political reasons for making the distinction between the two. Often it is the case that merely immoral behavior harms its "victims" much less than does criminal behavior. In other cases, it would be simply too difficult to put together the legal evidence one would need to prosecute cases of mere immorality. One example of immoral behavior that seems to fit these two descriptions is lying to one's spouse about an extramarital affair. Lying in such a situation is obviously immoral, but is not nearly as harmful as many of the harms the criminal law prohibits, and it is extremely difficult to prove (even more difficult than the affair itself, especially if only the two married people heard the lie). Still, it does seem to be true that even though there are immoral acts that are not criminal, criminal acts are usually immoral. Criminal acts, then, are immoral, but should be something more: They are explicitly forbidden in the law, they are subject to punishment, their results are especially harmful, and outlawing them does not unduly limit the individual liberties of citizens. As such, it would seem that criminal behavior could be understood as a *subset* of all immoral behavior.

Thus, it appears that all criminal behavior is immoral behavior, and there is no criminal behavior that is not also immoral. But is that really the case? Are there some acts that are criminal, but not immoral as well? Having a law on the books that outlaws a given action has a tendency to make us think of that behavior as wrong, and it is not long before we see that action as immoral as well as criminal. Consider, though, cases of firearm or drug possession. Possessing a firearm, especially an unlicensed one, is often a serious crime. Suppose, however, you carry a firearm for your own protection (even though you do not have a license for it), and never hurt, threaten, or even pose a risk to anyone else in the process. In such a case, it is hard to say exactly how that particular crime is immoral. Similarly, you could possess an illicit drug and never use or sell it, or intend to do so. This might seem pointless or stupid, but it is not clearly immoral. These examples of criminal actions that are not clearly immoral show that even though *most* criminal actions are also immoral, not *all* of them are.

The example of drug possession leads to a more difficult issue with respect to the relationship between crime and immorality. Suppose you believe that the only immoral actions are those that have some impact on other people. In other words, actions that affected no one other than yourself would be neither moral nor immoral in nature. In such a view, it would be okay (at least not immoral) to use drugs in situations that did not affect others (assume that the drug user does not attempt to drive, the drug user has no dependents who rely upon him or her or his or her income, the drug user doesn't use drugs in front of impressionable children, and so on). Others with different moral beliefs might draw the opposite conclusion: Drug use is always wrong, regardless of the situation. The question then is, which view of morality is the right one?

Consider tax evasion as another example. One could argue that it is immoral to be forced to pay taxes to an unjust or wasteful government. According to this view, not only is it all right to refuse to pay taxes, but governments violate individual rights when they force taxes on us.[4] On the other hand, one can argue that if you receive the benefits of everyone's paying their taxes (such as well-maintained roads and police protection), you are obligated to uphold your end of the deal and pay your part for those benefits. Otherwise, you take unfair advantage of those who pay their taxes in order to receive the same benefits without paying for them. Because the free rider shares none of the burden of taxes, but still enjoys the benefits of them, the burden of those who do pay their taxes would increase.

The possibility that two moral views can conflict on a given issue makes separating crime from immorality all the more difficult, but also all the more important. In order to run smoothly, governments need definite answers as to whether they should prohibit a given activity or guarantee individual rights to that activity. In addition, in a morally and religiously diverse society that respects freedom of religion and freedom of speech and conscience, it is crucial that the laws that apply to all of us allow independence of our various moral and religious views. Yet there may need to be limits to *behaviors* that emerge from such views. The issue of medical treatment for children, for example, illustrates a precarious balance among the rights of parents, children, adherents of the Christian Science religion, and the government. The fact that important social and political values exist along with moral values makes it necessary to distinguish between criminal and merely immoral behavior—as when we have to decide between treating parents as murderers or as devout followers of their faith.

The social and political values that help us to distinguish between criminal and merely immoral behavior also point to the particular issues that philosophers of crime seek to address. The political value of keeping governments from abusing their police power, for example, has led to philosophical theories that test whether punishment models are justified. What is more, the social and political value of having a legal system that is consistent in its use of key concepts drives the philosophical study of the General Part of the criminal law. Finally, the social and political necessity to apply principles consistently motivates the philosophical analysis of particular kinds of offenses under the heading of the Specific Part of the criminal law. I will now turn to these three main issues—punishment theory, the General Part of criminal law, and the Specific Part of criminal law—and the social and political values that drive them.

Box 6.2 • Faith Healing vs. Kids' Rights

Christian Scientists to Fight Bill Dropping Legal Shield for Parents

Gov. Owens, Colorado prosecutors and child-advocacy groups support the proposed striking of a section of a 1989 law that exempts some parents from prosecution if, for religious reasons, they withhold medical treatments from children who are in danger of dying or being disabled.

These proponents of equal protection for all children are pitted against the powerful lobbying of the Christian Science Church. Christian Scientists successfully inserted the exemption into the law in 1989.

The exemption-deleting bill that has created the new stir was introduced by Rep. Kay Alexander, R-Montrose, and Sen. Bob Hagedorn, D-Aurora, just days before 13-year-old Amanda Bates of Grand Junction died of untreated diabetes. Bates' parents are members of the General Assembly Church of the First Born, a centuries-old church that does not believe in medical treatments for illness or injury. Since 1974, 11 children of Church of the First Born members have died or been stillborn in Colorado after not receiving medical care.

Nancy Lofholm, *The Denver Post*, February 10, 2001.

Punishment Theory

The main way most philosophers deal with issues related to crime is through *punishment theory*. This is because philosophers do not attempt to describe crimes, or the criminal justice system, as they might be observed in society, but focus instead on how best to prevent, respond to, or exact retribution for crime. Though theories differ on which of these goals is more important, all view punishment as a way of achieving them. Philosophers define punishment as some harm or pain (usually a loss of liberty) inflicted on an individual who violates the criminal law. Generally speaking, punishment must be *for* something. If the legal system inflicted harm on an individual who did nothing wrong whatsoever, that would not be punishment, but something else altogether, such as state persecution.

Philosophers seek out justifications for systems of punishment for two very important reasons. The first reason I discussed above: Because punishment causes harm or pain to an individual, the state is not automatically entitled to impose punishment, but needs a good reason for putting its punishment model into effect. The second reason is that most systems of punishment do not strive to achieve one purpose or even one coherent *set* of purposes. This is because the criminal law (particularly in the United States and Britain) developed by responding to different social, cultural, and economic pressures throughout history. As a result, today's criminal law is made up of different statutes and court decisions, many of which stem from different conceptions of what the aims of punishment should be. Thus, one cannot rely on the law simply as it exists to help evaluate the purpose of punishment. Philosophers go one step further and argue that the lack of a coherent set of purposes in the criminal law as it is practiced highlights the need for a principled account of what the aims of punishment *should be*, which can make sense of the criminal law as it exists or can point to reforms that will address its incoherence.

The two most enduring and widely discussed theories for justifying punishment are deterrence and retributivism. In the sections to follow, I will discuss these two theories in some detail. While they are not the only theoretical justifications for punishment by any means, they have had the greatest influence on philosophers who seek to justify punishment or question its legitimacy.

Deterrence

The basis for deterrence theory is the moral theory of *utilitarianism*, brought to prominence in the late eighteenth and early nineteenth centuries by Jeremy Bentham and John Stuart Mill, which counts actions as moral when they promote the greatest good for the greatest number of people. In a nonutilitarian state, the authorities would inflict pain or suffering on the criminal without first calculating how the entire community will be affected, including the offender. Under a *deterrence model*, punishments are acceptable only if they prevent more suffering than they cause. According to deterrence theory, punishing a criminal sends the message to other would-be criminals that they can look forward to similar treatment if they commit similar crimes. Because it is generally the case that individuals want to avoid punishment, this threat of punishment serves to *deter*, or prevent, would-be criminals from committing similar crimes. If the theory is correct, punishing one murderer should deter at least a handful of would-be murderers, so that the benefit of deterrence (saving the lives of a handful of victims) outweighs the harm that punishment imposes on the murderer and actually produces more good than *not* punishing the murderer.

However, one can justify deterrence theory only if the state can effectively implement the theory in the real world. In other words, if a society's punishment does not actually deter would-be criminals, then it is impossible to justify that punishment on the grounds of deterrence, at least not in that particular society at that particular time. If would-be criminals, say drug dealers, are not deterred by the threat of punishment and continue to deal drugs, leaving the community no better off, then the authorities should stop punishing those kinds of criminals in that way, according to deterrence theory. The motivation for deterrence theory, after all, is to create the greatest good for the greatest number, and if a punishment does not do that—even if justice could be served in a few cases—deterrence theory would argue against the punishment, perhaps recommending a different type of punishment in its place.

Most people agree that at least one of the purposes of any system of punishment is to protect innocent victims from future crimes, but that there should be limits on the state's use of punishment. One disadvantage of deterrence theory is that it does a poor job of respecting such limits. On the one hand, excessive punishments such as torture could deter crimes ranging from murder to speeding; on the other hand, however, if punishing a crime with a minimal punishment would deter other individuals as effectively as a more severe punishment, then deterrence theorists would advocate the use of the less severe, less painful punishment. One problem with these scenarios is that they do not recognize any limits on how far the state should be allowed to go to achieve deterrence. For example, if the only effective deterrent against theft turned out to be cutting off the hands of thieves, and the benefits of drastically reducing occurrences of theft outweighed the pain and suffering put on those (very few) who received the punishment, then deterrence theorists would have little to say against punishing people in such a way. Another problem is that they say nothing about how much the criminal could be said to *deserve* a given punishment, based on the seriousness of the crime. Thus, if a two-year prison sentence would effectively deter murder (and was the least severe punishment achieving such a level of deterrence), then deterrence theory would maintain that a two-year sentence is as much punishment as a murderer should receive for his or her crime, even though many would argue that anyone who commits murder deserves more punishment than just two years in prison.

Retributivism

Based on the moral theory of eighteenth-century German philosopher Immanuel Kant, *retributivism* holds that punishment is justified only if the criminal did something to *deserve* the punishment. By seeking some form of *retribution*, or moral payback, for the crime, retributivism does not insist that punishment leads to the greatest good for the greatest number as deterrence theory does. For Kant, the criminal actions themselves justify the punishment. In fact, in laying out his retributivist position, Kant argued that even if you were certain that punishing a deserving criminal would do absolutely nothing for society generally, if the criminal deserves punishment, then it would be *wrong* to fail to punish him. To illustrate this point, Kant (1797:474) considers the most extreme example he can imagine:

> Even if a civil society were to be dissolved by the consent of all its members (e.g., if a people inhabiting an island decided to separate and disperse throughout the world), the last murderer remaining in prison would first have to be executed, so that each has done to him what his deeds deserve and blood guilt does not cling to the people for not having insisted upon this punishment; for otherwise the people can be regarded as collaborators in this public violation of justice.

Knowing that the punishment will not benefit society in any way (it cannot deter others, because as soon as the society dissolves there will be no others to be deterred; it cannot benefit society in the future because there will be no society to benefit in the future), Kant thinks that the criminal should be executed nevertheless, because the criminal deserves it and it would be wrong not to give him or her the deserved punishment.

The deeper explanation for Kant's view here is a bit tricky and philosophically controversial, but it goes as follows: For Kant, good moral rules are those one would choose for others as well as oneself, and autonomy (or the ability to make choices for oneself without others restricting what you can do) is a necessary precursor to acting morally. Kant combines these two features of his moral philosophy in a rather ingenious way to justify retributivism. He claims that in choosing to act in a given way, one implicitly decides that that way of acting is not only good for oneself, but for others to follow as well. So, when a murderer such as Albert DeSalvo, the "Boston Strangler," kills his victims, in Kant's view, he decides that killing constitutes a good way to act, a way that others should act as well, even with respect to him. In essence, then, by killing another person, the murderer has implicitly asked for someone else to kill him. Of course, criminals rarely think of their actions in this way, but that is irrelevant to Kant. For him, everyone, including criminals, *ought* to follow this kind of moral reasoning—if we did, we would live in a better world. Society's motivation to punish ought to be based on something like the Golden Rule: Do unto others as you would have others do unto you. As I noted above, this view has sparked considerable philosophical controversy, with philosophers noting, among other problems, that if we act in such a way that deliberately honors the murderer's choice, we seem to be endorsing her decision to murder, even though such behavior clearly violates Kant's idea of morality.

Retributivism has one clear advantage over deterrence theory, which is that it links the seriousness of the offense to the seriousness of the punishment, preventing either excessive or overly lenient punishment. Taken at face value, however, this link has odd implications. In Kant's view, it would seem that the death penalty would be the appropriate punishment for murder. Depending on how one feels about capital punishment, this may or may not strike one as an odd implication. Consider the counterexample of rape: Retributivism would seem to suggest that it is appropriate to punish a rapist by sexually violating him. Not only would these punishments fail to match up with the ways we normally treat such criminals, but the very possibility of such punishments also creates further, deeper difficulties for retributivism. For example, there is the issue of how the state would go about administering sexual assaults as punishments. In general, the eye-for-an-eye doctrine that retributivism seems to endorse would generate many serious difficulties for our penal system that would go beyond even the fundamental problems of cruel and unusual punishment.

Immanuel Kant, ca. 1790. *With permission of Johannes Gutenberg –Universität Mainz*

Beyond these general difficulties, retributivism's eye-for-an-eye approach creates specific problems in identifying the degrees of particular crimes. Consider the difference between first- and second-degree murder. Few would deny that premeditated murder is seriously wrong, and should be punished more severely than murder committed in the heat of passion. Nonetheless, retributivism, at least in its most basic form, would seem to recommend death as the appropriate punishment for both first- and second-degree murder because both result in death. Similarly, it is not clear what the punishments should be for voluntary versus involuntary manslaughter. If the appropriate punishment for either of these offenses is death, then retributivism would not seem to measure the deservedness of punishment very well. If the appropriate punishment is something else, Kant's view does not give us clear guidance on how we should go about figuring out what it should be. The point is that Kant's original conception of retributivism considers only broad categories of crimes, and does not consider the gradations within crime categories that we often find in the criminal law

In light of such specific and general problems, many philosophers have abandoned Kant's original conception of retributivism in favor of *proportional retributivism*. Proportional retributivism holds that the most severe crime should receive the most severe punishment, the second most severe crime should receive the second most severe punishment, and so on. Like retributivism in its original form, proportional retributivism accounts for the deservedness of punishment and matches degrees of punishment with levels of the harm caused by the offender. But proportional retributivism avoids a direct eye-for-an-eye approach by recommending less problematic forms of punishment (typically incarceration) and letting the punishment vary in degree (say, number of years in prison). It is important to note that despite its refinements, proportional retributivism is still more or less true to its Kantian roots: Given that the punishments for crimes are made explicit to the general public, a proportional retributivist can claim that the criminal chooses the punishment received because he or she chooses the crime, fully aware of the punishment associated with that crime—"you do the crime, you do the time." So once again, the idea is that because we respect the ability of individuals to make choices, we must give a criminal the punishment he or she chose when he or she decided to commit the crime.

Though proportional retributivism is an improvement over Kant's retributivism, it is not without its own difficulties, one of which is linking the severity of the punishment to the severity of a given crime. While proportional retributivism can explain why first-degree murder, for example, deserves more punishment than second-degree murder, it tends to leave open the question of how we can justify a *particular* amount of punishment for a particular crime (say, 20 years for first-degree and 15 for second-degree). Perhaps, as proportional retributivists might argue, such determinations are less important than ordering the relative severity of punishment in accordance with the relative severity of crime.

Criminal Law: The General Part

The *General Part* of the criminal law consists of fundamental concepts and requirements present in the criminal law. In analyzing the General Part, philosophers and legal theorists look for those concepts and requirements, such as what counts as a justification or an excuse or even an "act," that run throughout the law and ensure that they are consistent overall. Philosophers find these concepts and requirements interesting apart from their practical purpose in the law, because legal concepts pose challenging theoretical problems for them to consider.

Fundamental Concepts

There are many fundamental concepts under the General Part of the criminal law that invite controversy, but examples of particularly thorny ones include "intent," "act," "insanity," "duress," "ignorance," "diminished capacity," and "attempt." Philosophers have sought to define concepts like these since the ancient times of Aristotle, whose early work on moral responsibility preceded formal law as we know it today. The challenges of the General Part for contemporary philosophers now include social and political concerns in addition to the factor of moral responsibility

Take for example the concept of "attempt." A criminal attempt is most often defined as trying but failing to commit a crime. Merely preparing to commit a crime, however, is typically not considered a crime. So where should the criminal law draw the line between merely preparing to commit a crime and actually attempting to commit that crime? This question turns out to be particularly significant in cases in which the police apprehend a would-be criminal in the process of committing a crime. Suppose Joe, who has no prior record, legally buys ammunition with which he intends to shoot and kill his victim, Gary. Imagine further that Joe loads a gun with the ammunition and carries the gun, concealed in his jacket, to Gary's house with the intention of going there to kill Gary. Carrying a concealed weapon may itself be an offense for which Joe could be arrested, but up to this point, Joe's actions would not be considered attempted murder. Imagine, however, that Joe lies in wait behind Gary's car, gun drawn and ready to shoot. In some jurisdictions, lying in wait is considered an attempt, but in others, Joe would have to shoot and miss or merely wound Gary in order to be held liable for attempted murder, and even then, there would need to be some proof of his intent to murder.

Which treatment of this case is the correct one? Part of the argument against treating cases of lying in wait as attempts is that the law (and the police) should not interfere with the liberty of individuals unless they have done something clearly illegal. To allow the police to arrest individuals when they are merely contemplating or planning to commit crimes would punish people for their thoughts alone. Furthermore, arresting individuals before they do anything wrong prevents them from reconsidering and aborting the attempt (and thus avoiding punishment). On the other hand, you could claim that Joe, lying in wait with his gun drawn, is clearly dangerous and unlikely to reconsider. Given that one purpose of the criminal law is to protect citizens from crime, perhaps the police should be allowed to intervene and charge Joe with the crime that he seems likely to have committed if he had the chance.

Both sides of this argument consider the state's dual responsibility to Joe's individual liberty on the one hand, and to the community on the other, including Joe's potential victim and anyone else who might be endangered if he fired his weapon. The state's responsibility to protect individual liberty draws on arguments seeking to prevent the police from busting into people's houses unnecessarily or conducting random searches of transit commuters. The state's responsibility to the community prioritizes preventing dangerous behavior and promoting the safety of individuals in society. Each side of the debate offers powerful social and political reasons for the authorities to act aggressively or to back off entirely. Because the arguments concern individual rights versus public safety for the entire community, the moral responsibility of any particular individual is not centrally important. This is not to say, however, that moral responsibility is irrelevant with respect to issues in the General Part of the criminal law, but rather that social and political factors also play a role in defining the key concepts within the General Part.

Box 6.3 • Personal Searches a Case of Ride and Wrong˙

Two civil rights groups upset by unprecedented searches of backpacks and bags on Boston trains during the Democratic convention sued the regional transit authority yesterday, complaining that cops are violating passenger rights.

"Sporadic, half-hearted searches don't make me feel safer, only less free. It reminded me of a World War II movie," said Steve Spain, 47, who was heading from a homeless veterans' shelter where he works when he was randomly approached by Boston cops Monday. Spain refused to allow the search and was ordered off the train.

"I argued I paid my fare and should be allowed to ride, but I ended up walking two stops," said Spain, who is one of several passengers who have filed complaints with rights groups.

Kenneth R. Bazinet, *New York Daily News*, July 28, 2004.

Formal Requirements

The balance of social and political values along with moral responsibility is central to creating and assessing many of the *formal requirements* within the General Part. The power imbalance between the defendant and the state is the main reason for the rigorous safeguards of criminal procedure, the heavy burden of proof borne by the state, and the presumption of innocence. The criminal law's requirements are "formal" because they provide the structure to which all written laws must conform and because they provide very little in the way of substantive content. In other words, formal requirements identify the form the law must take, but say little about what the substance of the law must be. For example, the fact that every crime requires an act is a formal requirement, but the fact that we rank the act of murder as more serious than the act of theft points to a substantive feature of the criminal law. Formal requirements allow lawyers and philosophers to deconstruct the theoretical and practical elements within criminal laws and understand how they relate to the overall structure of the criminal law.

Foremost among the formal requirements are *actus reus* and *mens rea*, both of which are requirements for criminal liability, or guilt. *Actus reus,* or evil act, requires that the accused individual is the person who committed the act in question, and the state must demonstrate this before holding him or her criminally liable. Just as it sounds, *actus reus* requires an evil *act,* not merely an evil thought or plan, or even an evil omission that produces similar results. *Mens rea* requires that the individual must commit whatever evil acts he does with an evil mind. Under this requirement, the criminal act must spring from some malicious state of mind such as intent, knowledge, recklessness, or negligence, and cannot be accidental. To justify these two requirements in the law, philosophers invoke theories of moral responsibility and also consider how the law should serve as a social and political institution.

Consider the *actus reus* requirement: One argument for this requirement is that it is much more difficult for individuals to control their thoughts, emotions, and physical states (like diseases) than it is for them to control their bodily movements, so by requiring an actual act on the part of the criminal, *actus reus* allows individuals a more reasonable opportunity to avoid punishment. The discussion of the attempted murder example suggests the danger of allowing punishment for thoughts—one could be arrested just for thinking about murder. Even though the *actus reus* requirement includes features of moral responsibility (control and choice), it also appeals to broader political values (individual liberty, in the form of the reasonable opportunity to avoid punishment).

Philosophers use a combination of moral and political arguments to justify formal requirements. Consider the political *principle of legality,* which holds that the state can punish only behavior that is clearly prohibited in the criminal law. Moral responsibility alone does not justify this principle. The main rationale for the principle of legality is political: The law must be made public, and individual liberty must be maintained. Otherwise the authorities might invent reasons to lock up innocent individuals they don't like, giving the public no legal recourse to challenge the state (Husak, 1987).

To illustrate the protection of individual liberty within the principle of legality, consider the following example: Jake picks, dries, and smokes a plant that he believes is marijuana growing behind the office building in which he works. As he smokes it behind the office building, a police officer on patrol catches Jake in the act of smoking, seizes what is left of his "cigarette," and arrests him for possession of illegal narcotics. However, it turns out that even though Jake truly believes that the plant he was smoking is marijuana, the plant is actually a rare form of poison ivy. Upon closer analysis, the police discover that the plant Jake was smoking was not in fact an illegal drug at all. Because smoking poison ivy is not a crime, the police cannot charge Jake with possession of illegal narcotics. If moral responsibility were the only consideration, Jake would be guilty of at least trying to possess and use illegal drugs, but that is not the only consideration here. Even though Jake may be morally guilty, the principle of legality protects law-abiding individuals from unfair prosecution and from the state making the law up as it goes along. The idea is that the state should prioritize political (or legal) concerns over moral ones so that individuals can know in advance what actions the state will punish. This way individuals can willfully choose not to violate the law if they wish to avoid punishment. This principle allows individuals to do anything they like, including smoking the rare form of poison ivy (maybe some people find it refreshing), provided that behavior does not violate something explicitly forbidden in the criminal law.

It is important to note that the principle of legality involves a consideration of why political concerns need to take priority over moral ones. The argument is that legality, with its system of knowable laws, allows people to predict which behaviors carry a risk of punishment and which do not. This enhances their freedom and liberty to make choices. In other words, they can confidently choose among many behaviors that do not violate the law—more important, in a free society, than the wholesale enforcement of morality. So even the most obviously political of the formal requirements within the General Part of the criminal law involves some balancing of moral and political values, and in this way the relationship between morality and the law is given consideration.

Criminal Law: The Specific Part

The *Specific Part* of the criminal law gets its name from the fact that it focuses on specific crimes and the justifications specific to them. In essence, the Specific Part is the flip-side of the General Part of the criminal law. While the General Part tries to pick out general concepts and requirements that would apply to every crime, the Specific Part examines particular crimes and asks whether general principles within the criminal law can explain and justify them. As a result, the study of the Specific Part of the criminal law ultimately has the same goal as the study of the General Part: To identify those principles in the criminal law that can justify it as a whole, and provide a basis for changing aspects of the law that do not fit with those principles. Perhaps the most commonly discussed crime under the heading of the Specific Part is blackmail (see Box 6.4). One justification that theorists have offered for blackmail is that it involves *taking unfair advantage* of the victim. But this cannot be a justifying principle for the whole of the criminal law: There are many ways in which one may take unfair advantage of another (consider cheating in a family card game), many of them are perfectly legal, and as a society we may not want to discourage them. Nevertheless, the *unfair advantage principle* is valuable to the study of the Specific Part, as in the case of blackmail.

Box 6.4 • Case Study: Blackmail

The main problem with blackmail is that the action the blackmailer threatens to perform against his or her victim is not itself illegal. Take, for example, the case of Jim, a wealthy businessman who is cheating on his wife. When Jim's boss catches him in the act of cheating, she views the discovery as a potentially lucrative opportunity. A day or two later, she approaches Jim and demands that he give her a large sum of money, saying that if she does not get it, she will disclose the cheating to Jim's wife. The difficulty of justifying this as a crime is that the act that the boss threatens to carry out, revealing the adultery to Jim's wife, is not an illegal activity. So, if Jim refused to pay and the boss told Jim's wife of his cheating, no additional law (beyond blackmail) would be broken. In this way, blackmail is different from menacing, threatening assault, or extortion, all of which threaten to commit acts that are crimes. What is wrong with blackmail has nothing to do with the wrongness of the threatened behavior. As a result, the *harm principle* (which states that the law should prevent individuals from harming or threatening to harm others) does not apply. The task of the philosopher of crime, then, is to explain what exactly it is that is so wrong about blackmail that it should be criminalized.

If what is really wrong with blackmail is something other than the harm the blackmailer threatens, then what's wrong with blackmail must lie in the way the blackmailer goes about requesting the money. However, one could argue that Jim brought this kind of problem on himself by cheating on his wife, and he could avoid this kind of problem entirely by admitting his behavior to his wife. At worst, then, the boss is acting opportunistically on Jim's bad behavior. So what is so objectionable about a request for money such as the one the boss makes? Why is the fact that she takes advantage of the situation a *criminal* matter?

As I suggested above, philosophers and legal theorists have argued that the real problem with blackmail is that it allows an individual to take *unfair advantage* of someone else. This principle explains the wrongness of blackmail much better than the harm principle does. Still, the philosophy of the Specific Part of the criminal law demands not only that one provide an explanation of the underlying wrongfulness of a particular crime, but also that the explanation should explain most, if not all, of the other actions the criminal law prohibits. However, the Specific Part does not stop there: The principles studied by philosophers under the Specific Part of the criminal law must also be able to explain why other, noncriminal actions are *not* criminalized.

Consider, for example, the higher prices charged for gas by isolated gas stations on long, empty stretches of highway. Charging such prices takes unfair advantage of those traveling on the highway, many of whom will need gas by

---

Box 6.4, *continued*

that point or soon thereafter. We may think it unfair or evil to take advantage of people in such a way, but we may also feel that state regulation of gas prices—and all of the costs (both in terms of money and liberty) associated with such a bureaucracy—would be worse than allowing some gas stations to gouge their customers. So even though there is something clearly morally wrong with taking unfair advantage of other people, that principle is too broad—it would require criminalization of too many of our activities—to act as a general justifying principle within the criminal law. Furthermore, "taking unfair advantage" fails to capture what we think is really wrong with many other kinds of criminal activity: It would seem that there is something wrong with armed robbery, for example, beyond the fact that the armed robber "takes unfair advantage" of the fact that he has a gun and the victim does not.

Even though a principle against taking unfair advantage of others might fail to justify the criminal law as a whole, such a principle might still be close enough to the justification for enough criminal prohibitions that it can serve as one of a *coherent set* of principles, many of which overlap, and most of which fit with our moral leanings as a society. In this way, the law would seem to be like morality—no one principle sums it up easily, and the real issues within the law, at least from the point of view of philosophy, come down to disagreements about how competing principles should be weighed against one another. Within such a view of the law, taking unfair advantage seems plausible as a principled justification for outlawing blackmail, because it does capture, at least in part, what is wrong with a significant number of criminal activities, especially crimes such as insider trading (which is also frequently debated by philosophers). In addition, taking unfair advantage bears a close resemblance to other kinds of *taking*, like stealing, most killing (or taking a life), kidnapping, and even crimes of recklessness (taking unreasonable risks). In summary, such an argument defending the criminalization of blackmail would be reasonable from a philosophical point of view because it refers to a substantial part of the criminal law and because it can be applied to other types of crime as well.

Still, as should be clear from this discussion, the precise role that the unfair advantage principle (or any other, for that matter) can be said to play in the criminal law depends largely upon what other principles might compete with this principle. For this reason, particular questions within the Specific Part of the criminal law often consider more general accounts of what principles exist within the criminal law as well as of how the criminal law makes those principles work together (if it can be said to do so at all). In the end, the Specific Part, like the General Part, seeks to balance moral, political, and legal principles in order to make sense of the institution of the criminal law in rather broad terms or to suggest reforms where the institution fails to make sense.

Conclusion and Future Directions

Since the 1960s, when H.L.A. Hart's work helped spark the widespread study of the philosophy of law, the philosophy of crime, especially in the form of punishment theory, has become increasingly more commonplace in undergraduate curricula in the United States and the United Kingdom. Established in an American culture fascinated by crime and the law, that trend seems unlikely to reverse itself. At the same time, however, many top philosophers of law have turned recently from criminal to civil law. With respect to some topics within the criminal law, philosophers seem to have arrived at a general consensus or have argued themselves to a standstill. As a result, at present, there seems to be much less innovative work being done in the philosophy of criminal law and much more being done in the philosophy of civil law. As the graduate students of those top philosophers of law filter into undergraduate teaching positions over the next couple of decades, we may see a corresponding shift within the undergraduate curricula to address civil as well as criminal law. I suspect that the philosophy courses dealing with crime will not disappear completely, however, due to the cultural fascination we seem to have with crime. Nonetheless, a shift to address issues in both the civil and the criminal law, should it ever come, would be a good idea, because the civil law in the United States makes up many more of the statutes on the books and takes up many more of the court proceedings than do criminal cases.

Another factor that I believe will contribute to the continuing study of the criminal law within philosophy courses is the fact that the philosophy of crime is filled with thorny and controversial issues that remain the subject of some debate. Most of those issues arise in the search for the General and Specific Parts of the criminal law and in attempts to justify punishment. Even though these three categories may at first appear rather narrow in their scope, I hope that I have demonstrated the richness and complexity of these topics for philosophers. One can trace most of that complexity to the fact that philosophers of crime must be attentive to how moral, political, and legal philosophy bear on the issues at hand. This makes the philosophical study of crime especially challenging, because often, moral and political principles do not speak to the same issues, and even when they do, they do not always require the same things.

For all of its complexity and attention to nuanced distinctions, however, the philosophy of crime has one last thing going for it that should contribute to its staying power: It has tremendous practical importance. The contributions made by philosophers of crime influence not only the politicians who create, maintain, and reform the penal system, but also the judges and lawyers who practice, shape, and refine the criminal law. And despite the fact that some civil proceedings can have devastating effects on individuals and corporations, few of those effects are as serious as the loss of liberty that the criminal law regularly imposes on criminals. In the end, the philosophy of crime and the arguments it develops *matter* because an individual's liberty, a community's safety, and even justice in general hang in the balance.

Endnotes

1. I am not suggesting that the government *never* concern itself with lying. Philosophers of crime note that during criminal investigations and trials, perjury laws that prohibit people from lying make sense for two reasons: Lying threatens to undermine the legal process, and the law is enforceable in a practical sense because the authorities can compare inconsistencies in the evidence they have gathered.

2. Of course, philosophers have long debated and continue to debate whether human beings have free will. Many philosophers hold the position that causal factors (brain chemistry, environment, family upbringing, etc.) actually *determine* what actions an individual will perform, even if the person feels as if he or she can choose to act or not act in one way or another. If an individual's actions are determined in this way, then it would seem difficult to hold him or her responsible for those actions (as they were not up to the person or the result of his or her choices). It is important to note that there is no end in sight with respect to this debate, mainly because it is very difficult to prove either side true or false. For this reason, among others, philosophers concerned with issues of crime tend to assume that at least some criminals have free will and freely choose to commit crimes. My point here is not that philosophers are no longer interested in the debate, but rather that philosophers of crime specifically (and especially those who are philosophers of law) tend to begin with the assumption of free will.

3. Plato, *Republic,* Book IV, 423d-427c, esp. 425c-d.

4. For a most provocative and influential statement of this view, see Nozick (1974).

Suggested Further Reading

Bedau, H. (1982). *The Death Penalty in America*, 3rd ed. Oxford: Oxford University Press.

Dressler, J. (1995). *Understanding Criminal Law*, 2nd ed. New York: Matthew Bender.

Feinberg, J., and J. Coleman (eds., 2000). *Philosophy of Law*, 6th ed. Stamford, CT: Wadsworth.

Feinberg, J. (1970). *Doing and Deserving*. Princeton, NJ: Princeton University Press.

Fletcher, G.P. (1978). *Rethinking Criminal Law*. Boston: Little, Brown.

Fuller, L. (1964). *The Morality of Law*. New Haven, CT: Yale University Press.

Gross, H. (1979). *A Theory of Criminal Justice*. Oxford, UK: Oxford University Press.

Hart, H.L.A. (1961). *The Concept of Law*. Oxford, UK: Oxford University Press.

Hart, H.L.A. (1968). *Punishment and Responsibility*. Oxford, UK: Oxford University Press.

Husak, D. (1987). *Philosophy of Criminal Law*. Totowa, NJ: Rowman & Littlefield.

Kelly, J.M. (1992). *A Short History of Western Legal Theory*. Oxford, UK: Clarendon Press.

Murphy, J.G. (ed., 1985). *Punishment and Rehabilitation*, 2nd ed. Belmont, MA: Wadsworth.

Murphy, J.G (1979). *Retribution, Justice, and Therapy: Essays in the Philosophy of Law*. Boston: D. Reidel.

Murphy, J.G., and J. Coleman (1990). *Philosophy of Law*, rev. ed. Boulder, CO: Westview Press.

Patterson, D. (ed., 1996). *A Companion to Philosophy of Law and Legal Theory*. Cambridge, MA: Blackwell.

Wasserstrom, R. (1980). "Punishment." In R. Wasserstrom (ed.), *Philosophy and Social Issues: Five Studies,* pp. 112-151. Notre Dame, IN: University of Notre Dame Press.

Wolff, R.P. (1970). *In Defense of Anarchism*. New York: Harper and Row.

Woozley, A.D. (1979). *Law and Obedience*. London: Duckworth.

References

American Law Institute (1962). *Model Penal Code: Proposed Official Draft*. Philadelphia: American Law Institute.

Aquinas, St. Thomas (1993). *Treatise on Law: Summa Theologiaie I-Ii, Qq. 90-97*. Edited by R.J. Henle. Notre Dame, IN: University of Notre Dame Press.

Aristotle (1992). *The Politics*, rev. rep. ed. Translated by T.A. Sinclair. New York: Viking Press.

Austin, J. (1911). *Lectures on Jurisprudence*. 5th ed. Revised and edited by R. Campbell. London: J. Murray.

Austin, J. [1832] (1954). *The Province of Jurisprudence Determined*. Edited by H.L.A. Hart. London: Weidenfeld and Nicolson.

Dworkin, R. (1977). *Taking Rights Seriously*. Cambridge, MA: Harvard University Press.

Dworkin, R. (1986). *Law's Empire*. Cambridge, MA: Harvard University Press.

Hamilton, E., and H. Cairns (eds.) (1961). *The Collected Dialogues of Plato*. Princeton, NJ: Princeton University Press.

Hart, H.L.A. (1961). *The Concept of Law*. Oxford, UK: Oxford University Press.

Hart, H.L.A. (1968). *Punishment and Responsibility*. Oxford, UK: Oxford University Press.

Hobbes, T. [1651] (1985). *Leviathan*. Ed. by C.B. MacPherson. New York: Viking Press.

Holmes, O.W. [1881] (1938). *The Common Law*. Boston: Little, Brown.

Husak, D. (1987). *Philosophy of Criminal Law*. Totowa, NJ: Rowman & Littlefield.

Kant, I. (1965). *Methaphysical Elements of Justice*. Trans. by J. Ladd. Indianapolis: Bobbs-Merrill.

Kant, I. [1785] (1996). *Groundwork of The Metaphysics of Morals.* In M.J. Gregor (trans. and ed.), *The Cambridge Edition of the Works of Immanuel Kant: Practical Philosophy*, pp. 37-108. New York: Cambridge University Press.

Kant, I. [1797] (1996). *The Metaphysics of Morals.* In M.J. Gregor (trans. and ed.), *The Cambridge Edition of the Works of Immanuel Kant: Practical Philosophy*, pp. 37-108. New York: Cambridge University Press.

Katz, L. (1996). "Criminal Law." In D. Patterson (ed.), *A Companion to Philosophy of Law and Legal Theory*, pp. 80-95. Cambridge, MA: Blackwell.

Nozick, R. (1974). *Anarchy, State and Utopia.* New York: Basic Books.

Commentary

David O. Friedrichs

Philosophy is the original discipline. All forms of knowledge (as opposed to belief) are rooted in philosophical speculation. Most notably, in the Western tradition, the Classical Greek philosophers (e.g., Socrates, Plato, Aristotle) provided a fundamental foundation for the pursuit of knowledge. Although philosophy today occupies a relatively modest presence in the college or university curriculum, it continues to grapple with questions of transcendent importance to those in all other disciplines and fields. Certainly contemporary philosophers can assist us in understanding issues in other disciplines—for example, criminology—and can show us how to think more clearly about these issues.

This is one of the themes of Stephen Mathis's chapter, "Philosophy and Crime." He suggests that philosophers may also marshal arguments in favor of or against some laws, or some penalties. Of course, philosophers who adopt a specific position—for example, in favor of or against the death penalty—may sacrifice some level of respect from those who disagree with the position they take. Mathis in his chapter tends to emphasize how philosophers can provide answers to some of our core questions relating to crime and punishment. In another sense, though, I believe it is important to recognize that philosophy compels us to remain reasonably humble, to appreciate what we do not know and cannot fully understand. In this context, a favorite story recounted by the nineteenth-century Danish philosopher and theologian, Soren Kierkegaard, comes to mind. Kierkegaard ([1845] 1958:92-93) was sitting at a café one day, contemplating all the ways in which the geniuses of his time had discovered ways to make life easier for people. He wondered what contribution he might make. As he smoked his cigar and watched the servant girls go by, it suddenly occurred to him: he would help make everything difficult. And so it is with philosophers. In some respects, they help us to acknowledge how difficult it is, in the final analysis, to fully explain the nature of our existence and the behavior of human beings.

As an undergraduate, I minored in philosophy, while majoring in sociology, with a criminological specialization. Perhaps no undergraduate course made more of impression on me than a course on existentialism. It may be true that existentialism has not been in vogue for some good time now. But the key insights of existentialists, from Kierkegaard to Jean-Paul Sartre, open up a whole new way of thinking about our existence and our responsibility as human beings. "Existence precedes essence" is one of these key propositions. Human beings must recognize that it is up to them to give meaning to the world they find themselves inhabiting. Human consciousness means that human beings are different from things, and must take responsibility for their actions. To claim that one has no choice is to deceive oneself, to be in bad faith, in this view. Jean-Paul Sartre (1952) applied this framework to his massive exploration of the thief and criminal— and ultimately, the successful writer—Jean Genet, in his book *Saint Genet*. This work remains among the most original and provocative interpretations of criminality.

Philosophers continue to contend with questions that no other discipline has been able to answer decisively, or convincingly. Metaphysics, a branch of philosophy, is concerned with the ultimate nature of reality. The simplest construct on one enduring metaphysical issue is this: Is reality objective, or subjective? Is it "out there," or in the mind of the observer? This ancient question has some profoundly important implications for students of crime. Is crime best understood as an objective fact or as a subjective construct? In the latter interpretation, we focus especially on how some kinds of behavior came to be designated as criminal while other behavior, which would appear to be equally harmful or even more harmful, did not. Richard Quinney (1970), in his influential book *The Social Reality of Crime*, called attention to how crime as a category is socially constructed. Those with greater power in society are also in a position to shape the "reality" of society, and typically do so in a way that is skewed to protect their interests and values. This fundamental insight underlies many theories in criminology, particularly those that fall into the subgrouping of "conflict theories."

The question of whether humans have a free will, in some meaningful sense, or whether such a belief is an illusion, and human behavior is determined by various internal and external forces, is also a key question that philosophers have contended with over a period of thousands of years. Stephen Mathis, in a footnote in the chapter you have just read, suggests that philosophers of crime and law are no longer especially interested in this question. On some level, though, the question remains central to how we think about criminals, how we respond to them, and how we evaluate our own choices. The two basic positions on this question are known as volunteerism and determinism (with intermediate positions classified as soft voluntarism and soft determinism). This ancient question cuts to the heart of a criminological concern: Do those who engage in criminal acts do so vol-

untarily, or because various forces "determine" their behavior? Historically, the criminal law in our tradition has adopted the voluntarist position,
and generally assumes that those who break laws do so willfully and voluntarily, are responsible for their actions, and must be punished accordingly.
However, there are some recognized exceptions to this general assumption,
such as underage status or serious mental illness, taking the form of legally
recognizable insanity. On the other hand, a massive body of social scientific
research over a period of more than a century has demonstrated the impact
and influence of many different factors on human behavior. Early in the
twenty-first century, with all of our large body of knowledge on crime
and criminal behavior, I do not believe we can assert with complete confidence that we wholly understand why those who commit crimes do so,
and to what extent—if at all—they do so "voluntarily" in any truly meaningful
sense. As a society, we may have no practical alternative to assuming that
most mature individuals have chosen to break the law, and can accordingly
be held accountable for their actions. But it does not follow from this that
we can claim to know that this assumption is correct, or is an illusion on
some level.

If we adopt the conventional assumption that humans are capable of
making meaningful choices, philosophy also calls our attention to another
critical question: Are we generally obliged to comply with law, and legal
orders? And under which circumstances—if any—are we justified in not
complying with law? This question goes to the legitimacy of a legal order,
or the extent to which it is deserving of compliance. Mathis, in his chapter, addresses some aspects of the complex relationship between law and
morality, and the moral validity of some laws and some punishments. The
legitimacy-of-law question is another dimension of this complex relationship. The concept of legitimation, or validity, has been investigated by
political scientists, sociologists, and psychologists, among others, who
have been interested in the grounds for legitimating a legal order, and the
specific attributes and attitudes of those who comply and fail to comply with
law. Within the discipline of philosophy, the reasoning of Henry David
Thoreau, Mahatma Gandhi, and Martin Luther King Jr.—to name three celebrated proponents of civil disobedience who went to jail rather than
comply with unjust or bad laws—has been of interest. Military and civilian
subordinates within any legal order are generally expected to comply with
orders by those higher in the chain of command, but how does one dis-
criminate between valid orders and evil, or criminal, orders? This has also
been a question of some interest to philosophers. In a related vein, if a central mission of any criminal justice system is to realize justice and to achieve
just outcomes, what are the proper criteria for establishing whether this
objective is met? Some aspects of this key philosophical question are
explored in Mathis's chapter.

Finally, some mention should be made of that branch of philosophy
known as epistemology, which investigates the forms, sources, and limits

of knowledge. All that we know or claim to know about crime, criminals, and criminal justice, is based on some form of knowledge. Such knowledge comes to us in many different ways, and from many different sources. We should always be conscious of the enduring philosophical question here—famously addressed by Plato, among others, in ancient times—of what our knowledge is based upon, and the reliability or validity of what we claim to know. Sir Francis Bacon ([1620] 1960:47-49), in the seventeenth century, identified what he characterized as "idols" that interfere with our ability to know the world scientifically. These idols include: Idols of the Tribe, or the human tendency to impose artificial order on the world; Idols of the Cave, or the human tendency to be influenced by our particular background; Idols of the Marketplace, or the distortions that take place in representing our observations accurately, through our choice of words; and Idols of the Theater, or the tendency to see the world as some great thinker of the past said we should. It seems to me that these "idols" still play a significant role in any effort to describe, explain, and predict about criminality, crime, and criminal justice, in a disinterested manner.

Altogether, then, criminology students are well-advised to attend to philosophy in the course of their education, and to keep philosophical questions in mind as they pursue an understanding of crime. Philosophy can advance our understanding; philosophy also reminds us of the ultimate limitations on our understanding. Perhaps that great, philosophical novelist, Fyodor Dostoevsky, in his *Notes from Underground* (1864), was correct when he suggested that as human beings we really do not want a full understanding of our behavior and actions, we do not want to be "piano keys" simply played upon by forces beyond our control, we do not want to live by formula, and we do not want to live in a "Crystal Palace"—or utopia—where we cannot stick out our tongue. But we can benefit from knowing as much as possible about criminality, crime, and criminal justice, even if we should neither expect—or perhaps even hope—to know everything about these topics.

References

Bacon, F. [1620] (1960). *The New Organum and Related Writings.* New York: Macmillan.

Dostoevsky, F. [1864] (2004). *Notes from Underground.* New York: Everyman's Library.

Kierkegaard, S. [1845] (1958). *The Journals of Kierkegaard.* Edited and translated by Alexander Dru. New York: Harper & Row.

Quinney, R. (1970). *The Social Reality of Crime.* Boston: Little Brown.

Sartre, J. [1952] (1963). *Saint Genet.* New York: New American Library.

Chapter Seven

Religious Studies and Crime

Edwin C. Hostetter

In the commentary that follows this chapter, noted criminologist Howard Zehr discusses how the field of criminology, in general, has tended to ignore the discipline of religious studies and its importance in understanding crime. There are three main reasons why, in this case as in many others, too little knowledge can be a dangerous thing. First, a potential area for study that has just begun to receive attention among criminologists is the relationship between *religiosity*, or the prominence of religion in one's life, and crime. Recent studies have been formulated to examine the possible link between religious life and law-abiding behavior. Such studies focus on the role that religion plays in teaching individuals to respect *sacred* beliefs or divine law, which is taught within churches or other places of worship and influence individuals to engage in behaviors that are consistent with those beliefs. Are adults who regularly attend church less likely to commit crimes? Are children who are raised in religious environments less likely to become involved in delinquent activities?

Second, a related area for study, and one which Zehr, in particular, has examined, has to do with the creation and acceptance of *secular* laws, or laws proscribed by civil societies that come from governmental entities such as legislatures and courts. To what extent have secular laws found justification in sacred teachings? When and where have religions affected the creation of laws? Related questions have to do with the fact that secular laws represent societies, not religions, and therefore transcend differences across religious beliefs. Yet issues involving religious beliefs in the United States, for example, often remain active in the public forum long after secular laws become established in the legal system. Good examples of conflict between church and state in the United States are the continuation of vehement disagreement on either side of *Roe v. Wade* or the use of capital punishment.

A third argument for not ignoring religion is the union of the first two points: How does the experience of religion, which generally first occurs in childhood, predispose individuals to accept not only sacred rules of conduct within their religious community but also civil laws proscribing behavior in the larger society? Do the moral teachings of the church, temple, or mosque sensitize individuals to accept the imposition of laws more generally? Do children who develop an understanding of "sin" in the Christian tradition, for example, have a similar understanding of "crime" in the legal sense? In communities where "ex-communication" is part of the religious tradition, such as Catholicism and the Amish culture, does the philosophy of *retribution*, or imposing moral payback on offenders, become an accepted justification for secular law? Where religious traditions that accentuate atonement and restitution have existed, as in many native and indigenous societies, does the legal philosophy of *restitution*, or achieving a satisfactory closure for the victim, tend to have more influence in the criminal codes of those societies?

As they exist today, the two academic disciplines of criminology and religious studies may appear, at first glance, to be completely independent of one another, yet examples of overlapping interests abound. Consider the following two cases:

> On a recent New Year's Eve near Houston, Texas, a man slapped his wife during an argument about her drinking problem. Three weeks later, a judge sentenced him to 12 months' probation—and ordered him to take a yoga class during that time. Yoga is a regimen of physical exercise and spiritual meditation that has its roots in the Hindu religion in India. The bending and stretching poses, along with deep breathing techniques, are designed to instill feelings of peacefulness in those who faithfully adhere to the practice of yoga. "It's part of anger management," said the judge. "I thought [yoga] would help him realize that he only has control over himself" (Tilghman, 2004). Meanwhile, in Albuquerque, New Mexico, followers of Uniaode Vegetal, a Brazilian religion, claimed that a local law prohibiting their use of an exotic tea during religious ceremonies was a violation of a 1993 federal law that protects such religious practice. Adherents of this faith maintained that the tea, brewed from the ayahuasca root, produces a dreamlike state that is essential to their religion. (Willing, 2004)

These cases illustrate two ways in which the disciplines of religious studies and criminology overlap. The first case shows how the criminal court can co-opt or integrate certain religious practices into secular criminal proceedings. The second case demonstrates the legal dominance of the secular court over the exercise of a specific religious ritual. The right to free speech, including the practice of one's religion, is subordinate to the civil law in a secular society such as the United States, which enforces a separation of church and state. In contrast to the secular model found in the United States and in many countries throughout the world, *fundamentalist* societies, such as Iran and Sudan, are governed by religious orthodoxy and make little or no distinction between divine law and the laws enforced by the courts.

Scholarly Methods and Theories

The study of religion in academic or nontheological settings is a modern trend whose roots lie mainly in the Enlightenment Era. European scholars first made observations of "exotic" religious customs and rituals during the sixteenth century, and by the nineteenth century, a significant number of Indian and Chinese philosophical and doctrinal texts, such as the *Vedas* in the Hindu religion, were being translated into European languages. Certain theories on the origin of religion were proposed at that time as well. The discipline of religious studies was born in an intellectual atmosphere that allowed scholars to analyze religion from a point of view that was not necessarily either spiritual or antispiritual. No longer satisfied with merely guessing about the origin of religion, early anthropologists based their theories on *observation*. These early scholars investigated contemporary "primitive" religions and used *cross-cultural methods* to reanalyze reports of religious life during ancient times. The goal was to describe, compare, and explain spirituality's history, diversity, and persistence in all civilizations. Later, many anthropologists were reluctant to simply assume that cultural patterns of contemporary tribal societies were valid indicators of prehistorical tribal life, and instead placed scholarly emphasis on the function of religion in their own contemporary era.

Today's scholars in religious studies use systematic methods to understand the various meanings that religions attach to the sacred world. Religious studies, as a scholarly discipline, is characterized by a variety of methodologies. For example, scholars might translate religious texts from their original ancient languages so that the earliest traditions can become more widely known. They might conduct *textual criticism*, or critical readings of religious writings, using standard methods of *literary analysis* to describe the genre or style of the text, or to determine authorship, source material, or historical context. Source critics have enhanced our understanding of the Bible, including the book of Isaiah, a complex text in Jewish scripture in which scholars identified the contributions of three distinct authors, separated by time and place and writing for different audiences. Literary analysis might explore common themes, focus on character analysis, or compare literary elements using multiple texts. *Critical analysis* of religious texts involves the study of contradictions or inconsistencies within a religion's texts, or comparing sacred texts' accounts of history, for example, with nonreligious sources of information that provide alternative historical or scientific explanations.

Scholars of *comparative religion* compare characteristics of different religions. Their research might discuss both similarities and differences among various religions' writings and practices. Some religion scholars conduct *ethnographic studies*, or fieldwork that involves directly observing religious actions and interviewing participants. Ethnography is used to find out what religious persons say about their faiths and observe how the faiths are practiced within religious communities. For example, ethnographers have demonstrated how the spirituality of the Nuer tribe in East Africa, which lacks a formal government, nonetheless inhibits crime by compensating the injured and using ritual sacrifice to demonstrate purification and reintegration of the offender.

One recently completed project in the field of comparative religions was the Pluralism Project led by Diana Eck (1993). Through interviews with urban residents around the United States, this project attempted to map the diversity of religions in the United States and learn how different religious communities coexist in a diversified society. The project addressed three questions: What do specific American cities now look like, religiously? How are the various religious traditions of Hinduism, Buddhism, Islam, Sikhism, and so on changing as they become established in the American context? And how is the culture of the United States changing as a consequence of the various religious traditions? The recent diversity of immigrants moving to the United States has raised new questions about beliefs and cultural practices in our multireligious society. For example, most Americans probably do not think of Houston, Texas, in this way, but the Pluralism Project found that it is the only city in the United States with a comprehensive plan for designing Islamic places of worship. The Islamic Society of Greater Houston has divided the city into eight geographic zones, with a main mosque and satellite mosques proposed throughout the city (Eck, 2001).

In relation to crime, the study of religion covers myriad topics, including moral behavior and moral authority. For example, German economist Max Weber (1864-1920) emphasized how religious values are translated into social sanctions through conceptions of the sacred, which lend credibility to socially imposed norms. British anthropologist A.R. Radcliffe-Brown (1881-1955) portrayed religion as a system of ritualized behaviors and shared symbols that enabled human beings—by establishing common moods and motivations in people—to live harmoniously and collectively. However, it was French sociologist Emile Durkheim (1858-1917) who first became aware that respect for sacred things essentially equaled respect for moral authority. He saw how closely a society's religious symbols were integrated with the group's moral sentiments. Religious beliefs sanctify norms of conduct and provide justification for adhering to them, while religious rituals elicit attitudes strengthening the awe in which such norms are held. For example, certain African tribal beliefs warn that if relatives turn their backs on orphaned children, they will be punished supernaturally by the child's deceased father—using the fear of being eternally haunted to discourage the abandonment of children. Thus, religion offers a strategic basis for social control and stability in the face of deviant tendencies and dangerous impulses. Stated another way, religion frees people from unchecked desire and binds them ethically within a community. Durkheim wrote: "That is why penal law is not alone essentially religious in origin, but indeed always retains a certain religious stamp. It is because the acts that it punishes appear to be attacks upon something transcendent" (1949:100). Durkheim went so far as to locate the essence of religion in the identity of the social group. Durkheim argued that religion developed in order to encourage social cohesion and give meaning to social institutions, such as public religious holidays, that express the rhythm of collective activity and ensure its regularity. He never doubted that group consciousness is as real as individual experiences and that religion is a moral force, created in a group process, that binds groups together. Wherever there are groups or societies of individuals, their concerns about crime and justice will intersect with the subject of religion. The remainder of this chapter will attempt to show how spiritual traditions have defined what constitutes criminal behavior, inhibited criminal behavior, and shaped the punishment for criminal behavior.

Buddhism, Christianity, and Islam

The following examination of religion, transgressions, and crime will mainly cover comparisons and contrasts among sacred texts and contemporary practice in three world religions: Buddhism, Christianity, and Islam. These major faiths were chosen to represent the study of religion because they are global and are not fundamentally tied to a particular ethnicity, minimizing the difficulty of separating "religion" from "ethnic culture." Buddhism, Christianity, and Islam will serve as useful spiritualities to study because their texts, although given different interpretations depending on the culture or society that practices those faiths, tend more than others to represent religious, as opposed to cultural, beliefs. Our attention will focus on mainstream interpretations of each tradition, although it should be noted that alternative interpretations beyond the scope of this chapter may be equally valid. The material will be divided into three sections: (1) laws, transgressions, and crimes, (2) punishment, and (3) restorative justice.

We will begin our comparison of three religions with a brief outline of the sacred teachings of Buddhism, Christianity, and Islam. The Theravada strain of Buddhism is the oldest of the three religions. Theravada Buddhism was founded by Siddhartha Gautama, who was not a god, notably, but the son of a king living in northeast India. Gautama was born around 566 BCE and at the age of 35 he became an enlightened person (that is, a "Buddha") and subsequently founded the religion known as Buddhism. Gautama's disciples spread his teachings to the rest of Asia and eventually to Europe and the Americas. Unlike *theistic* religions, which assume the existence of a god, Buddhism does not believe in a god or deity as the ultimate reality or higher power. In Gautama's day, the Indian people worshipped and offered sacrifices to many gods to relieve their burdens and nevertheless great suffering persisted, which he observed with deep concern. After his enlightenment experience, Gautama preached the "Four Noble Truths," which became the core of Buddhism: (1) There is suffering. (2) The cause of suffering is desire. (3) There is a way to overcome desire and become free from suffering. (4) The eightfold path, which guides its followers to resist desires and material attachments and actively respond to human suffering, leads to *nirvana* or freedom from suffering. The eightfold path consists of "right" understanding, thoughts, speech, action, livelihood, effort, mindfulness, and concentration.

Box 7.1 • Buddhism

When you practice whether bowing or sitting or chanting, there is a moment where the self is forgotten and when the self is forgotten, it is a realization experience. What has been forgotten is the concept of the self, and because you have forgotten the concept of the self, you have become one with everything, or one with the universe (research subject quoted in Eck, 1994).

Christianity, the second oldest religion of the three that we are examining here and the faith with which most Americans identify, is approximately 2,000 years old. Jesus was born in Palestine and was persecuted by Roman emperors because he taught the existence of God and in doing so, challenged the emperors' positions as ultimate rulers on earth. At the age of 33, Jesus was executed by the Romans but, according to his disciples, was raised from the dead by God three days later. His disciples—called Christians—worship him as the anointed one, or "Christ," and the son of God, especially in Europe, the Americas, and Africa. For Christians, belief in Jesus as the Christ is necessary for human salvation, or the cure for sin. Through him, people are saved from eternal damnation. But left to their own devices, humans are not capable of saving themselves. In Roman Catholic Christianity, for example, forgiveness and salvation are possible as long as sinners confess and atone for their misdeeds.

Islam is the youngest of the three religions. Muhammad, who was born into a merchant family in western Arabia around 570 CE, did not begin to preach until after his fortieth birthday. Muhammad received a series of divine visitations from the archangel Gabriel about *"islam"* (or submission) to *Allah*—the Arabic word for God. Muslims believe that Muhammad recorded the word of God, as transmitted to him by Gabriel, in the *Quran*, the holy book which became the basis for the religion of Islam. Islamic practice requires affirming a core belief in God; praying five times daily; paying an alms tax for the poor; fasting during the ninth month, known as Ramadan; and traveling on pilgrimage to Mecca, in Saudi Arabia. Most of Muhammad's Muslim followers now populate Asia, Africa, and Europe.

All three religions speak of encouraging virtuous actions and commitment to religious practice and preach religious laws and rules that expressly prohibit certain behaviors. Buddhists must refrain from harming any living being, taking what is not given, misusing the senses, engaging in wrong speech, and taking drugs or drinks that cloud the mind. Christians believe in the Bible's Ten Commandments, which forbid killing, adultery, stealing, bearing false witness, and coveting or desiring what belongs to others. In the *Quran,* similar Islamic prohibitions include, among other things, squandering wealth, killing one's children for fear or want, committing adultery, or killing any person Allah has protected.

Laws, Transgressions, and Crimes

As we consider how different religious texts examine crime and law, a couple of questions are important to consider. First, to what extent do religious teachings about immorality and transgressions or sins, based on sacred texts, continue to guide beliefs and practices about crime today? Second, how do the different religious perspectives relate to one another? Some people believe that each religion is an alternative path to a common destination of sacred truth, while others claim that their religion provides the only correct spiritual path to salvation.

All three religions discussed above have something to say about the definition of law, meaning the religious laws adhered to within their spiritual communities. Christianity and Islam share the common claim that law comes from God. Theravada Buddhism, however, does not profess a god or deity as the ultimate reality, and consequently does not teach that law can be transmitted either directly or indirectly by such a divine being. Rather than rely on divine law, Theravada Buddhists assert that there is a certain standard of truth to which laws on earth should conform. Ashoka, a Buddhist emperor who ruled India between 200 and 300 BCE, worked devoutly to meet the standard of truth. He promoted impartiality in legal procedures and punishments, and he commissioned officers "to work among prisoners to distribute money to those who have many children, to secure the release of those who were instigated to crime by others, and to pardon those who are very aged" (as quoted in Nikam and McKeon, 1959:59). Ashoka was the first king to issue a number of Buddhist edicts, or laws governing conduct, which were posted on rocks and pillars across India so that the Indian people would become familiar with them. Because many of his people were illiterate, Ashoka appointed ministers to read these statutes to his subjects.

Religious scholars of Christianity have examined, to some extent, the origins of "human" or secular laws as an outgrowth of divine teachings about morality and "sin." Timothy Gorringe (1996) considered the differences between crimes, or violations of human law, and sins, or immoral acts, as taught within religious scripture. Gorringe found several different meanings of these two terms in Christian teachings: (1) Crime and sin are innately identical acts and differ only in the type of response they provoke, meaning that some acts are criminalized while others are not. Governments punish *crimes* but stay away from criminalizing any remaining *sins* only because they find some political advantage in doing so. (2) Crime is a subset of the broader category of sin. Crimes are those sins that violate not only divine laws, but human laws as well. Every crime is a sin, but not every sin is a crime. (3) Crime and sin exist independently and also overlap, depending on the circumstances. Some sins, such as theft, breach legal obligations and become crimes as well as sins. The commission of a crime, when it willfully ignores an existing public law, breaches moral obligations and becomes a sin.

Arguing that none of these propositions is complete because none accounts for the possibility of unjust laws, Gorringe has suggested a modified combination of the second and third definitions: Breaking a *just* law yields a crime, and hence a sin at the same time. Breaking an unjust law, however, may be a crime, because it is a violation of the law, but is not a sin, because the law was unjust to begin with. Finally, in Christianity, an act of rebellion against God alone, such as blasphemy, would be considered a sin but not a crime because it is forbidden in the religious community but not in the secular community (Gorringe, 1996).

Christianity at its roots espouses a concern for the relatively powerless at the hands of the powerful, and this concern is expressed by Biblical law. For example, Christians believe that a crime is more severe when an official abuses his or her authority in the perpetration of the crime. The same is true when either the transgressor or the victim is famous or wealthy (Eltz, 1967). Christianity also makes the observation that individuals' moral character can be negatively shaped through exploitation and deprivation, which supports the belief that criminal behavior has social causes. Nevertheless, Christians generally concede that a person's background or psychological state cannot be the sole reason for her or his transgressions.

Box 7.2 • Christianity

"What it boils down to for me is that I was born in America in the middle of the twentieth century, as at that time a "Negro," and brought with me the heritage of slavery and the black church. Jesus Christ then becomes a figure that represents liberation, spiritual freedom, hope, and certainly a relationship to people who are down-and-out, on the fringes. So Jesus Christ is my friend, and a historical figure that invites hope." Claudia Highbaugh (interviewed in Eck, 1994).

Buddhists hold nearly the same outlook on crimes by the powerful as Christians. Buddhist teachings specifically caution against corrupt leaders who might inspire their subordinates to emulate their corruption (Ratnapaia, 1993). Buddhists also believe that social injustice, such as the unequal distribution of property, leads to poverty, which in turn encourages theft and even murder. Consider the fictional tale of King Dalhanemi, who suffered the consequences of social inequality when the people turned to crime and disorder under his rule. The sacred document *Digha Nikaya* reports: "Thus, from the not giving of property to the needy, poverty became rife, from the growth of poverty, the taking of what was not given increased, from the increase of theft, the use of weapons increased, from the increased use of weapons, the taking of life increased—and from the increase in the taking of life, people's life-span decreased, their beauty decreased" (as quoted in Walshe, 1995:399-400). Islam contains similar themes and states that governments, corporations, and individuals must care for the poor so they will not be compelled to commit theft and, ultimately, because it is God's will.

In Islam, the basis for morality can be found in the *Sharia,* or divine law. As in Christianity, illegal and criminal behaviors *per se* are not discussed differently in the *Sharia* from what is unreligious, unethical, or immoral. The *Quran* as well as the *Sunna,* or early "customs" did not anticipate all behaviors in any situation, so prior to the tenth century, Muslim followers learned to use *analogical reasoning* or *ijtihad* to determine, by analogy, if a given deed had violated the divine law. If needed, Muslims often called on trained interpreters of the law to draw analogies between the situation in question and the material found in the *Quran* and *Sunna.* Following the tenth century, the use of *ijtihad* came to an end. Muslims concluded that the development of Islamic law was complete by then and that *Sharia,* determined to be absolute, required no further independent interpretations based on *ijtihad.*

Muslims believe strongly that their cultural environment should reflect their religious values of right and wrong. In Muslim culture, what is right is encouraged and assisted, such as modesty in dress, while what is wrong is discouraged and diminished, such as mixed-gender gatherings. Muslims believe that the inner urge to commit crime is suppressed by such public examples of moral conduct, as well as protection of the poor. For example, Islamic law condemns those merchants who hoard food. By law, food merchants cannot capitalize on opportunities to monopolize and charge higher prices but are forced to sell to consumers at reasonable prices to avoid oppressing the public (Lippman, McConville, and Yerushalmi, 1988:37). Fraud in weights and measures is equally condemned; it is identified outright as theft. Significant exceptions to the Islamic laws of theft or fraud include the taking of such "impure" items as wine, pigs, or dogs: "There is no amputation [cutting off a hand] if what was stolen was impurity (which cannot constitute property) such as wine, or a pig or dog, or the skin of an animal not ritually slaughtered. But if the container of the wine was worth the minimum amount, amputation follows" (Williams, 1971:151).

The changing nature of religion, law, and culture is illustrated in studies of Islamic law in contemporary Muslim societies. During the 1970s and 1980s, the legislative bodies of several Muslim countries, including Saudi Arabia, Libya, Pakistan, Iran, and Sudan, introduced *Sharia,* or Islamic divine law, into their criminal code, so that divine law replaced parts of the existing legal code. As a result, the legal codes of these countries have at least in part returned to the early period when Islam was first established 1500 years ago, with serious consequences. For example, Saudi Arabia's Ministry of Justice, which is based on *Sharia,* was created by King Faisal in 1970 and oversees more than 300 *Sharia* courts. The Supreme Judicial Council approves all sentences of death, amputations for theft crimes, and stoning for adultery. The African nation of Libya has recently restored the right of the next of kin of a murder victim to choose between demanding retaliation (death to the murderer) or "blood money" (payment from the murderer). While not yet carried out in Pakistan, stoning and amputation are now legally accepted forms of punishment. In Iran, sentences of stoning for sexual offenses were imposed during the 1970s and 1980s. Iranian laws include rules that guide the infliction of retaliation by the victim, compensation for homicide and injury, and flogging for some 50 offenses—for example, operating a car without a driver's license. During the 1970s, Sudan introduced a penal code by which most offenses were to be punished with public flogging, imprisonment, and/or a fine. At least 100 Sudanese have had their limbs amputated, and several more have been crucified.

One further note about Islam and other recently established religions in contemporary U.S. society has to do with crimes committed against religious believers by those who are threatened by their mere presence. In the reaction to the tragic events of September 11, 2001, the attention on religion was unmistakable: increased hate crimes against Muslim Americans, property damage to mosques, shootings, and even murders. The fact that many Americans knew little if anything about Islam became obvious when Sikhs, who are not Muslims, were targeted for anti-Muslim hate crimes. Religions that have been recently established in the United States have a physical presence that may be construed as threatening to some. Today there is often dramatic architecture used to showcase temples, mosques, and churches, unlike 20 years ago, when the first generation of American mosques, for example, were inexpensively—and for the most part, invisibly—housed within unmarked warehouses,

Hsi Lai Temple (Hacienda Heights, California). *With permission of Robert Marinelli, Jr.*

storefronts, or gymnasiums. During the 1980s and 1990s, visually striking Islamic mosques were constructed around the country, as were multimillion-dollar Hindu temples and, perhaps most notably, the architecturally dominating Hsi Lai Temple in Hacienda Heights, California, a Buddhist temple that was fought by neighbors initially, but which is now perceived as a magnificent addition to the landscape (Eck, 2001).

Punishment

The relationship between contemporary societies' criminal sentencing codes and their dominant religions' philosophies of punishment is an area for future study but, to date, it has not received much attention by academic scholars. However, it is possible to discern the underlying philosophies used in law and criminal justice within the sacred teachings of our three religions, particularly retribution, deterrence, and rehabilitation. The philosophy of restorative justice will be considered in the following section.

Determining the appropriate punishment for a given crime is always a complicated matter in the criminal justice system. A reading of sacred religious texts suggests that establishing principles to guide the choice of punishment has been very important to followers of each religion. Buddhists believe that we have lived multiple lives in the past and anticipate the possibility of continued lives into the future, offering multiple chances to achieve enlightenment but at the same time increasing the possibility that commission of a misdeed will lead to increased suffering, or failure to achieve enlightenment. Meritorious behavior in this life will result in less suffering in the next one, but criminal behavior will result not only in the possibility of punishment in this lifetime, but in a future life of suffering. Within Buddhist monastic codes, punishments for moral transgressions are proportionate to each transgression. Severe penalties match severe violations; minor penalties match minor violations. More broadly, whether king or slave, all Buddhists suffer the consequences of violating religious law, such as being deprived, at least temporarily, of the "karmic reward" of enlightenment. Yet one's past behavior and lifestyle—that is, one's character—bear on the penalty one might receive for an offense. How an accused individual's friends have conducted themselves—that is, the company he or she keeps—is also weighed, along with the individual's intention. If the alleged offender has confessed to wrongdoing, her or his punishment may be reduced. There are many stories in the ancient texts that portray criminals who renounce material possessions and convert to lives of pious observance.

Buddhism is not a single religious tradition but instead has been influenced by different cultural traditions. Tibetan Buddhism, whose spiritual leader is the Dalai Lama, is a religion that is concerned with a broad range of humanitarian and environmental causes. Tibetan Buddhism is associated with the refugee Tibetan community, which is currently in exile due to the Chinese occupation of Tibet in 1959. Prior to the Chinese takeover, the Tibetan system for punishing offenders was based on a premodern *theocracy,* or "rule by the deity," represented by religious leaders who claimed to represent the divine on earth. The system dictated differential treatment according to the socioeconomic status of the victim. Although equal punishment of perpetrators for similar crimes is possible, or in principle, ideal, there is deliberate inequality that may be perceived as discrimination in terms of the social standing of the victim.

The punishment model developed in Tibet is shown in Box 7.3. Under this model any type of punishment could be awarded for any type of crime. Tibetan law codes contained only a few passages that directly correlated specific infractions with specific punishments. Each type of offense was considered to be the product of its own detailed factors: the circumstances of the crime, including location, time of year, the presence of a mob; the position—social category, occupation, gender, age, rank, record of previous crimes, and wealth—of both the victim and the accused; and the mental state of the accused, including motivation and intent.

Box 7.3 • Tibetan Buddhist Punishment Rankings Based on Victims' Social Status

Category of crime victim	Examples of crime victim	Amount of monetary payment
High	Dalai Lama Monks	80-200 sung*
Medium	Government workers Landowners	40-60 sung*
Low	Blacksmiths Executioners	5-20 sung*

*A sung equals approximately one ounce of gold or silver, usually a coin.

Adapted from Rebecca Redwood French, *The Golden Yoke: The Legal Cosmology of Buddhist Tibet*. Ithaca: Cornell University Press, 1995, 114.

The Tibetan interpretation of Buddhism is unique among Buddhists because its direct translation into law, unlike other Buddhist societies, retained a strongly monastic element from the eighth century CE. In other contemporary Buddhist societies, the favored punishments tend to be fines or imprisonment. Fines, in particular, are levied for abortion, drinking alcohol, and slander. The penalty in the case of some offenses is losing one's right to vote in political elections. When probation is the consequence, it is usually supervised by a network of family members and neighborhood residents

(Bhagvat, n.d.; Ratnapala, 1993). Buddhist philosophy on prisons allows for *incapacitation*—that is, penitentiaries that protect the community by incarcerating lawbreakers—but more significantly, for *rehabilitation*: to educate offenders and change them for the better (Ratnapala, 1993).

One purpose of the Tibetan model was *restitution*—to compensate victims for their losses financially. Financial payments demanded from defendants were distributed to victims in an attempt to rectify the possible social harm caused by the crime. Another purpose of punishment was *deterrence*—to impress upon criminals the grievousness of their acts so that they would not repeat their offenses, and to impress upon the public at large the wrongfulness of criminal behavior. The compensation for murder depended upon the social level of the victim, and the punishment for victimizing government officials or landowners was at least three times higher than for victimizing blacksmiths or executioners, while the punishment for murdering a religious leader or monk was at least twice that of a government official.

Similarly in Islam, characteristics of the victim such as gender or religion partly determine the sentence imposed on the offender. For instance, only half the compensation can be demanded for the murder of a woman, a Jew, or a Christian, compared with a male Muslim (Juynboll, 1914:292). Punishment also varies depending on the victim's age. In Islam, both deterrence and retribution are underlying themes. Homicide normally results in capital punishment, and assault and battery is punished by the infliction of pain equivalent to the physical injury. If either crime is unintentional, however, less severe consequences may replace the customary execution or mutilation. Lighter punishments are also imposed if people kill or wound when they have a right to do so: for instance, a man who catches his wife's rapist or a woman who finds a burglar in her house. Accidental killing leads to paying a certain amount of money or goods of equivalent value to the surviving kin. For example, the Islamic holy book, the *Quran*, states:

> It is unlawful for a believer to kill another believer, accidents excepted. He that accidentally kills a believer must free one Muslim slave and pay blood-money to the family of the victim, unless they choose to give it away in alms. If the victim be a Muslim from a hostile tribe, the penalty is the freeing of one Muslim slave. But if the victim be a member of an allied tribe, then blood-money must be paid to his family and a Muslim slave set free. He that lacks the means must fast two consecutive months. Such is the penance imposed by God: God is all-knowing and wise. (Dawood, 1990:92)

In Islam, accidental wounding also leads to paying a compensatory fine. Full compensation is charged for a singular body part that is hurt, such as a nose. One-half compensation is charged for doubles, like a foot; one-fourth for an eyelid; 10 percent for a finger; and one-thirtieth for a knuckle (Juynboll, 1914:292). Even if the harm was deliberate, retaliatory execution or mutilation is not imposed in cases in which a father or a teacher kills a child through corporal discipline, nor where a father or a male guardian kills a female who is guilty of unlawful sexual intercourse. Similarly, injury brought either by a free person onto a slave or by a man onto a woman does not invoke the right to retaliation (Lippman, McConville, and Yerushalmi, 1988).

Islamic law is very specific as to crimes involving private conduct. For example, the *Quran* prescribes stoning to death for married people who commit adultery. The unmarried individual who sleeps with a married person might be punished by death too, or else by mutilation or imprisonment. However, if neither person is married to others and they are found having sex together, the punishment is merely a whipping. Regardless of the circumstance, both the man and the woman experience an identical punishment. If they are not guilty but were falsely accused of illicit lovemaking, then the accuser is penalized with 80 lashes from a whip. The *Quran* dictates that the punishment for adultery should be witnessed by a crowd, which upholds the doctrine of deterrence. Thus, when punishment is imposed in a public manner, it is intended that the fear it generates will prevent people from imitating the offenders.

Like Muslims, early Christians found deterrence and retribution to be useful principles in implementing punishment, particularly in the use of the death penalty during the first 500 years of the last millennium. Besides bringing revenge on murderers and making it impossible for them to kill again, many Christians believed that executions persuaded others not to take human life without justification. As stated by Roman theologian Saint Augustine in 414 CE:

> Surely, it is not without purpose that we have the institution of the power of kings, the death penalty of the judge, the barbed hooks of the executioner, the weapons of the soldier, the right of punishment of the overlord, even the severity of the good father. All those things have their methods, their causes, their reasons, their practical benefits. While these are feared, the wicked are kept within bounds and the good live more peacefully among the wicked. . . . It is not without advantage that human recklessness should be confined by fear of the law so that innocence may be safe among evil-doers, and the evil-doers themselves may be cured by calling on God when their freedom of action is held in check by fear of punishment. (as quoted in Parsons, 1951-56, 3:293)

In the early development of the American colonies, the Christian religion supported a punishment model that was based on retribution—that a punishment ought to match the crime, and that a perpetrator must pay for the crime—in other words, that imposing suffering on an offender is just and good. A weaker form of retributivism emphasized the value of punishment as an authoritative expression of society's moral condemnation for the wickedness involved in the offense (Gorringe, 1996). Despite the dominance of retribution as a guiding philosophy of punishment, Christianity—

influenced by Quaker principles and perhaps driven by labor needs in the colonies—played a major role in the development of the philosophy of *rehabilitation*, or achieving change in the offender through a planned program of intervention within the criminal justice system. Since the mid-seventeenth century, the Quakers (also known as the Society of Friends) were at the forefront of the movement to substitute the penitentiary for cruder sanctions, like corporal or capital punishment, with the aim of encouraging the offender to repent through contemplation.

During the nineteenth century, Quakers in particular lobbied for every prisoner to have an opportunity to reflect penitently on her or his misdeeds and to follow the guidance of one's inner light toward achieving a restored life. Because the teaching of spirituality through prison chaplains had become a regular element within prisons in predominantly Catholic and Christian nations since the sixteenth century, prison fellowship organizations spread the idea that reform was a very desirable by-product of imprisonment, with the hope that the community would offer forgiveness to repentant and reformed offenders (Durham, 1988; Hoekema, 1986).

Box 7.4 • Forgiveness

Of all Pope John Paul II's global journeys, the one of a few miles to a Rome prison in late December may be the most remembered. It was a journey of forgiveness. In meeting with Mehmet Ali Agca, the gunman who tried to kill him, John Paul was telling the world that the bullets that didn't destroy his body didn't harm his soul either.

A photograph of the visit, displayed on front pages around a planet starved for news of compassion, showed John Paul and Agca in a prison cell. They sat and talked under barred windows. Between this Christian and Moslem, reconciliation was stronger than any steel. Forgiveness is a force, not a gesture.

In John Paul's religion of Christianity, forgiveness is the ethic of non-retaliation that is perhaps the most central and most radical expression of faith. Christ died forgiving his killers. He took to the end what he had been teaching all along. When Peter asked if forgiving an offender seven times was enough—thinking no doubt he would be praised for his liberality—he was told no, it must be "seventy times seven." In other words, forgiveness is a token unless it is unlimited.

Colman McCarthy, "Pope John Paul II's Mission of Mercy," *The Washington Post*, January 8, 1984.

The development of the penitentiary in the United States had a false start with the introduction of solitary confinement, which was motivated by themes of repentant change in Christian religions but in practice was more retributive than rehabilitative (Allard and Northey, 2001). At the end of the eighteenth century and the beginning of the nineteenth, the Quakers of Philadelphia influenced city officials to approve the "Pennsylvania system" of imprisonment, which emphasized solitary confinement. Prior to that time, the most well-known model of individualized confinement was the Hospice of San Michele, erected in Rome by Pope Clement XI in 1704, which was historically significant because it kept inmates isolated and separated. The Quakers were impressed by this model and believed that applying individual treatment to all convicts would best accomplish the reform of criminals in the United States. Not only was solitary confinement expected to serve as a form of punishment, it was hoped to encourage contrite reflection and protect the new prisoners from becoming influenced through contact with the more sophisticated and hardened convicts. Rehabilitation could be completed through the enlightenment of religious instruction, the discipline of individual labor, and support from outside visitors.

In 1796, a few individual cells were built in Philadelphia's Walnut Street Jail. Later, in 1821, when a new institution, the Eastern State Penitentiary, was scheduled for construction in eastern Pennsylvania, the authorities chose a program of absolute solitary confinement, which was modeled after the Walnut Street Jail. The Eastern State Penitentiary held each inmate in a monastic-style cell with access to its own adjacent yard. Every prisoner entered her or his yard at different times. Water pipes were erected on the outside of cell walls to prevent prisoners from tapping out communications. In order to maintain complete silence, wardens wore socks over their shoes—and leather straps covered food-cart wheels. An austere atmosphere of silence, solitude, meditation, and isolation was created. By 1834, however, the practice of strict isolation was already losing support, and the Eastern State Penitentiary officially abandoned solitary confinement in 1913, for a variety of practical reasons. Running such an individualized prison proved to be prohibitively expensive. Income from inmate work in exclusively small trades (mainly shoemaking) did not cover the expenses of incarceration. Additionally, frequent claims that solitary confinement drove inmates to the point of insanity also contributed to ending the practice (Schmid, 2003).

During the twentieth century, the U.S. punishment philosophy experimented with rehabilitation models that were based on psychological and social work interventions. Mid-century rehabilitation advocates were influenced by the possibilities of psychiatry and social work, which were growing disciplines during the early part of the century, and prison therapeutic models were developed that emphasized counseling and other forms of treatment. Even while rehabilitation was the leading rationale for punishment, the philosophies of retribution and deterrence continued to play a role. Critics of rehabilitation began to raise objections about viewing crime as essentially pathological. Some disagreed with the theory of rehabilitation and argued that the philosophy of retribution needed to predominate instead. Others were concerned that under rehabilitative models, the length of incarceration was left open-ended and determined by rehabilitative as opposed to retributive goals.

Box 7.5 • Re-establishing Community

An increasing number of people are coming to see that any method of correction that is based in punishment—whatever the conditions and justifications for its use—is just another form of violence. Far from having the potential for helping people to heal personally and to restore their severed relationships, it disables and deconstructs them, thereby destroying the possibility of re-establishing community for those whose lives have been disrupted by harm.

Dennis Sullivan and Larry Tifft, *Restorative Justice: Healing the Foundations of Our Everyday Lives* (2001), p. viii.

Restorative Justice

As the quote by Dennis Sullivan and Larry Tifft above indicates, a different way of thinking about the notion of justice in the United States has occurred in the area of *restorative justice*—a *reconciliatory* response to handling criminal cases that addresses the needs of victims, communities, and offenders. This approach has been incorporated into program models for offenders in Vermont, Florida, and other states, and it is a primary component of the "Balanced and Restorative Justice" model used by many states' juvenile justice systems. Other U.S. programs that contain elements of restorative justice include the Victim Offender Reconciliation Program and the Victim Offender Mediation Program (which was initially tested with property crimes but later extended to serious crimes). In Canada, Community Chaplaincies and Circles of Support are initiatives that involve the faith communities in a more significant role with both offenders and victims.

In general, the practice of restorative justice involves five basic principles (Kurki, 1999):

1. Crime is more than a violation against the state's laws or authority.

2. Crime involves disruption to the victim and community as well as to the offender.

3. Harm is caused to the victim and community that must be repaired.

4. The victim, community, and offender should work together to determine the appropriate response to the crime, giving the formal criminal justice system a secondary role.

5. The response to the crime should be based on the needs of the victim, community, and offender.

Over the last couple of decades, restorative justice has evolved from an abstract concept to a coherent set of principles, and the philosophy has encouraged many new models in criminal justice such as *victim-offender mediation* and *family group conferencing* for offenders. Unlike retributive justice, which is concerned with the punishment the offender deserves based on the amount of harm caused by the crime, in restorative justice the focus is on the offender's repair of the harm he or she has caused to the victim and community. Restorative philosophy addresses a major gap in retributive philosophy, which is that after the court establishes the guilt of the offender, the criminal justice system can achieve the goal of retribution without any further contact with the victim. Additionally, the offender can serve out a sentence, say in prison, without addressing any of the needs of the victim, the community, or of his or her own. Restorative justice has roots in many religious traditions. (For an excellent overview of various religious traditions and how they fit into contemporary thinking about restorative justice, see Hadley, 2001.) For the purpose of the case study below, we will focus on one specific restorative justice program that fits within the teachings of Christianity.

Box 7.6 • Case Study: Restorative Justice

In the Christian concept of justice, the voice of the victim is the primary one. Forgiveness of the offender by the victim ("turn the other cheek") is an essential process for overcoming the devastation of crime. The act of forgiveness can repair fractured human relations and prevent endless cycles of violence, which is our natural response to victimization. Nonetheless, in practice, Christian traditions have tended to endorse retributive rather than restorative justice due to the retributive legacy of the Roman legal system, which was absorbed into the largely Christian culture of the Middle Ages. However, the association of Christianity with retribution was confronted over the past 30 years by the Christian faith communities, which encouraged a number of initiatives in many countries that supplemented retribution with restoration.

In Christian scriptures, restorative justice is founded on principles of healing and reconciliation. It restores the lives of God's children through repentance on the part of offenders and forgiveness on the part of victims or their survivors, in cases of murder. Restorative justice promotes both the repair of harm caused by crime and the active involvement of communities. The wrongdoer is made to know and feel the injury he or she has caused and to make her or his victim whole again to the degree possible. This is done through accountability measures such as *restitution*, or direct payment of fines to the victim, and victim-offender mediation. The community has a say in how offenders are dealt with, helps them readjust to life in society, and provides an environment for victims of crime to once again feel safe. Restorative justice also extends to inmates' families, who are adversely affected by the separation of incarceration and often need assistance in dealing with the situation.

Box 7.6, *continued*

Many organizations reflect restorative justice principles. *Justice Fellowship* is a nonprofit organization of Christians whose goal is to reform the American criminal justice system by reflecting these biblically based principles of restoration. Founded in 1983 as a subsidiary of *Prison Fellowship Ministries*, Justice Fellowship maintains a presence in local, state, and federal jurisdictions. It works with key policymakers to change the way current criminal justice agencies are administered. It has lobbied to extend the practice of religious freedom within prisons, supported victims' rights legislation, assisted with the design of restitution policies and procedures, and drafted standards for correctional programming and probationary supervision.

One particular example of its efforts has to do with prison employment opportunities. Because inmate idleness is destructive, Justice Fellowship has provided congressional testimony in favor of expanding job opportunities behind bars. Prison work programs are believed to be an essential part of changing offenders' lives so that they leave prison better than how they enter. Meaningful employment teaches inmates skills and values that will aid them in leading productive lives in the free world. Consistent with restorative justice, earned wages should be diverted according to the harm that the offense caused the victim, contribute toward supporting the offender's family, pay some of the costs of incarceration, and accumulate as "gate money" for disbursement upon release. Of course, work programs must be accomplished without displacing already employed workers in the community.

Conclusion and Future Directions

Throughout this chapter I have examined the relationship between the moral and the legal and have shown how religious beliefs and practices influence ideas about crime and punishment. Criminal justice is essentially religious in origin, because the acts it punishes attack the sacred realm as well as the profane. Religions believe laws should conform to a transcendent (if not divine) standard of truth. Establishing principles to guide the choice of penalty has also been very important to spiritual individuals and groups. The leading philosophies of punishment—deterrence, retribution, rehabilitation, and restoration—have roots in sacred religious beliefs.

While punishment tends to emphasize retribution and deterrence, religions also teach that criminal behavior has social causes besides personal ones. Thus the environment should be shaped to encourage obedience to societal rules rather than tempt disobedience. Many religious organizations promote rehabilitation of the offender in order to educate and reform her or him. The offender must make amends for criminal behavior by repairing the harm done but at the same time be reintegrated into the community as a whole citizen. Ideally, forgiveness by the victim will enhance the process of overcoming crime's devastation.

Underway among scholars and other professionals is an examination of the support religion provides for the contemporary restorative justice movement, which addresses the needs of victims, communities, and offenders based on religious principles such as those described in the case study above. Scholars of religion who are concerned with crime will watch this pursuit with interest. Restorative justice emphasizes healing the emotional/psychological wounds that crimes have caused to victims and communities. It expects offenders to make amends for their criminal behavior by repairing the harm they have done, but restorative justice also seeks to reintegrate offenders into their communities as whole, productive, and contributing citizens (Prison Fellowship International, n.d.). One example of a focus on religion vis-à-vis restorative justice was an eight-day research retreat in 1998 in British Columbia sponsored by the Social Sciences and Humanities Research Council of Canada. The retreat was attended by scholars, justice professionals, crime victims, and ex-offenders, all of different faiths. Speakers and attendees addressed the possibility that spiritual traditions of conflict resolution, such as Native American "circle sentencing," might be imitated in criminal justice practices by governments around the world.

Basic to a Native American concept of "offense" is the recognition by all parties that something has happened that has disrupted the ongoing harmony of the group. It is the function of a *sentencing circle* to restore that harmony. In this ceremony, usually under the leadership of an elder, people are seated in a circle. It typically accommodates a judge (without formal robe), a prosecutor, a defense attorney, a courtworker, a probation officer, an alcohol/drug agent, a crime prevention coordinator, the offender, the victim, and the victims' and offenders' family members. All community members are invited to attend and participate. The "circle" process allows each individual to speak from his or her perspective and to have his or her concerns considered. The tone of reconciliation that develops among the members of the circle is necessary to resolve the conflict between the victim and the offender, and it also develops positive relationships among the support providers who will later oversee that the agreed-upon resolution is adhered to by the offender. For example, a first-time offender convicted of breaking and entering a home and stealing money might be ordered to return the stolen money to the victim, wear an electronic monitor, attend counseling for a serious gambling addiction, and fulfill community service by speaking to youths about the dangers of gambling.

The positive working relationship among the "circle" members offers community cohesiveness that is essential for healing to take place. The resulting community sentencing plan normally involves commitments by both the offender and the community, and the sentencing plan is supervised by a probation officer or a community support person. The purpose of the sentence is to promote a positive reintegration of the offender into the community and to promote healing and support for the victim. It restores a sense of wholeness to the community so the people can begin to make a future again.

Despite concerns elsewhere about protecting victims' identities, members of one community have developed this approach even for dealing with reintegration after sexual assault, and they treat everybody impacted: victims and offenders and the families of both (Blue and Blue, 2001).

In 2003, B'nai Brith Canada, a Jewish organization, had the opportunity to implement restorative justice principles (Schmidt, 2003). The former Canadian chief of both the Assembly of First Nations and the Federation of Saskatchewan Indian Nations had referred to Jewish people as a "disease," and he implied that the Nazis had done right when they exterminated six million Jews. He later apologized with remorse and resigned from several official posts. Meanwhile the local justice department launched criminal proceedings against the chief, but said it would consider a restorative justice proposal if the police recommended that charges should be pressed. The justice department proposed that if the aboriginal leader agreed to take part in healing and sentencing circles, a hate-crime investigation into his anti-Semitic comments would be halted. In return, Jewish leaders promised to visit Indian reservations to learn more about life there, and Indian leaders accepted an invitation to visit Israel over the summer. B'nai Brith Canada's executive vice president assessed the situation in this way: "Indeed there is a silver lining to all this."

Suggested Further Reading

Bhagvat, D.N. (n.d.). "Early Buddhist Jurisprudence." *Studies in Indian History*, no. 13. Poona, India: Oriental Book Agency, n.d.

Day, T.P. (1982). "The Conception of Punishment in Early Indian Literature." *Editions SR*, vol. 2. Waterloo: Wilfrid Laurier University Press for the Canadian Corporation for Studies in Religion.

French, R.R. (1995). *The Golden Yoke: The Legal Cosmology of Buddhist Tibet*. Ithaca, NY: Cornell University Press.

Gorringe, T. (1996). *God's Just Vengeance: Crime, Violence and the Rhetoric of Salvation*. Cambridge Studies in Ideology and Religion, vol. 9. Cambridge, UK: Cambridge University Press.

Hadley, M.L. (ed, 2001). *The Spiritual Roots of Restorative Justice*. SUNY Series in Religious Studies. Albany: State University of New York Press.

Jacob, W., and M. Zemer (eds., 1999). "Crime and Punishment in Jewish Law: Essays and Responsa." *Studies in Progressive Halakhah*, vol. 9. New York: Berghahn Books.

Kurki, L. (1999). *Incorporating Restorative and Community Justice into American Sentencing and Corrections*. Research in Brief, Sentencing Corrections: Issues for the 21st Century. Washington, DC: U.S. Department of Justice, National Institute of Justice.

Lippman, M., S. McConville, and M. Yerushalmi. (1988). *Islamic Criminal Law and Procedure: An Introduction*. With a foreword by M. Cherif Bassiouni. New York: Praeger.

Ratnapala, N. (1993). *Crime and Punishment in the Buddhist Tradition.* With a foreword by Richard H. Ward. New Delhi: Mittal.

Speller, A. (1986). *Breaking Out: A Christian Critique of Criminal Justice.* London: Hodder & Stoughton.

Van Ness, D.W. (1986). *Crime and Its Victims.* With a foreword by Charles W. Colson. Downers Grove, IL: InterVarsity Press.

Witte, J. Jr. and F. S. Alexander (eds., 1988). "The Weightier Matters of the Law: Essays on Law and Religion." *American Academy of Religion Studies in Religion*, no. 51. Atlanta: Scholars Press.

References

Allard, P., and W. Northey (2001). "Christianity: The Rediscovery of Restorative Justice." In M. L. Hadley (ed.), *The Spiritual Roots of Restorative Justice*, pp. 119-143. SUNY Series in Religious Studies. Albany: State University of New York Press.

Bhagvat, D.N. (n.d.). *Early Buddhist Jurisprudence.* Studies in Indian History, no. 13. Poona, India: Oriental Book Agency.

Blue, A.W., and M.A. Rogers Blue (2001). "The Case for Aboriginal Justice and Healing: The Self Perceived through a Broken Mirror." In M.L. Hadley (ed.), *The Spiritual Roots of Restorative Justice,* pp. 57-80. SUNY Series in Religious Studies. Albany: State University of New York Press.

Dawood, N.J., trans. (1990). *The Quran,* 5th rev. ed. London: Penguin Books.

Durham, W.C., Jr. (1988). "Religion and the Criminal Law: Types and Contexts of Interaction." In J. Witte Jr. and F.S. Alexander (eds.), *The Weightier Matters of the Law: Essays on Law and Religion*, American Academy of Religion Studies in Religion, no. 51. Atlanta: Scholars Press.

Durkheim, E. (1949). *The Division of Labor in Society,* trans. George Simpson. Glencoe, IL: Free Press.

Eck, D.L. (1993). "The Challenge of Pluralism." *Nieman Reports* "God in the Newsroom" Issue, Vol. XLVII,(2)Summer.

Eck, D.L. (2001). *A New Religious America.* New York: Harper Collins.

Eck, D.L., and the Pluralism Project (1994). *On Common Ground; World Religions in America.* New York: Columbia University Press (CD-Rom).

Eltz, L.A. (1967). "Crime (Canon Law)," in *New Catholic Encyclopedia,* 19 vols. New York: McGraw-Hill, 4:453.

French, R.R. (1995). *The Golden Yoke: The Legal Cosmology of Buddhist Tibet.* Ithaca, NY: Cornell University Press.

Gorringe, T. (1996). *God's Just Vengeance: Crime, Violence and the Rhetoric of Salvation.* Cambridge Studies in Ideology and Religion, vol. 9. Cambridge: Cambridge University Press.

Hadley, M.L. (ed.,2001). *The Spiritual Roots of Restorative Justice.* SUNY Series in Religious Studies. Albany: State University of New York Press, 2001.

Hoekema, D. (1986). *Rights and Wrongs: Coercion, Punishment, and the State*. Selinsgrove, PA: Susquehanna University Press.

Juynboll, T.W. (1914). "Crimes and Punishments (Muhammadan)." In J. Hastings (ed.) *Encyclopedia of Religion and Ethics*, vol. 4. New York: Charles Scribner's Sons.

Lippman, M., S. McConville, and M. Yerushalmi (1988). *Islamic Criminal Law and Procedure: An Introduction*. With a foreword by M. Cherif Bassiouni. New York: Praeger.

Nikam, N.A. and R. McKeon, (eds. and trans., 1959). *The Edicts of Asoka*. Chicago: University of Chicago Press.

Parsons, W. (trans., 1951-56). *Saint Augustine: Letters*. NY: Fathers of the Church.

Prison Fellowship International (n.d.). "What is Restorative Justice?" *Centre for Justice and Reconciliation*, available from http://www.restorativejustice.org/rj3/intro_default.htm.

Ratnapala, N. (1993). *Crime and Punishment in the Buddhist Tradition*. With a foreword by Richard H. Ward. New Delhi: Mittal.

Schmid, M. (2003). "'The Eye of God': Religious Beliefs and Punishment in Early Nineteenth-Century Prison Reform." *Theology Today* 59:546-58.

Sullivan, D. and L. Tifft (2001). *Restorative Justice: Healing the Foundations of Our Everyday Lives*. Monsey, NY: Willow Tree Press.

Schmidt, S. (2003). "Indian, Jewish Leaders Meet: Healing Circle Proposed for Ahenakew." *Gazette* (Montreal), (January 9, final edition):A9.

Tilghman, A. (2004). "Man's Sentence: Probation, Yoga," *Houston Chronicle* (January 22, three star edition):A.17.

Walshe, M. (1995). *The Long Discourses of the Buddha: A Translation of the Digha Nikaya*. Somerville, MA: Wisdom.

Williams, J.A. (ed., 1971). *Themes of Islamic Civilization*. Berkeley: University of California Press.

Willing, R. (2004). "Courts Asked to Consider Culture." *USA Today*, (May 25):A.03.

Commentary

Howard H. Zehr

In the preceding chapter, Edwin C. Hostetter points out that criminology, like most other academic disciplines, has largely overlooked religious perspectives and factors. This neglect is unfortunate, he argues, because the various religious traditions have much to say about crime and justice and, moreover, have profoundly influenced their societies' attitudes about these topics. Definitions and understandings of crime and justice do not exist "out there" in some concrete form. Rather, they are constructed in various ways through experience and culture and even for societies that are today largely secular, religions have played—and continue to play—a role in shaping these understandings. Without an understanding of these religious perspectives, then, our picture is incomplete.

I want to expand on this fact by briefly looking at history using Christianity as an example. I will then note some of my current areas of interest as examples of topics for which an understanding of religious perspectives may be important.

In my book *Changing Lenses: A New Focus for Crime and Justice* (1990:95-157), I explain that early developments in Western law and theology influenced each other. I argue that as a result of this interaction, a kind of "historical short-circuit" took place that skewed our understanding of Christianity's views on punishment all the way to the present day. Over several centuries, certain Christian theological concepts were taken out of context, helping to shape and support a legalistic, punitive, and authority-centered view of justice within newly developing Western legal systems. The disproportionate focus on punishment in turn influenced the way scripture was understood, resulting in a tendency to see God as an angry, vengeful judge and to emphasize punitive rather than restorative themes in the Bible.[1] Even today, this punitive theology continues to influence the current legal system.

Timothy Gorringe (1996) of the University of Exeter has developed this historical interpretation, first by showing how deeply the Western legal system and a distorted Christianity mutually reinforced each other, and then by examining the way that a violent, punitive perspective in Christianity,

237

through its theology and rituals, reinforced these themes in Western culture generally. Gorringe focuses on the Catholic tradition, the dominant religion in the West before the sixteenth century, when the basic outlines of theology and law were emerging. Richard T. Snyder (2001) does the same for the Protestant tradition that emerged after that era, arguing that a similar process in mainstream Protestantism explains the contemporary West's prevailing culture of punishment. Gil Bailie (1995) further examines the way that a distortion of Christianity reinforced—rather than reduced, as the New Testament Gospel actually intended—the use of violence as a just response.

In short, I argue that a distortion of Christian theology played an important role in shaping our current understandings of crime and justice such as these:

- Crime is defined by law-breaking rather than harm to actual people.

- Victims—the ones actually harmed—are not central to justice processes.

- Crime is essentially against a central authority—God and/or state. Thus crimes are defined as offenses against the state—for example, *U.S. v. McVeigh.*

- Above all, offenders must get their "just deserts," and what they deserve is punishment—i.e., justice is essentially about punishment.

- Mercy is not part of justice but is something separate, a mitigation of the harshness of justice.

- Forgiveness is irrelevant to justice and, when sought, it is often seen as a process of forgiving oneself or of seeking God's forgiveness rather than an obligation the offender owes to another person.

- Violence is justified as a response to violence.

The last point, that you fight violence with violence, is important for criminology. Quinney and Wildeman (1991:40) argue that criminology has been preoccupied with justifying punishment:

> From its earliest beginnings in the eighteenth century Enlightenment, the primary focus of criminology has been on retribution, punishment, and vengeance in the cause of maintaining an existing social order. . . . The historical drift in criminological theory has been that if crime is violent and wrecks violence on our fellows and our social relationships, then the effort to understand and control crime must also be violent and repressive.

If it is true that religion has influenced the most basic, and often unconscious, assumptions underlying criminological thinking, then religion is an important area for study. Indeed, Dutch criminologist Herman Bianchi (1994) argues that as concerns the problem of justice, it will take renewed doses of Christian theology simply to undo the distorted cultural assumptions that were shaped in part by the Christian tradition.

The relationship between Christianity and punishment is relevant not only to the West but to the rest of the world as well. Through colonialism, the spread of Christianity, and, more recently, through the globalization of Western culture, most of the world has been influenced by Western ideas and law. Indeed, Western legal systems were forced on other societies, thus displacing traditional justice and conflict-resolution processes. My graduate students, who come from Buddhist, Islamic, and other religious traditions around the world, often find these observations about the imposition of Western law helpful to understanding their own cultures. Moreover, they often see restorative justice—my primary area of work—as a framework that helps them to legitimate and strengthen those traditional approaches to justice that have been repressed or even lost.

Religion, then, is important in helping us understand current realities. Using restorative justice as an example, Hostetter suggests that religion may also point toward a remedy. Indeed, today's restorative justice field did originate in the religious community, although it is now an international movement that has evolved far beyond its religious roots. The origins of the restorative movement were Christian, but people from other religions—Buddhist, Muslim, Jewish, and so on—are finding that it also resonates with their traditions (Hadley, 2001).

Finally, let me briefly note three areas of personal interest that may suggest important directions for restorative justice, religion, and crime:[2]

1. Having worked with many crime victims, I believe that one of their basic justice needs is to be "vindicated." Part of what this entails is that we all have a need to "settle the score." In the U.S. legal system we tend to see that as punishment—returning harm for the harm done—but this assumption is in part culturally determined, and there are other ways to find vindication that offer deeper satisfaction to the victim. As I argued above, religions are part of this cultural matrix, so a more complete understanding of the role of religion in shaping our cultural assumptions may help us to further examine and better address victims' judicial needs.

2. James Gilligan (1996) argues that violence is an effort to do justice, or to undo injustice. In other words, many offenders are, or see themselves as, victims of punishment, and their violence is a way to seek justice, to be vindicated for their victimization. If this it is true, then an understanding of the role of punishment in our culture, and its place in religion, may help us to understand not only justice but also the motivation for criminal behavior.

3. Although the Western world tends to deny this, I believe that the dynamics of honor versus humiliation and shame versus respect are important keys to understanding offending, victimization,

and the counterproductive impact of our criminal justice system on both victims and offenders. Similarly, the dynamics of shame, and its opposite, respect, may be key to constructing a justice process that really "works." Indeed, I have been arguing that restorative justice is essentially about respecting people, their needs, and their obligations. Religions have much to say about, and have helped to shape, these ideas.

These are just a few suggestions. The point that Hostetter and I are making is that religion is an important factor in many people's lives—myself included—but even when it is not, it plays an important role in shaping our cultural attitudes and assumptions about crime and justice. It is essential, then, that religious study be a part of criminological study.

Endnotes

1. For a re-examination of punitive and restorative themes in the Christian New Testament, see Chris Marshall, *Beyond Retribution* (2001).

2. I explore these themes in "Journey to Belonging" (2002).

References

Bailie, G. (1995). Violence Unveiled: Humanity at the Crossroads. New York: Crossroad.

Bianchi, H. (1994). *Justice as Sanctuary: Toward a New System of Crime Control.* Bloomington, IN: Indiana University Press.

Gilligan, J. (1996). *Violence: Reflections on a National Epidemic.* New York: Random House.

Gorringe, T. (1996). *God's Just Vengeance: Crime, Violence and the Rhetoric of Salvation.* Cambridge, UK: Cambridge University Press.

Hadley, M.L. (2001). *The Spiritual Roots of Restorative Justice.* Albany, NY: State University of New York Press.

Hoekema, D. (1986). *Rights and Wrongs: Coercion, Punishment, and the State.* Selinsgrove, PA: Susquehanna University Press.

Marshall, C.D. (2001). Beyond Retribution: A New Testament Vision for Justice, Crime, and Punishment. Grand Rapids, MI: Eerdman's.

Quinney, R., and Wildeman, J. (1991). *The Problem of Crime: A Peace and Social Justice Perspective.* Mountain View, CA: Mayfield.

Snyder, T.R. (2001). The Protestant Ethic and the Spirit of Punishment. Grand Rapids, MI: Eerdman's.

Zehr, H. (1990/95). *Changing Lenses: A New Focus for Crime and Justice.* Scottdale, PA: Herald Press.

Zehr, H. (2002). "Journey to Belonging." In E.G.M. Weitekamp and H. Kerner (eds.), *Restorative Justice: Theoretical Foundations*, pp. 21-31. Devon, UK: Willan.

Chapter Eight

Conclusion: Toward an Interdisciplinary Understanding of Crime

Bruce A. Arrigo

Fyodor Dostoevsky, the nineteenth-century Russian novelist imprisoned for four years in a Siberian prison camp for alleged political crimes, is often quoted as saying that "the degree of civilization in a society can be judged by entering its prisons." While prisons can indeed tell us much about the values of a society, crime in general—its definition, what we believe to be the causes, and how a society reacts to it—allows us to observe not only civilization but other dimensions of social and intellectual life. These dimensions, or themes, relate to crime and also pertain to fundamental—and unresolved—questions about human existence. In this chapter, I consider how these fundamental themes within the human experience, mediated through six academic disciplines, shape our conceptions of crime.

The purpose of this book is to provide students, practitioners, policy analysts, and researchers with a sharper and clearer vision for understanding crime. This was accomplished through a thoughtful assessment of crime from within the history, logic, language, and values of six different academic disciplines. Overall, then, each of the substantive chapters in this volume represents a state-of-the-art analysis, informed by sociology, economics, psychology, biology, philosophy, and religious studies. To be sure, accomplishing the book's principal goal is no small feat and, justifiably, readers may still wonder whether their attempt at understanding crime has been advanced in any appreciable way.

For example, while sociology may tell us that structure, process, and conflict are important factors that affect crime, and while economics may argue that matters of production, efficiency, and opportunity are essential to the analysis of crime, we learn little, if anything, about how these two very different criminological perspectives interrelate. The same may be said about the other conceptual perspectives that make up this book. In short, the six disciplines examined in the preceding chapters *independently* offer considerable information about crime, its origins, and its control; however, the relationships that exist (if any) among the disciplines have not yet been discussed. Not surprisingly, then, this omission leaves us with a somewhat underdeveloped understanding of crime.

The problem, however, is not unique to this volume. Indeed, efforts to establish unifying theories about crime abound in the literature (e.g., Barak, 1998a; Bernard, 1983; Hagan, 1985; Henry and Lanier, 1998; Henry and Milovanovic, 1996; Hirschi, 1979; Messner, Krohn, and Liska, 1989; Quinney, 1977; Wilson and Herrnstein, 1985). While these and other efforts tend to focus on the best way for organizing theoretical integration, it is the sociological perspective that typically informs these endeavors.

In the present volume, however, conceptual integration is complicated by the wide diversity of disciplines. Simply stated, in an effort at better understanding crime, this book crosses the academic boundaries of the social, behavioral, and natural sciences, as well as the humanities. Thus, given the book's organization, any attempt at theoretical synthesis has to occur from within an *interdisciplinary* framework. Once again, we are confronted with a formidable challenge in our understanding of crime.

One useful method for integrating knowledge in criminology is known as *thematic convergence* (Arrigo, 1999, 2002, 2004; Lynch, 1999). Thematic convergence is an analytical tool that reveals where and how different theories about crime, which come from distinct disciplines, interrelate. In theoretical thematic convergence, "criminological theories [are] grouped together on the basis of key conceptual points of correspondence" (Arrigo, 2000:9). This attempt at theoretical consolidation reveals how "the theories themselves are similar" (Barak, 1998b:xv) by stepping back and examining themes that underlie the theories.

The process of thematic convergence endeavors to enhance our knowledge of crime through a "fusion of knowledge," based on commonly held beliefs, rather than a "fission of criminological thought" or competing theories about crime (Arrigo, 2000:9; Barak, 1998a:190). Knowledge of interdisciplinary themes, rather than discipline-based theory, is the central organizing feature of the integrative effort. For our purposes, then, what is at stake is whether the book's six substantive chapters contribute to a *conceptual synthesis* about crime—whether they *collectively* tell us something noteworthy about the human condition and, by extension, of social life. If they do, then the subject of crime, as a product of our lives and as a specific academic inquiry, can help us to better understand the society we shape and that shapes us.

Admittedly, relying on the six substantive chapters for guidance in thematic convergence may be something of an oversimplification, resulting in a misguided, if not an altogether faulty, assessment. For example, we could question whether the authors (and their commentators) adequately represent the discipline about which they write. This critique challenges the author's reliability. Moreover, we could question the completeness of the chapters, the balance of the coverage, and the accuracy of the disciplinary-specific analysis. This critique challenges my conclusions' validity. Finally, we could question the strategy of thematic convergence itself, arguing that it produces little more than an arbitrary collection of interesting, though limited, ideas whose generalizability is questionable. This critique challenges my own biases.

These concerns are all understandable. However, this chapter is something of a tentative exploration, not previously undertaken, into the area of criminological integration. Thus, it is in the spirit of intellectual discovery that I consider these ideas. At the outset, I duly note this chapter's limits linked to validity, reliability, and bias. Moreover, those themes of convergence that I will identify are presented as suggestive and conditional. Thus, the framework that I develop is intended, at best, to call attention to potential conceptual linkages, and to a promising interdisciplinary model of criminological understanding. It is my hope that initiating this tentative interdisciplinary model will compel future scholars to build on the speculative insights that I develop here.

This chapter is divided into three principal sections. First, I will have more to say about the method of thematic convergence and the logic of conceptual synthesis. In particular, I will discuss how the subject matter of the six chapters was reviewed, how the identified themes were selected, and how the integration of underlying concepts about crime underscored both activities. Second, I will present one level of analysis—the *existential theme,* which relates to an understanding of the human condition—and how it is linked to the disciplines' conceptions of crime. Third, several implications from this chapter are outlined, specifically as regards the future of understanding crime from an interdisciplinary model of thematic convergence and conceptual synthesis. While my observations are meant to be merely suggestive, they nonetheless are an effort to rethink how the phenomenon of crime can be discussed by college students. In particular, my comments in the third section will focus on how the topic of crime profoundly relates to the human experience and to social life. This will be made evident by taking an integrative approach in analyzing the social and, behavioral, and natural sciences, as well as the humanities.

Method of Inquiry

From the strategy of thematic convergence, I consider two main questions regarding the six chapters: (1) How do the authors describe the intellectual approach under review? and (2) What sorts of discipline-specific questions guide the authors' understanding of crime? Let me now briefly discuss both of these concerns.

The first question above emphasizes the overall approach the authors take in presenting their arguments. For example, the chapter on psychology maintains that this discipline is a "science" and, as such, offers a positivist interpretation of the field. The chapter is therefore based on the doctrine of positivism, including the logic of empiricism, objectivism, and quantification. Conversely, the chapter on religious studies appeals to the "sacred writings" of a given society, which assert that crime and punishment should conform to transcendent (if not divine) laws. Thus, this chapter is founded on the logic of textualism, spiritualism, and culture. What is important here for purposes of the exercise on thematic convergence is that not only are the disciplines themselves distinct (e.g., psychology versus religious studies) but so, too, are the intellectual approaches the respective authors employ. In order to develop a unified model of interdisciplinary criminological understanding, it is necessary to account for these differences.

The second question identified above considers how a given discipline's specific research questions inform a theory's overall approach to understanding crime. To illustrate, philosophy seeks to develop justifications for why laws and punishments should or should not exist. In this respect, then, the discipline of philosophy assesses forms of argumentation, types of reasoning, and evaluative models in its critique of crime. Contrastingly, biology addresses evolutionary processes in all life forms, including those biosocial factors that contribute to a person's likelihood for engaging in criminal or delinquent conduct. As such, the discipline of biology understands the origin and nature of crime based on the interaction of brain functioning and the biosocial correlates of criminal behavior. Recognizing the unique questions that underscore how a specific discipline interprets the phenomenon of crime is essential to establishing an interdisciplinary strategy of thematic convergence.

Linked to the manner in which I review the six individual chapters is the process by which I identify various themes. My reading of the six substantive chapters focuses on each discipline's content and the author's framing of the subject matter. However, when locating points of thematic convergence, I deepen my analysis by examining how each discipline treats common themes. Locating instances of convergence that span the six academic approaches is very much a part of the overall consolidation process. Fundamental to this activity is the selection process itself, which produced the themes under consideration here.

Given the interdisciplinary nature of the thematic convergence exercise and the extent to which the social, behavior, and natural sciences, as well as the humanities, inform this endeavor, I deliberately chose the strategy of thematic integration. Further, I emphasize a macro-level, rather than a situational, assessment of thematic points of agreement located across the six disciplines. By exploring general commonalities, I am able to discuss broad domains of knowledge that are important to all disciplines. What makes this enterprise so appealing is that the core assumptions underpinning diverse disciplinary approaches to crime can be discussed using a common vocabulary, making it possible to articulate a more fully developed model of interdisciplinary criminological understanding (Arrigo, 2002). Moreover, the chapter will demonstrate how the study of crime illuminates several of the *existential tensions* so pivotal to human affairs and civic life. For purposes of this chapter, five *existential themes*, depicted as polarities, inform the interdisciplinary exercise:

1. determinism versus freedom
3. logic versus emotion
4. objectivity versus subjectivity
5. truth versus meaning
6. scientism versus humanism

Finally, conceptual synthesis, based on a fusion of knowledge, is identified as the essential component of the thematic convergence strategy. Integration of theory, by comparing and synthesizing the concepts that underlie various theories, is relevant to both an assessment of the subject matter in the individual chapters and to the general work of thematic convergence. In our attempt at understanding crime, conceptual synthesis involves a careful and deliberate reading of how different theories distinctively converge on each of the five existential themes. If I can show how discipline-specific theories converge around important issues of the human condition, then these five existential themes, as forms of knowledge, represent points of similarity in which the respective theories can be integrated.

Understanding Crime: Toward an Interdisciplinary Model of Thematic Convergence and Conceptual Synthesis

I begin by briefly describing each of the five existential organizing themes, which represent tensions about what we know and how we know it, that are significant to human affairs and civic life. I then examine the themes in relation to each discipline's specific theories about crime and general approach to knowledge-building by situating each discipline within five dichotomies representing the existential themes identified above. While my judgment may be something of an exaggeration or "forced fit," the overall exercise nevertheless suggests important differences among the values inherent in the discipline-based theories about crime. My analysis is based on the insights contained in this volume's six substantive chapters, as presented by the various authors and their commentators, and is summarized in Box 8.1. The table in Box 8.1 depicts the relationships among the six disciplines' perspectives on crime as well as the five existential themes. It is important to note that this organizing framework allows us to compare the underlying, and often taken-for-granted, assumptions within these intellectual points of view. Theoretical criminological scholarship has recently argued in favor of this sort of conceptual organization because it allows us to rethink, advance, and deepen our knowledge about crime (e.g., Arrigo and Williams, 2005; Williams and Arrigo, 2004).

Box 8.1 • Understanding Crime: An Existential Thematic Inquiry

	EXISTENTIAL THEMES				
	Determinism vs. Freedom	Logic vs. Emotion	Objectivity vs. Subjectivity	Truth vs. Meaning	Scientism vs. Humanism
ACADEMIC DISCIPLINE					
Sociology	crime = product of social forces	structure and process explanations	cause and effect, linear logic, and rationality	statistics, rationality, and measurement	social environments and criminal behavior
Economics	crime = product of utilitarian choices	law of maximum utility	rationality; utility theory	opportunity, production, and costs and benefits	market probabilities and criminal behavior
Psychology	crime = product of psychopathology	profiling offenders	quantification, prediction, and control	hypothesis testing, and scientific method	personality and behavioral typologies
Biology	crime = product of evolutionary patterns in (all) humans	brain function and competitive victimizing behavior	forensic neuroscience and crime correlates	statistical, natural science method	biosocial and social learning correlates of criminal behavior
Philosophy	crime = product of ontological crises	balance gov't and individual interests	the logic of justification	evaluative method; types of reasoning	understanding fairness, harm, desert, and individual liberties
Religious Studies	crime = product of deviant tendencies and dangerous impulses	sacred writings and religious practices	textual criticism; cultural inquiry of truth	transcendent and divine standard	spiritualism; culture; identity

The theme of *determinism versus freedom* is well documented in theoretical and philosophical criminology (Pfohl, 1994; Williams and Arrigo, 2005). Dating back at least to the Greeks, especially Plato, and explicitly presented in Cesare Beccaria's classic work, *On Crimes and Punishments* (1764), questions about responsibility for one's (criminal) wrongdoing have figured prominently in much social thought throughout the ages (MacKenzie, 1981; Pappas, 1995). Within criminology, this existential tension between determinism and freedom assesses where the assignment of moral blameworthiness or legal accountability can and should lie, given one's delinquent or criminal behavior. Borrowing from the philosophy of Beccaria and the utilitarianism of Jeremy Bentham (1996), classical criminology argued that people were rational pleasure seekers and pain avoiders whose actions were *freely chosen* based on a careful and deliberate weighing of the benefits and costs for engaging in criminality. However, much of modern criminology, dating back to the pioneering work of founding positivists such as the biology of Cesare Lombroso (1889, 1912) and Enrico Ferri (1900), claimed that a host of physiological, psychological, economic, and social forces, external to one's control, led to delinquent or criminal conduct (Beirne, 1993). Thus, the person's criminality was understood to be *determined*, rather than freely chosen (Williams and Arrigo, 2005). Considerable debate surrounding the appropriate assessment of responsibility for the offender's conduct continues today.

The existential theme of *logic versus emotion* represents the underlying rationale wherein questions about crime, law, punishment, and deviance are identified, pursued, and examined (Pfohl, 1994; Williams and Arrigo, 2004). *Logic* embraces linearity, stasis, order, predictability, control, and sameness; *emotion* embraces nonlinearity, change, disorder, unpredictability, fluidity, and difference (Arrigo, 1995). To date, this tension has not been the subject of criminological discussions, except in studies that seek to investigate the taken-for-granted assumptions of theoretical criminology (Arrigo and Williams, 2005; Einstadter and Henry, 1995; and for applications in law and social control see, Williams and Arrigo, 2002). Logic has likely dominated discussions of crime in academic disciplines because the traditional notion of disciplinary analysis itself emphasizes identifying patterns in phenomena and building knowledge in a linear progression.

The theme of *objectivity versus subjectivity* represents the preferred "voice" and method by which a particular criminological critique unfolds. *Objectivity* is linked to such values as neutrality, impartiality, statistical measurement, and quantification. *Subjectivity* is associated with such values as culture, narrativity (how a story is told), qualitative reasoning (relying on verbal or spatial facts rather than numerical ones), and intuition. Philosophically informed studies in criminology have recently investigated the objectivity–subjectivity dichotomy (DiCristina, 1995), including influential works in constitutive theory (Henry and Milovanovic, 1996), cultural criminology (Ferrell, 2002; Ferrell and Sanders, 1995; Hayward and Young, 2004), and postmodernism (Arrigo, Milovanovic, and Schehr, 2005; Milovanovic, 2003).

The *truth versus meaning* dichotomy points to the existential goal of any academic inquiry. *Truth* refers to the certainty of reason, the exactness of knowing, and the absoluteness of our existences. In short, truth signifies that foundational realities are authoritatively definable. Conversely, *meaning* refers to the inconsistency of reason, the fluidity of knowing, and the mutability of our existences. In short, meaning signifies that identities are negotiated and that reality is temporary. Efforts to discuss this dichotomy in criminology are mostly linked to sociological understandings of the creation of crime and deviance, through shared meanings in social settings, including ethnomethodology, symbolic interactionism, and labeling theory (e.g., Dotter, 2004).

The *scientism versus humanism* polarity represents the various forms of knowledge underpinning discipline-specific theories about crime. At issue here is the particular framework from within which a given theory interprets crime and criminal wrongdoing. As an unstated assumption about a particular theory and its method, the scientism–humanism dichotomy draws attention to the type of knowing pursued by each disciplinary perspective. *Scientism* endorses a kind of knowing that has explanatory and predictive properties, and that is testable, verifiable, and falsifiable. *Humanism* supports a type of knowing that has sense-making and culturally bound properties, and that is built on wisdom and experience, interpersonal truths, and intersubjective understanding. Philosophically informed works in criminology have only recently examined this tension (Arrigo, 1999; Arrigo and Williams, 2005; DiCristina, 1995).

Based on this brief review of the five existential themes, or dichotomous forms of knowledge, outlined above, it is now possible to identify where and how the six discipline-specific perspectives concerning crime uniquely relate to these dichotomies. Again, for purposes of simplicity, each perspective is generally located on one end of each polar dichotomy based on the presentation of the theories by the various authors and their commentators. At issue here is the manner in which the different conceptual frameworks concerning crime individually endorse the theme under consideration. If it can be shown that one uniform identification process can be applied across the distinct disciplines, then conceptual synthesis built on the logic of thematic convergence will deepen our understanding of crime as consolidated within a multidisciplinary model.

Sociological Criminology

Although sociological criminology acknowledges that people are responsible for their behavior, much contemporary research, and many of the sociological theories, regard crime as a product of various forces beyond the individual's control. This means that the principal rationale for understanding crime is based on investigating the structure and process of criminal wrongdoing and the wayward actions of transgressors. As such, sociology maintains that crime can be socially constructed, as well as predicted, controlled, and prevented. To substantiate this claim, criminologists informed by the insights of sociology, methodologically quantify and measure (e.g., study crime and victimization rates). By remaining impartial, truth is a product of objective, cause-and- effect, linear, and rational models of statistical inquiry. Indeed, the truth about crime is a matter of scientific rigor, precision in the research methods employed, and the reliability and validity of data. For most sociologists, knowledge about crime comes from what is testable, verifiable, and falsifiable. As such, it is the social environment, that is, the social world inhabited by humans, to which these criminologists turn when seeking to explain and predict about crime and its control.

Economic Criminology

Economists concerned with the phenomenon of crime locate its source in the choices individuals make. Utilitarian theory, as derived from economics, states that people behave in a manner that enables them to maximize their utility or well-being. Economic criminologists argue that, as a freely chosen action, the conduct of criminals is mostly rational. Marginal analysis sees would-be transgressors as calculating the costs and benefits of committing crime. They weigh such factors as utility, opportunity, and efficiency. Wanting to logically predict the outcome of their action, would-be offenders ask themselves such questions as: Will I or will I not get caught? Will the rewards I receive from the criminal act be better than the punishments that will follow if I get caught? Given that economists regard crime as an ascertainable, rational, and utilitarian outcome, they see criminal conduct as determined by likely outcomes. Factors such as unemployment rates and crime, poverty and crime, and the costs of crime all figure prominently into the economic analysis. In this way, the truth about criminal wrongdoing is attributed, with some precision and certainty, to differences in social opportunities, matters of economic production, and the calculus of rewards versus punishments. Not surprisingly, then, economic criminologists turn to the vagaries of market forces, labor dynamics, and various decision-making probabilities as a way of knowing, explaining, and predicting crime.

Psychological Criminology

Criminal responsibility in psychological criminology is attributed to the offender's psychopathology. Dangerous and deviant tendencies, traced to personality deficits, biological abnormalities, arrested development, cognitive impairments, and clinical disorders, are seen as deficiencies of the mind and, thus, are understood to be mostly outside the individual's control. In order to comprehend the link between these psychological factors and crime, criminologists, persuaded by the insights of psychology, create offender typologies. These typologies are created from an assemblage and cataloguing of personality and behavioral data, emphasizing such things as methods of victim selection, characteristics of the perpetrator and/or crime, and facilitators associated with the criminal event (e.g., the use of alcohol, other drugs, pornography). Methodologically speaking, then, understanding human behavior for the psychological criminologists depends largely on the precision with which such typologies are developed, quantified, and measured. Ultimately, these profiling efforts are designed to predict offender "types" and to control the commission of crime. As such, psychological criminologists maintain that by constructing testable hypotheses built around exacting methods of scientific inquiry, true and accurate portraits can be obtained of the arsonist, rapist, serial murder, terrorist, stalker, and so on. In this way, psychological criminologists can assess the degree of explanation and prediction of the behavioral and personality typologies.

Biological Criminology

Biologists who study crime maintain that its cause and persistence is a result of evolutionary patterns and/or biochemical factors involving the brain. Although individuals are mostly seen as being responsible for their actions, their biosocial patterns (including those involving social learning) determine a person's probability of engaging in delinquent or criminal conduct. In order to examine these probabilities, biological criminologists turn to "competitive victimizing tendencies"—behaviors correlated with specific aspects of brain functioning that result from exposure to male-typical levels of testosterone (e.g., suboptimal arousal, episodic dyscontrol). By systematically assessing these tendencies, predictability, control, and stability are achieved, especially with respect to understanding the biological traits or evolutionary patterns that underlie certain forms of criminal behavior. This is the principal rationale that informs biological criminology. Not surprisingly, then, statistical measurement, quantification, value neutrality, and objective analysis methodologically structure biological investigations of crime. One compelling example of the biological approach is forensic neuroscience and its evaluation of the correlates of criminal behavior (e.g., testosterone levels, skin conductivity, slow brain wave patterns, mesomorphy). Thus, the truth about crime from the biological perspective relies on the tenets of natural science and the precision of the research methods employed. Ultimately, biological criminology supports a type of knowing built around testable, verifiable, and falsifiable models of inquiry. These are models that seek to understand, predict, and explain (likely) offending based on brain functioning and the discrete biological and social learning conditions that contribute to it.

Philosophical Criminology

From the perspective of philosophy, criminal behavior is the product of unresolved crises in human existence and civic life. How governments deal with and respond to crime, how people interpret individual liberties, and how the law imposes punitive sanctions, represent some of the contentious issues in assigning responsibility for criminal wrongdoing. In this respect, then, philosophy's commitment to personal freedom is at the same time conditioned by those governmental institutions—the police, courts, and prisons—that restrict or prevent a person's independent choice-making. Philosophy's dual consideration of personal freedom and personal constraint—informed by an ordered, reasoned, and linear rationale—entails the deliberate use of the logic of justification. The logic of justification, as an analytical method of inquiry, offers insight into evaluating the merits of competing concerns. When seeking to justify certain principles, the use of evaluative insight accounts for culture, narrative, and emotional decisions because philosophers assume that reality is situational, knowledge is imprecise, and reason is fluid. Achieving evaluative insight means searching for meaning using such methods as hypothetical argument and deductive reasoning. Thus, for the criminologist persuaded by the wisdom of philosophy, how society should deal with and "know" crime is a function of interpersonal truths, intersubjective understandings, and humanistic obligations to offenders, victims, and the community to which both are bound.

Religious Studies and Criminology

For the discipline of religious studies, crime is a product of a person's deviant tendencies and dangerous impulses. However, assigning moral blameworthiness for one's criminal behavior first entails a consideration of the sacred writings and religious practices of a given culture or group. This is because religion offers a strategy for promoting social control and social order in the face of one's wayward conduct. The underlying assumption informing how a culture's sacred texts and rituals relate to an individual's transgressions has to do with the difference in how religious groups recognize their sacred dimensions. Across each religion, there is uniqueness among the various theologies and the moral precepts informing the community of believers. Precisely because religion is defined as people's beliefs and practices relative to sacred things, ascertaining the "voice" of the sacred within a given culture is essential to understanding that culture's regard for delinquency and crime. For criminologists who work within this framework, textual criticism, cultural inquiry, narrative accounts, personal experience, and qualitative sense-making are all valued methods. This is because meaning, rather than truth, is the ultimate goal of such investigations. To substantiate meaning, religious studies scholars call for interpersonal and intersubjective standards of knowing, or standards that rely on reciprocally interacting subjective views of the transcendent and divine. These are fluid and mutable ways of knowing, ways in which culture, spiritualism, and identity figure prominently. As a result, knowledge about crime and criminals is culturally bound, humanistically conceived, and experientially pursued. Religious studies, then, reminds us that systems of laws and punishment are fundamentally steeped in moral values that affirm religious beliefs.

Implications

As I demonstrated in the previous section, it is quite possible to conceptually integrate discipline-specific theories about crime through the strategy of thematic convergence. In doing so, I combined forms of knowledge with the goal of broadening our understanding of five existential themes related to crime. Central to this endeavor are questions about *what we know*, *how we know*, and *who we are*. As we have seen, each perspective regarding crime—whether from the social sciences, the behavioral sciences, the natural sciences, or the humanities—deepens our appreciation for several basic concerns about human existence and civic life. In this respect, then, crime, as a product of culture, helps us to understand the society that profoundly shapes us and that we shape.

With this in mind, it is now necessary that I evaluate the strategy of thematic convergence, particularly in regard to understanding crime. Indeed, in order to build on what I have said thus far, it is not enough to merely identify the relationship between existential themes and their connection to the work of thematic convergence; a more complete interdisciplinary model of criminological understanding requires that we consider two other levels of inquiry.

In this section I make some preliminary observations regarding the usefulness of thematic convergence and conceptual synthesis. In particular, I consider the *institutional and operational themes* that translate and mediate the abstract existential considerations explained above. For my purposes the *institutional themes* are:

1. reality construction
2. power and the distribution of resources
3. race, ethnic, and gender dynamics
4. the nature of justice

An Interdisciplinary Model of Understanding Crime: The Institutional Level

Linked to the existential themes of thematic convergence are questions about institutional values and how discipline-specific theories apply these values in understanding crime. *Values* are belief systems; they are a collection of core ideas and principles about a certain phenomenon. For our purposes, the phenomenon under consideration is crime. Specifically, our interest is in the values that influence what the different criminological perspectives say about the way criminal justice institutions should function. Obvious examples of criminal justice institutions are the police, the courts, corrections, and juvenile justice agencies. Others include psychiatric, public health, social welfare, housing, chemical dependency, and veteran's affair agencies. Together, these institutions represent a vast organizational source for responding to the problems that stem from crime. Analyzing the institutional values inherent in the various disciplines not only tells us a great deal about their view on crime, it also helps us in constructing an interdisciplinary model of thematic convergence.

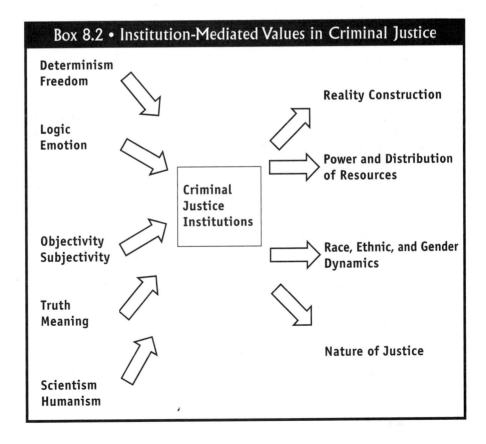

Box 8.2 • Institution-Mediated Values in Criminal Justice

Determinism
Freedom

Reality Construction

Logic
Emotion

Power and Distribution
of Resources

Criminal
Justice
Institutions

Objectivity
Subjectivity

Race, Ethnic, and Gender
Dynamics

Truth
Meaning

Nature of Justice

Scientism
Humanism

Different perspectives on crime—biology, philosophy, economics, etc.—are influenced by particular values in regard to criminal justice institutions. Although frequently unstated, these values show us how the six disciplinary perspectives play out their existential themes. As a practical matter, then, it is necessary to identify and explain these core institutional values.

The institutional theme of *reality construction* refers to how discipline-specific theories about crime interpret the workings of various criminal justice institutions. Certain disciplinary understandings of crime can challenge institutional realities, while others affirm those same realities. Further, institutional realities change from place to place and time to time, ensuring very different perceptions, and thus, responses to the following questions: Are law and politics separate entities? Does the juvenile justice system ensure that delinquent youths benefit from the same constitutional rights guaranteed for adults? Has the medical establishment demonstrated that mental illness and dangerousness are objective, empirically grounded, preventable psychiatric conditions, or are they just products of culture? Is it best for society to continue its campaign against illicit drug use or should some illegal substances be decriminalized? Should there be a federally mandated right to decent, affordable, and safe housing, or does this unduly burden taxpayers, transforming the country into a welfare state? Questions such as these are not easily answered; however, each of the six disciplinary approaches to crime can be examined in light of the values it endorses and privileges, concerning the workings of criminal justice institutions.

The institutional theme of *power and the distribution of resources* examines the values each discipline-specific theory assigns to the capitalist political economy. Of particular concern here is how each theory interprets the workings of criminal justice institutions in an era of hyperconsumerism, privatization, and increased use of the mass media. Given these economic and political conditions, we are concerned with such questions as: Is there a "prison industrial complex" that has supplanted state control of decisions involving the punishment of criminal offenders with for-profit bureaucratic interests? How do private correction companies, who are in the business of providing detention and correction services to federal, state, and local governments, support the economy? If the poor and disenfranchised are disproportionately processed through the police, the courts, and correctional systems, as compared with people in the middle and upper classes, to what extent is this a matter of disparities in wealth and access to life opportunities (e.g., education, housing, employment, etc.)? To what extent should the government be involved in controlling environmental, corporate, and white-collar crime, given that these offenses cause the most personal and financial devastation to society? The approaches to crime presented in this volume, implicitly or explicitly, embrace certain values in regard to these politically and economically influenced institutional concerns. As such, the theme of power and the distribution of (scarce) resources warrant greater attention in any interdisciplinary approach to understanding crime.

Race, ethnic, and gender dynamics have to do with institutional beliefs about multiculturalism and diversity. At issue here is the way in which discipline-specific theories regarding crime interpret the agency-based responses to women, persons of color, and other so-called "protected" groups. This concern extends to both victims as well as offenders. The important questions in this regard include: To what extent, if at all, does the culture of law enforcement and the socialization of police officers promote institutional racism? Are murders committed by women apt to be victim-precipitated homicides (killings in which the victim's actions contributed to the incident) and, if so, do the courts understand the gendered construction of crime? In what way does the USA PATRIOT Act of 2001, intended to deter and punish terrorist acts by enhancing law enforcement investigatory tools, unfairly target and profile people of certain ethnic groups (e.g., people of Middle Eastern descent) and how, if at all, do these practices violate their civil liberties? The disciplinary approaches to crime presented throughout this book support discrete values regarding issues of race, ethnicity, and gender, and the criminal justice system's response to them. The theme of diversity and multiculturalism, then, is one practical organizing strategy by which to conceptually integrate the different criminological frameworks at the institutional level.

Reality construction, power and the distribution of resources, and race, ethnicity, and gender dynamics, are significant for establishing a fourth institutional theme, that of the *nature of justice*. Each discipline-specific theory maintains certain core values about the place of justice in society, especially in relation to how criminal justice institutions function to achieve this end. Concerns for justice involve matters of fairness, reasonableness, equity, proportionality, opportunity, interest balancing, and the like. Concerns for justice draw our attention to social and political inequality. Pertinent questions in this regard include: In what way is the criminal law structured to guarantee due process for all citizens? To what extent does prosecutorial and judicial discretion—the right of federal administrative agencies and judges to do as they think fit, but prudently, at opportune times—serve the best interests of society and those individuals impacted by it? Under what conditions does capital punishment promote the administration of justice?

Consider the case of the Los Angeles Police Department, whose overwhelming gang problems inspired a 2004 ballot measure that would have increased sales tax by one-half of 1 percent in order to hire more police officers. The measure was defeated due to opposition from African-American segments of the community, who protested not the tax increase, but the increase in police because of recent negative experiences of many with police officers (Rabin, Fausset and Minaya, 2004). In June 2004, the televised police beating of a black suspected car thief refueled the distrust toward police by blacks and their community leaders, which built up over many years, despite professed efforts by Police Chief William J. Bratton to reduce the impact of race on public perceptions about crime control (Leovy, 2004).

The disciplinary theories considered in this book should be reviewed as a basis for understanding the unique values they promote in relation to these sorts of institutional questions about justice. Undertaking this task is useful because it furthers the integrative exercise of thematic convergence.

An Interdisciplinary Model of Understanding Crime: The Operational Level

Both existential knowledge (i.e., how we know, what we know, and who we are) and institutional values (i.e., belief systems, core principles of criminal justice agencies) that inform the six disciplines, presented above, serve important thematic and integrative purposes. The institutional level demonstrates the usefulness of working from the theme-building strategy of conceptual synthesis. The operational level, on the other hand, assesses the interdisciplinary approach to understanding crime very pragmatically.

The operational level of analysis examines the practical endpoints where existential concerns and institutional values intersect. At this level, criminal justice programming and policy are established, implemented, and evaluated.

As a way of organizing various conceptual frameworks about crime, the operational level addresses the roles and interests of three main groups:

1. the offenders

2. the victims

3. the community to which the offenders and victims belong

At issue here is how the respective theories interpret each group's role in relation to crime and its control. As with my previous comments about institutional values, my observations regarding the operational themes are meant to highlight the utility of the interdisciplinary approach to understanding crime.

The *role of the offender*, as an operational component, is concerned with whether criminals possess redemptive capacities. The relevant questions are: To what extent is desistance possible? To what extent is recovery from criminality possible? In what contexts is rehabilitation of the offender likely? Under what conditions is healing likely to occur? What circumstances facilitate offender insight? Each discipline-based perspective can be organized on the basis of these operational questions. Indeed, although the position taken by the different perspectives toward the role of the offender is likely to vary, the programming and policy agendas that these perspectives support are based on their notions about the offender's prospects for reform and salvation.

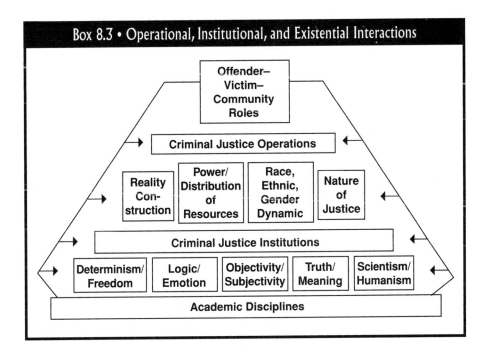

The second operational component, the *role of the victim*, examines whether those individuals harmed by crime can make peace with the wrongs perpetrated against them by others. Is forgiveness likely? What factors are essential to ensuring mercy? What circumstances must be addressed in order to achieve reconciliation between the victim and offender? Is overcoming the fear that follows victimization possible? The perspectives on crime described throughout this volume can be consolidated by examining the unique position each takes on these operational questions. Again, programming and policy recommendations resulting from these perspectives on crime are based on whether the victim's transformative commitments to resolution, closure, and recovery are deemed likely by each academic discipline. Analysis of the victim's role goes a long way toward grounding the existential commitments and the institutional values integral to establishing a sensible interdisciplinary model of crime.

The *role of the community* as an operational component in understanding crime entails assessing how society promotes offender-victim recompense from the unique vantage point of each discipline-specific theory. Is restitution possible? Is victim-offender mediation emphasized? Is restorative justice pursued? Are victim-offender reconciliation programs supported? Conversely, are other, more punitive forms of retribution promoted? Are boot camps, electronic monitoring, and other intermediate sanctions advanced as policy? Are determinate and mandatory sentences recommended? Is the death penalty regarded as a viable option for redressing the criminal actions of offenders on behalf of victims? Mindful of their unique existential leanings and their particular institutional values, academic disciplines from the social sciences, the behavioral sciences, the natural sciences, and the humanities make programmatic investments in offender-victim recompense. Exploring these investments is useful to understanding crime from an interdisciplinary model of thematic convergence and conceptual synthesis.

Conclusions

In this chapter I have endeavored to comprehend crime from within an interdisciplinary framework. Existential concerns, institutional values, and operational investments are all pivotal to this enterprise. Although there are other ways of consolidating discipline-based theories about crime, my approach pays particular attention to the distinct ways in which six disciplines—sociology, economics, psychology, biology, philosophy, and religious studies—collectively can be organized around the existential, institutional, and operational themes that tell us about the human condition and our civic life.

My strategy of thematic convergence demonstrates how crime itself is an effective tool for understanding disparate perspectives on crime. Moreover, this approach facilitates a richer appreciation for the social world that people shape and that shapes them. As a practical matter, then, studying crime is a powerful way to explore the relationships among culture, self, and society, and the various existential, institutional, and operational forces that sustain these relationships.

Crime and justice educators, especially those who represent a wide spectrum of disciplinary perspectives, would do well to rethink their treatment of crime. I maintain that it is not enough to *independently* explain the sociological, economic, psychological, biological, philosophical, and religious studies models that exist in the criminological literature. While this approach is appealing and useful in its own right, it is not sufficient if the aim is to broaden and deepen society's knowledge about criminality.

This aim, however, can be realized through an *interdisciplinary* approach. To be sure, if our knowledge about crime is to be appreciably advanced, then the next generation of practitioners and theorists must be equipped with the intellectual resources that foster this progress. The work undertaken in this book by the editors, chapter authors, and commentators represents their concerted effort to facilitate and achieve this noteworthy goal. Developing a practical interdisciplinary framework is intellectually original, intriguing, and challenging. In this chapter I have endeavored to contribute directly to this interdisciplinary effort at understanding crime.

References

Arrigo, B.A. (1995). "The Peripheral Core of Law and Criminology: On Postmodern Social Theory and Conceptual Integration." *Justice Quarterly*, 12:447-472.

Arrigo, B.A. (ed.) (1999). *Social Justice/Criminal Justice: The Maturation of Critical Theory in Law, Crime, and Deviance.* Belmont, CA: Wadsworth.

Arrigo, B.A. (2000). "Social Justice and Critical Criminology: On Integrating Knowledge." *Contemporary Justice Review*, 3(1):7-37.

Arrigo, B.A. (2002). "Critical Criminology, Existential Humanism, and Social Justice: Exploring the Contours of Conceptual Integration." *Critical Criminology: An International Journal*, 10(2):83-95.

Arrigo, B.A. (2004). "Prospects for Justice at the Law-Psychology Divide: An Agenda for Theory, Research, and Practice." In B.A Arrigo (ed.), *Psychological Jurisprudence: Critical Explorations in Law, Crime, and Society*, pp. 201-230. Albany, NY: State University of New York Press.

Arrigo, B.A., D. Milovanovic, and R.C. Schehr (2005). *The French Connection in Criminology: Rediscovering Crime, Law, and Social Change.* Albany, NY: State University of New York Press.

Arrigo, B.A., and C.R. Williams (eds.) (2005). *Philosophy, Crime, and Criminology*. Urbana-Champaign, IL: University of Illinois Press.

Barak, G. (1998a). *Integrating Criminologies*. Boston: Allyn & Bacon.

Barak, G. (1998b). *Integrative Criminology*. Brookfield, VT: Ashgate Dartmouth.

Beccaria, C. (1764/1963). *On Crimes and Punishments*. H. Paolucci (trans.). Indianapolis: Bobbs-Merrill.

Beirne, P. (1993). *Inventing Criminology*. Albany, NY: State University of New York Press.

Becker, H. (1963). *Outsiders: Studies in the Sociology of Deviance*. New York: Free Press.

Bentham, J. (1996). *An Introduction to The Principles of Morals and Legislation*. J. Burns and H. Hart (eds.). New York: Oxford University Press.

Bernard, T.J. (1983). *The Consensus-Conflict Debate: Form and Content in Social Theories*. New York: Columbia University Press.

DiCristina, B. (1995). *Method in Criminology: A Philosophical Primer*. New York: Harrow and Heston.

Dotter, D. (2004). *Creating Deviance: An Interaction Approach*. New York: Altamira Press.

Einstadter, W., and S. Henry (1995). *Criminological Theory: An Analysis of its Underlying Assumptions*. Fort Worth, TX: Harcourt and Brace.

Ferrell, J. (2002). *Tearing Down the Streets: Adventures in Urban Anarchy*. New York: St. Martin's Press.

Ferrell, J., and C. Sanders (ed.) (1995). *Cultural Criminology*. Boston: Northeastern University Press.

Ferri, E. (1900). *Criminal Sociology*. New York: D. Appleton.

Goffman, E. (1963). *Stigma*. Englewood Cliffs, NJ: Prentice Hall.

Hagan, J. (1985). *Modern Criminology: Crime, Criminal Behavior and its Control*. New York: McGraw-Hill.

Hayward, K.J., and J. Young (eds.) (2004). "Cultural Criminology." Special Issue of *Theoretical Criminology: An International Journal*, 8:259-386.

Henry, S.D., and M.M. Lanier (1998). "The Prism of Crime: Arguments for an Integrated Definition of Crime." *Justice Quarterly*, 15(4):609-629.

Henry, S.D., and D. Milovanovic (1996). *Constitutive Criminology: Beyond Postmodernism*. London: Sage.

Hirschi, T. (1979). "Separate and Equal is Better." *Journal of Research in Crime and Delinquency*, 16:34-38.

Leovy, J. (2004). "Beating of Black Suspect Puts Bratton's Race Inroads to Test." *The Los Angeles Times*, (June 28):A.1.

Lombroso, C. (1889). *The Criminal Man*, 4th ed. Torino, Italy: Bocca.

Lombroso, C. (1912). *Crime: Its Causes and Remedies*. Montclair, NJ: Patterson Smith.

Lynch, M.J. (1999). "Working Together: Towards an Integrated Critical Criminological Model for Social Justice." *Humanity & Society*, 23(1):68-78.

MacKenzie, M. (1981). *Plato on Punishment*. Berkeley, CA: University of California Press.

Messner, S.F., M.D. Krohn, and A. Liska (eds.). (1989). *Theoretical Integration in the Study of Deviance and Crime: Problems and Prospects*. New York: State University of New York Press.

Milovanovic, D. (2003). *Critical Criminology at the Edge: Postmodern Perspectives, Integration, and Applications*. Westport, CT: Praeger.

Pappas, N. (1995). *Plato and the Republic*. New York: Routledge.

Pfohl, S. (1994). *Images of Deviance and Social Control: A Sociological History, 2nd ed.* New York: McGraw-Hill.

Quinney, R. (1977). *Class, State, and Crime*. New York: David McKay.

Rabin, J., R. Fausset & Z. Minaya (2004). "Wary Blacks Voted No to More Police." *The Los Angeles Times*, (November 10):A.1.

Schur, E.M. (1971). *Labeling Deviant Behavior*. New York: Harper & Row.

Williams, C.R., and B.A. Arrigo (2002). *Law, Psychology, and Justice: Chaos Theory and the New (Dis)Order*. Albany, NY: State University of New York Press.

Williams, C.R., and B.A. Arrigo (2004). *Theory, Justice and Social Change: Theoretical Integrations and Critical Applications*. Norwell, MA: Kluwer Academic/Plenum.

Williams, C.R., and B.A. Arrigo (2005). "Philosophy, Crime, and Theoretical Criminology: An Introduction." In B.A. Arrigo and C.R. Williams (eds.), *Philosophy, Crime, and Criminology*. Urbana-Champaign, IL: University of Illinois Press.

Wilson, J.Q., and R.J. Herrnstein (1985). *Crime and Human Nature*. New York: Simon & Schuster.

About the Contributors

Bruce A. Arrigo teaches criminology at the University of North Carolina at Charlotte. He received his Ph.D. in Administration of Justice from the Pennsylvania State University. He has authored or edited 20 books and has published well over 100 peer- reviewed articles, book chapters, and scholarly essays. He is a Fellow of the American Psychological Association and a Fellow of the Academy of Criminal Justice Sciences.

Albert K. Cohen is Emeritus Professor of Sociology at the University of Connecticut. He is the author of *Delinquent Boys: The Culture of the Gang* and *Deviance and Social Control*. He is a Past President of the Society for the Study of Social Problems and the recipient of the Edwin H. Sutherland Award from the American Society of Criminology.

Francis T. Cullen, Ph.D., Columbia University, is Distinguished Professor of Criminal Justice at the University of Cincinnati. He is a Past President of the American Society of Criminology and the Academy of Criminal Justice Sciences. His research interests are in the areas of criminological theory, correctional policy, and the control of corporate crime.

Deborah W. Denno is Professor of Law at Fordham University School of Law. Professor Denno received her J.D. and her Ph.D. in criminology from the University of Pennsylvania.

Lee Ellis teaches sociobiology at Minot State University in Minot, North Dakota. He received his Ph.D. in criminology from Florida State University. He is coauthor (with A. Walsh) of *Biosocial Criminology: Challenging Environmentalism's Supremacy* and *Criminology: A Global Perspective*.

David O. Friedrichs is Professor of Sociology and Criminal Justice at the University of Scranton. He is the author of *Trusted Criminals: White Collar Crime in Contemporary Society* and *Law in Our Lives: An Introduction,* editor of *State Crime,* and author of some 100 journal articles, chapters, and essays.

Susan Guarino-Ghezzi is Professor of Criminology at Stonehill College in Easton, Massachusetts. She received her Ph.D. in sociology from Boston College. She is coauthor (with E. Loughran) of *Balancing Juvenile Justice*, founder of "Make Peace with Police," and former Director of Research at the Massachusetts Department of Youth Services.

Edwin C. Hostetter teaches religious studies at McDaniel College in Westminster, Maryland. He received his Ph.D. in near eastern studies from Johns Hopkins University.

Kimberly Kempf-Leonard teaches criminology and sociology at the University of Texas at Dallas. She received her Ph.D. in criminology from the University of Pennsylvania. Her work has brought innovation to measurement of diverse topics, including criminal career patterns, gender bias, racial disparity, insider trading, judicial decisionmaking, and theories of crime and justice. She is probably best known for her applied research aimed at improving juvenile and criminal court processing.

L. Thomas Kucharski is Associate Professor of Psychology at John Jay College of Criminal Justice in New York City. He received his Ph.D. in psychology from the University of Rhode Island. He was previously Chief Psychologist at the Metropolitan Correctional Center in New York City, forensic psychologist at Bridgewater State Hospital (in Massachusetts), and Director of Mental Health and Forensic Services of the Westchester County Department of Corrections.

Stephen Mathis teaches philosophy at Wheaton College in Norton, Massachusetts. He received his Ph.D. in philosophy from the University of Kansas.

Robert A. Rosenthal received his Ph.D. in economics from Boston University. He teaches economics at Stonehill College in Easton, Massachusetts, and serves as a consultant and expert witness in the field of forensic economics.

C. Gabrielle Salfati received her Ph.D. in Investigative Psychology from the University of Liverpool, UK. She is an international expert on crime scene analysis and offender profiling of homicide and sexual offenses, based in the Department of Psychology at John Jay College of Criminal Justice at City University of New York.

A. Javier Treviño teaches sociology and criminology at Wheaton College in Norton, Massachusetts. He received his Ph.D. in sociology from Boston College. He is a past President of the *Justice Studies Association,* Editor of the *Law & Society* series for Transaction Publishers, and author of *The Sociology of Law: Classical and Contemporary Perspectives.*

Lode Walgrave is Professor of Criminology at the Catholic University of Leuven (in Belgium). He served as President of the International Association for Juvenile Criminology. He is the editor of *Restorative Justice and the Law, Repositioning Restorative Justice,* and (with G. Bazemore) *Restorative Juvenile Justice.*

Howard H. Zehr teaches sociology and restorative justice at Eastern Mennonite University in Harrisonburg, Virginia. He received his Ph.D. in European history from Rutgers University. He has authored numerous books including *Crime and the Development of Modern Society: Patterns of Criminality in Nineteenth Century Germany and France; Changing Lenses: A New Focus for Crime and Justice;* and *The Little Book of Restorative Justice.*

Index